EVIL
by Design

**INTERACTION DESIGN TO
LEAD US INTO TEMPTATION**

Chris Nodder

WILEY

Evil by Design: Interaction design to lead us into temptation

Published by
John Wiley & Sons, Inc.
10475 Crosspoint Boulevard
Indianapolis, IN 46256
www.wiley.com

ISBN: 978-1-118-42214-4
ISBN: 978-1-118-45225-7 (ebk)
ISBN: 978-1-118-65481-1 (ebk)
ISBN: 978-1-118-65497-2 (ebk)
Manufactured in the United States of America
10 9 8 7 6 5 4 3 2 1

Library of Congress Control Number: 2013934763

To my wife, Mel, for putting up with me during the crunch times; and my dog, Sheila, for giving me the best excuse for taking breaks during those same crunch times.

Credits

Acquisitions Editor
Mary James

Senior Project Editor
Adaobi Obi Tulton

Technical Editor
Dan Lockton

Senior Production Editor
Kathleen Wisor

Copy Editor
Apostrophe Editing Services

Editorial Manager
Mary Beth Wakefield

Freelancer Editorial Manager
Rosemarie Graham

Associate Director of Marketing
David Mayhew

Marketing Manager
Ashley Zurcher

Business Manager
Amy Knies

Production Manager
Tim Tate

Vice President and Executive Group Publisher
Richard Swadley

Vice President and Executive Publisher
Neil Edde

Associate Executive Publisher
Jim Minatel

Project Coordinator, Cover
Katie Crocker

Compositor
Maureen Forys,
Happenstance Type-O-Rama

Proofreader
Nancy Carrasco

Indexer
John Sleeva

Cover Image
Chris Nodder

Cover Designer
Ryan Sneed

Background Images
Ryan Sneed

About the Author

Chris Nodder is the founder of Chris Nodder Consulting LLC, an agile user experience consultancy that helps companies build products that their users will love.

Chris also runs the QuestionableMethods.com website, which gives lean and agile teams the tools they need to run their own user research; and he is a Lynda.com video author. He presents on user experience topics at international conferences.

Before starting his own consulting business, Chris gained invaluable experience working with some of the best companies in the industry. He was a director with Nielsen Norman Group, a premiere international user research company, for 5 years. He also worked for 7 years as a senior user researcher at Microsoft Corp.

He has a background in psychology and human-computer interaction.

About the Technical Editor

Dan Lockton specializes in design for behavior change—understanding and influencing the use of products and services for social and environmental benefit. For his Ph.D. Dan developed the *Design with Intent Toolkit*, a pattern library for designers working in this emerging field. He is a senior research associate at the Helen Hamlyn Centre for Design, Royal College of Art, London, and does consultancy through his company, Requisite Variety.

Acknowledgments

The User Experience Dream Team: Jakob Nielsen for giving me the opportunity to test out some of the ideas in this book as a Nielsen Norman Group conference keynote; Don Norman for suggesting the title of the book and writing a wonderful introduction; and the benign trickster Bruce "Tog" Tognazzini for his inspirational story-telling.

The people at Wiley: especially Mary James, who first suggested I turn these ideas into a book; Adaobi Obi Tulton for keeping me (somewhat) on track; and San Dee Phillips for making my tenses agree, my punctuation perfect, and my English American.

The indispensables: Dan Lockton not just for setting me straight with technical edits but also for providing some great examples and new directions; Scott Berkun for giving me insights into the craziness of ever deciding to write a book; all the anonymous online reviewers; and finally all the companies and individuals who unintentionally provided the examples used in this book.

Contents

Foreword

SLOTH, PRIDE, ENVY, GREED, LUST, ANGER, GLUTTONY. What? I'm supposed to design for these traits? As a human-centered designer, I should be repelled by the thought of designing for such a list. What was Chris Nodder thinking? What was his publisher thinking? This is evil, amplified.

Although, come to think of it, those seven deadly sins are human traits. Want to know how people really behave? Just read the law books. Start with one of the most famous set of laws of all, the *Ten Commandments*. Every one of those commandments is about something that people actually did, and then prohibiting it. All laws are intended to stop or otherwise control human behavior. So, if you want to understand real human behavior, just see what the laws try to stop. The list of seven deadly sins provides a nice, tidy statement of fundamental human behavior, fundamental in the sense that from each of the deadly sins, one can derive a large list of less deadly ones.

But why should design be based on evil? Simple: Starting with evil means starting with real human behavior. This doesn't mean that the result is evil: It means that understanding what each sin represents adds to an understanding of people. And good design results from good understanding. This is Chris Nodder's great insight: Human frailty provides a great learning experience, illustrative examples that teach fundamental principles. And just as all fundamental principles can be used for good or evil, Nodder's principles can be used in either way.

There are obvious benefits to society in using the lessons learned from the sins to enhance design processes for the good of humankind. But there are also benefits to understanding how those who are less scrupulous than you or me use these same principles for nefarious purposes, defrauding people, or perhaps just causing them to buy things they do not need at a price they cannot afford. What possible benefits? The more the tactics are understood, the more readily they can be identified and resisted, fought against, and defeated.

Nodder has done a superb job of distilling and explaining. Fun to read, insightful to contemplate. Maybe he did too good a job—I am now far better equipped to do evil than I was before I read the book. But I'm also better equipped to notice when others apply these principles to me; and they do, many times a day, as I browse the Internet, click links, or wander the streets of my little town in the Philistine area called Silicon Valley; resisting temptations of greed, lust, and gluttony as I watch the natives feeding at outdoor cafes; buying at fancy glass-encased stores selling tantalizing electronic sin toys; passing the offices of venture capitalists along the way, with fancy, unimaginably expensive and powerful automobiles parked in front (in a city where the speed limit is 25 miles per hour, and it is rare to go even that fast). Which sins are on constant display? Every one of them.

The seven sins are all around us, easy to spot. But the designs that apply the underlying behavioral forces that underpin the sins are harder to discern. That's why we need this book.

Thank you Chris for providing insight coupled with fun. Teaching deep insights into human behavior together with valuable guidelines and frameworks for applying them is a blessing—57 blessings, one for each design pattern that Nodder has derived from the seven sins. Learning from sins. Pleasure from sins. A wonderful combination.

So yes, buy the book. No, don't download it for free: That would be sinful.

Don Norman
Nielsen Norman group
Author of *Design of Everyday Things*
Palo Alto, California

Introduction

IN MARK TWAIN'S CLASSIC book, *The Adventures of Tom Sawyer*, Sawyer convinces others to do his work for him by making the chore of painting a fence seem instead a desirable job. His friends beg to be involved.

> Tom said to himself that it was not such a hollow world, after all. He had discovered a great law of human action, without knowing it—namely, that in order to make a man or a boy covet a thing, it is only necessary to make the thing difficult to attain.

MARK TWAIN, *THE ADVENTURES OF TOM SAWYER*, 1876

Designers work hard to control the emotions and behaviors of their users. Truly great websites—good or evil—use specific techniques to get users to perform the desired task time and time again. Success in web design is most often measured in terms of how many users beg to be involved; creating, sharing, commenting, or purchasing.

Evil designs and their virtuous counterparts

Design is about persuasion. Marketers first codified many of these persuasive behaviors in the mid-1930s. It took until the turn of the century for economic researchers and psychologists to work out why people respond to these behaviors in the way they do. Now you can learn how to apply this knowledge in interaction design.

Sites capitalize on our weaknesses. Sometimes their intentions are good, but mainly they do this for "evil"—in other words to profit at our expense. The best sites manage to make us feel good at the same time.

Learning from the best

Controlling people's behavior for financial gain is not a new concept. Casinos do it, politicians do it, and marketers do it. Here, we consider human foibles and the manner in which they can be exploited into the digital age: How do we influence behavior through the medium of software?

We will draw many examples from existing apps and websites. The creators of these products may have been unaware of the psychological underpinnings of their design decisions. Indeed, they may not have intended to be truly evil in their implementations. However, the end results are often wonderful advertisements for evil by design.

Like a good magic trick, the best examples are the ones where you don't even realize that people are being manipulated until it's pointed out to you. When you understand the reasons why users respond the way they do, you'll appreciate even more how clever some of these "tricks" actually are and marvel at the beauty of some of the evil designs.

Defining evil design

We must differentiate between evil design and plain stupidity. Often, a lazy or ill-thought-out design can infuriate us. However, it takes a truly well-conceived evil design to make us come back for more.

Stupidity isn't evil. People who create bad designs because they don't know any better or because they are lazy aren't being evil. Evil design must be intentional. In fact, as you'll see in the various chapters, there is often a lot of planning involved in creating an evil design that truly works.

The idea behind evil design is that people enter willingly into the deal, even when the terms are exposed to them. Confidence tricksters are another group who control behavior for gain, but they take things a stage further than evil design by hiding the true outcome of the activity.

Stupidity is sloppily coded error messages that don't explain what's wrong, or how to fix it. Those dialog boxes are frustrating but benign. A con is software that promises to remove viruses but instead infects your computer. This is evil masquerading as good—and if users manage to see behind the mask, they will be dismayed. Evil design works on a different level, by convincing customers that the value proposition is in their best interest (financially or emotionally) and by persuading customers to participate even if they are aware of the imbalance in the outcome.

So evil design is that which creates purposefully designed interfaces that make users emotionally involved in doing something that benefits the designer more than them.

Human weakness: The seven deadly sins, and how sites leverage them

It seems only fitting to lay out the contents of this book according to the vices that sites exploit to attract and engage with users. Thus, the subsequent chapters group design techniques under the headings of the Seven Deadly Sins.

Throughout history, philosophers and religious scholars have categorized human weakness as a set of "sins." The Seven Deadly (unforgivable) Sins are Pride, Sloth, Gluttony, Anger, Envy, Lust, and Greed. Each chapter in this book addresses one of these sins, pointing out the human characteristics that enable software designers to create persuasive interfaces that appeal to each weakness. Using examples from contemporary web design, you will be able to see how the sin is exploited both for good and for evil. Each characteristic is accompanied by design patterns that give you simple rules to apply these same techniques in your own work.

This book concludes with a discussion about ethics. Not the heart-wrenching moral dilemma of whether to use any of these evil-by-design patterns, but instead an acceptance that they are being used already today. Knowing how to recognize these patterns enables you to turn them to your advantage both as a consumer and as a designer of software and websites.

Pride

Humility makes men like angels; Pride turns angels into devils.

SAINT AUGUSTINE

PRIDE ISN'T THE SIN IT USED TO BE. In the 4th Century, Evagrius of Pontus claimed that pride was the primary sin among the seven, and the one from which all others stemmed. By the time of Thomas Aquinas in the 13th Century, it was seen in a more measured manner—some pride was acceptable, but a surfeit was still a sin. In the 21st century, with the advent of social media, it appears that we more often ask, "Have you no pride?" when confronted with yet more drunken party photos, as if pride is a positive attribute that arbitrates in matters of taste.

These days, the sense in which pride is bad is probably best summed up by the word *hubris*—arrogance, loss of touch with reality, overestimating one's capabilities, thinking that you can do no wrong. In the Greek tragedies, hubris leads the hero to pick a fight with the gods and thus be punished with death for his insolence. These days, it's called overextending your credit.

Of course, the aim in this book isn't to bemoan the lack of humility in modern society but to see how sites leverage this human weakness.

Misplaced pride causes cognitive dissonance

Harold Camping, the owner of familyradio.com, has been wrong a couple of times in the past. He predicted that the world would end on May 21, 1988—then again on September 7, 1994, and subsequently on May 21, 2011, before settling for October 21, 2011. After the world steadfastly refused to stop turning on each of these dates, you'd think that Harold would call it quits and stop believing that the Rapture was imminent. You'd also think that the large number of his followers who sold or gave away all their possessions or spent their life savings on advertisements for the event(s) would be embarrassed or upset. Although a small minority expressed disappointment each time, most continued to believe Harold. Why?

It's all about how the brain manages to rationalize or resolve two conflicting concepts: a state called *cognitive dissonance*. For example, people know that smoking kills, but they continue to smoke. These dissonant thoughts don't work well together. People resolve the issue by removing one of the two conflicting concepts. Quitting tobacco is much harder than rationalizing that smoking is unlikely to kill you because you are a healthy individual, and anyway, everyone dies of something. In other words, changing your opinion (that smoking can kill you) is much easier than changing your behavior (smoking). So the dissonance is resolved by rationalizing your opinions, even if that leaves you believing something strange.

In Harold's case, each time he could demonstrate how his calculations (based on interpretation of scripture) had been slightly wrong. By admitting a small personal failing, he managed to refocus his followers' actions around the new date. For his followers, it was much easier to accept that their leader had forgotten to add a couple of years in his equation than to believe that their Rapture-targeted behaviors were misaligned or even laughable. The deeper they were involved in Harold's prophecies, the more pride they had at stake, the more cognitive dissonance they had to resolve, and so the more likely they would be to grasp on to any explanation that Harold could provide.

However, after his October 21, 2011 prophecy, Harold stopped providing new dates and seemed to be somewhat chastened.

> *The question constantly arises, where do we go from here? Many of us expected the Lord's return a few months ago, and obviously we are still here. Family Radio is still operating. What should be our thinking now? What is God teaching us? In our Bible study over the past few years, we came to the conclusion that May 21 and October 21 were very important dates in the Biblical calendar. We now believe God led us to those dates, but did not give us complete understanding. In fact, we did not understand at all the correct significance of those*

two dates. We are waiting upon the Lord, and in His mercy He may give us understanding in the future regarding the significance of those two dates.

Maybe this new outlook is partially due to his award of the 2011 Ig Nobel mathematics prize (jointly with several other prophets) for "teaching the world to be careful when making mathematical assumptions and calculations."

Provide reasons for people to use

If you expect that users will be conflicted about the product or service you offer, provide them with many reasons they can use to resolve cognitive dissonance and keep their pride intact.

Online, cognitive dissonance can be brought about by effects such as *buyer's remorse*, in which the purchaser struggles to justify the high purchase price and their desire for an item in comparison to their subsequent feelings of the item's worth.

Sites help users resolve this cognitive dissonance by giving them reasons and evidence that bolster their satisfaction with the product (positive reviews; images of famous people using the product; and promises of hard-to-quantify benefits, such as social approval brought about by using the product) rather than letting them resolve the dissonance by returning the product.

The Best Made Company sells axes. One of its models was exhibited by the Saatchi Gallery in London, instantly turning it from a utilitarian object into a work of art. Painting stripes on the handle in limited numbers per design added to the exclusivity and thus desirability (see also the Tom Sawyer effect, in the chapter on Gluttony).

Lowes is a hardware company that also sell axes. At Lowes, a similar hickory handled felling axe costs $30. The $30 option comes with a lifetime guarantee, so why would you choose the $300 version? Mainly because Best Made offers many superlatives that help to ease cognitive dissonance. Its product description reads more like a manifesto to the outdoors lifestyle than a listing of features.

If you were to point out to owners of this axe that they'd just paid about ten times too much money for something used to chop wood, they would have plenty of ammunition to fire back. Clever marketing on the bestmadeco.com site turns a utilitarian purchase into a search for exclusive art, thus resetting customers' pricing expectations. Continuing the marketing message through to the packaging of the item ensures that it is reinforced when customers receive the goods and every time they look at the product subsequently.

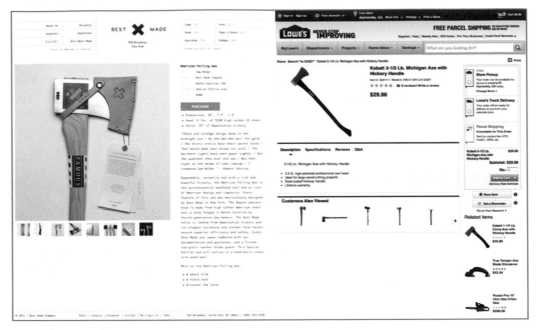

Buyer's remorse: You can spend $300 or you can spend $30. In both cases you get a hickory handled felling axe. (left image: bestmadeco.com, right image: lowes.com)

To prevent buyer's remorse, get customers to imagine the experiences they'll have with your product or the way that others will react when they see the customer using your product. Take the customer in their mind's eye to a contented future with the product and then make them look back on the current time as a pivotal decision point.

Continuing with the axe example, consider this quote on the About Us page: "Best Made Company is dedicated to equipping customers with quality tools and dependable information that they can use and pass down for generations. We seek to empower people to get outside, use their hands and in doing so embark on a life of fulfilling projects and lasting experiences." These words are aimed at making you jump into the future and look back on now. How could you *not* buy something that promises a fulfilling life full of lasting experiences?

To resolve buyer's remorse if it still happens, the trick is not to hide the return path, but to make it easier for customers to resolve the dissonance by changing their opinions instead. Because people are biased to see their choices as correct (see the description of confirmation bias in the Change Opinions pattern that follows), any supporting evidence can reinforce the initial opinions that led them to choose your product, help them rationalize their decision, and thus leave them happier with their initial choice. It is therefore important to use the same style of messaging throughout the site, from product pages through to the support and warranty/returns sections, and on all other collateral such as documentation sent with the product.

How to provide reasons

» Give purchasers plenty of reasons to want your product. Provide testimonials, reviews, and lifestyle images. Help them visualize a rosy future that includes your product. This is just as important after the purchase as before. Don't have a glossy sales page and a dull support page. Make it clear to existing owners that they did the right thing.

» Add something cheap but unique to your product offering. Best Made place their axe in a wooden crate lined with "wood wool" (shavings). This costs them comparatively little but boosts the appeal of the product by giving owners self-reassuring evidence that they received something special.

» Hire good product packaging and site designers. Presentation—how the product looks—can determine its price point. Utilitarian or bohemian?

Social proof: Using messages from friends to make it personal and emotional

Pride means caring what friends think about us and our activities. We're proud when our friends praise us for something we've done, and upset if our friends disapprove. Much of our behavior is determined by our impressions of what is the correct thing to do. Our impressions are based on what we observe others doing.

Those others don't have to be our friends. In a new situation we may follow the cues of total strangers. Most of those strangers could also be new to the environment, but we still make the assumption that they have a deeper understanding of the situation. Experts, celebrities, existing customers, and even the "wisdom of the crowd" can all serve as drivers for how we behave. This influence is known as *social proof*: "If other people are doing it, it must be right."

If we see a tip jar full of bills, we are more likely to tip. If we see a nightclub with a line outside, we're more likely to think it's a popular venue. If we see a restaurant full of happy people, we're more likely to think that eating a meal there would be worthwhile. That's why baristas "prime" their tip jars in cafes, why nightclubs keep a slow-moving line outside even if the club is quiet inside, and why restaurants seat people at the window seats first thing in the evening.

It doesn't hurt Apple to have long lines outside its stores on product release days. (Well, except for the Chinese release of the iPhone 4S, in which there was such a large crowd that the police made the stores cancel the release.) This just provides additional social proof that Apple's products must be worth having because so many people line up to buy them.

The line outside the Chicago Apple store on a cold morning two weeks after white iPads were first released. The fact that people were prepared to stand outside at least half an hour before opening time for the vague possibility that this store had some iPads in stock projects strong social proof that Apple's products must be worth having.

Dispel doubt by repeating positive messages

Hearing the same positive message several times from different trusted sources can provide the social proof that helps users form a decision.

In 1969, Stanley Milgram was running studies looking at conformity. He's best known for a study in which he determined that subjects would give supposedly lethal shocks to another person if told to by an authority figure. However, he also ran slightly more benign studies that looked at how influence varies with different numbers of sources. He had a paid helper stand on a busy sidewalk and look up at the (empty) sky. He noted that approximately 40 percent of people passing would also look up. With two confederates, that number rose to 60 percent. When he paid four people to stand together and look up, around 80 percent of people passing would also look up.

If more people are doing something, it lends additional credibility to the activity. If you hear about the same product from several different sources, you tend to attribute more positive views to it than a product you were unfamiliar with. In other words, familiarity doesn't breed contempt, it breeds reassurance.

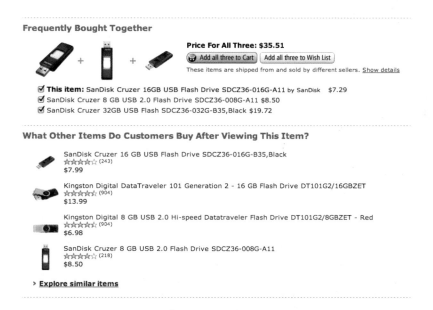

Showing what others bought and what is frequently bought together serves as two additional social proof reinforcements for the item on the page. (amazon.com)

People rely on social proof more when they are unsure what to do. New users, people shopping for infrequent or unfamiliar purchases, or people seeking expertise are all likely candidates for social proof persuasion.

To give customers several converging statements that add to social proof, sites also provide white papers of case studies, indications of how popular a particular item is (number sold, number left in stock, or even a "sold out" label), recommendations for complementary products or accessories, and product reviews.

Testimonials are another type of social proof. If you offer testimonials, make sure they come from people who appear qualified to make the statements, and that you give enough details about these people so that a reader can validate that they exist.

Because the information from each of these sources complements the other sources, and because they appear in different places around the site, users tend not to notice that the same basic message is repeated to them in different ways each time.

It's important that the social proof examples you use guide people in the direction that you want. Making it clear that a large group of people engage in the behavior you *don't* want (even if you emphasize it only to say "don't do this") legitimizes that behavior in people's minds and may provide social proof in the wrong direction. For instance, a campaign against teen drinking that tries to shock by saying what proportion of teens drink may work for adults, but will have the opposite effect on teens. ("Hey—all the others are doing it, so why don't I?")

The best forms of social proof come from outside the direct sphere of influence that a site has. Reading positive statements about a product or company on a supposedly neutral third-party site can have greater social proof outcomes than reading the same statements on the company's site. By 2011, only 13 percent of consumers purchased products without first using the Internet to review them. More customers think it's important to get reviews from other consumers than from professional reviewers or consumer associations.

This has led to the rapid growth of pay-to-blog advertising and sponsored posts. Companies exist to match advertisers with bloggers (inblogads.com, weblogsinc.com, sponsoredreviews.com, reviewme.com, payperpost.com, and blogsvertise.com), and a whole army of bloggers exists to take advantage of these paid endorsements. Many are in the home, family, and parenting blog categories and on tech "review" sites.

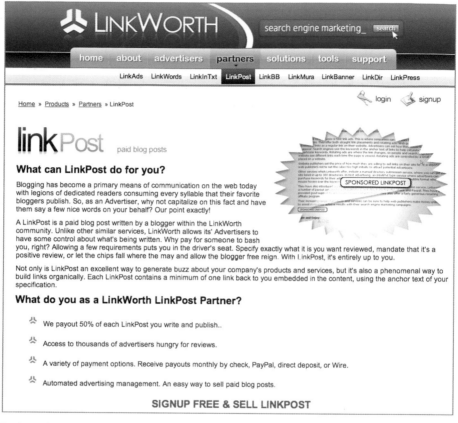

LinkWorth is just one of many companies who match advertisers to bloggers. The pseudo-originality of the blog post—each one written by a different blogger, but on the same theme—increases search engine optimization and adds social proof. (linkworth.com)

The proliferation of for-pay blogging caused concern about both the impartiality of reviews written online and also the blurry line between commercial sites and blogs that were basically shills for an organization.

In 2009 this led the Federal Trade Commission (FTC) to update its testimonial and endorsement guidelines for the first time since 1980.

When there exists a connection between the endorser and the seller of the advertised product [that] might materially affect the weight or credibility of the endorsement (i.e., the connection is not reasonably expected by the audience) such connection must be fully disclosed.

The maximum fine is $11,000—although this seems to be aimed more at celebrities on talk shows than at mommy bloggers. Now the industry has several different yet similar codes of conduct, all aimed at allowing bloggers to receive money from advertisers for giving honest opinions. The money hasn't disappeared, but the honesty (and the fact that blog posts are sponsored) should be more apparent.

The fact that bloggers can leave less favorable reviews probably won't even harm sponsors considerably. Only 4 percent of people would change their mind about a product or service after reading one negative review, and it takes three negative reviews before the majority of users would change their minds. The proportion of reviews can also play a role: Three negative reviews may mean very little in comparison to 300 positive reviews.

How to use social proof

» Try to create several statements that back up the same general positive concept about your product or service. Users are more likely to believe you if they hear several variations on the same theme.

» Get statements placed on different sources or sites. Seemingly impartial reviewers have more credibility, and hearing the same statement from multiple sources also improves social proof.

» Place statements at locations on the site where they'll be seen by new users, people shopping for infrequent or unfamiliar purchases, or people seeking expertise.

» Describe your process, product, and so on as the accepted norm—for instance, the industry standard or reference item. Being seen as a standard gives the product implied social proof.

» Work with common stereotypes of behavior—if it's commonly held that people will do X in situation Y, then reinforce that stereotype to your advantage, as it plays to social proof.

» Use site statistics to impute social proof—for instance "70 percent of our business comes from client referrals" demonstrates that clients like the business enough to recommend it to others.

» Make sure the social proof example you use emphasizes your desired behavior rather than trying to dissuade people from the opposite behavior. Don't even raise the opposite behavior as an option.

Personal messages hit home

Messages aimed directly at the user grab attention. Messages that come from friends and trusted others have even more effect.

To reach Hanakapiai Beach on Kauai in the Hawaiian islands, you have to hike a couple of miles along the beautiful but up-and-down Kalalau trail along the Na Pali coast. The visual reward makes the hike worthwhile, and it would be unfair to spoil it for you by showing you photos here. Instead, I'm going to show you photos of the warning signs that you see just before you reach the beach.

On the left is the series of three official signs. Each is carefully crafted to give a depiction of the dangers that await you, backed up by stern sounding warnings. That clean, official, indirect voice keeps things passive and impersonal and thus relatively easy to ignore.

On the right is the unofficial sign, found just a few yards further down the trail. Obviously hand-carved by a concerned amateur, this sign talks less about the natural features of the beach and more about the outcome: "Killed? Yikes!" This more personal approach (backed up with near real-time updates on the death toll) is much more likely to hit home with passing hikers.

Back in the tech world, Jimmy Wales' "personal appeal" to raise funds for Wikipedia has a positive effect on donations. Wikipedia runs annual fund raising drives, and in 2011 the banner ads it used to accompany the fund raising were crafted through a series of A/B comparison tests to ensure maximum click through, followed by appeal pages designed to tell a story that would maximize conversion and donation amounts.

Please read:
A personal appeal from
Wikipedia founder Jimmy Wales

Wikipedia's A/B tests allowed them to work out that the most effective messages came from Jimmy Wales (the founder and public face of Wikipedia) and included a trustable explanation as to why the donations were needed. Thus, it came as close to being "personal" as is possible from a person that donors had probably never met.

Social networking sites use pseudo-personal messages in an attempt to drive viral adoption. For instance, Google+ tells you your friends have invited you, so you feel like it's a recommendation from them to use the service. All that actually happened was that your friend added your e-mail address to their Google+ Circles.

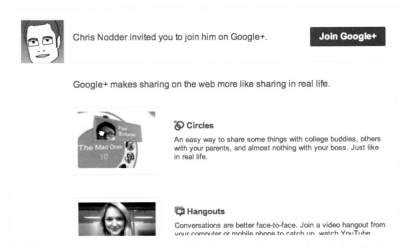

Did Chris really invite me to join him? No, he just added me to his circles. But it sounds more like a recommendation this way.

After you sign up and add some people to your own circles, you perpetuate the social proof effect. In addition, when you reciprocate with an "add," Google informs the person who first added you that "they want to hear from you."

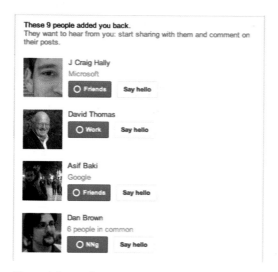

The recipients of my "invitation" now apparently want to hear from me. Wow, I'd better start using the service more diligently!

Even more insidious is LinkedIn and Facebook's habit of using your name and likeness in ads seen by your friends and contacts saying that YOU recommended/used/did this thing, so your contacts should, too.

An e-mail from LinkedIn uses my connections' names and likenesses to convince me to do something. If all of these respectable professionals are doing it, maybe I should be too.

Interestingly, Facebook first tried this in 2007 with its Beacon product. It bombed because it was hideously intrusive, to the point of sharing details of purchases that individuals made at third-party sites on their Facebook walls. After much public outcry it was shut down in 2009.

facebook

Sponsored Stories in Marketplace

Select "Sponsored Stories" at http://www.facebook.com/ads/create.

Story type		Story content	Who sees it
Page Like	Mike Fretto and Mary-Jane Faul like Southwest Airlines. / Southwest Airlines · Like	Someone liked your Page directly from Facebook or from the Like Box on your website at any point in time.	The friends of your fans.
Page Post Like	Fidji Simo likes adidas Soccer's album FC Dallas 4/17/11. / FC Dallas 4/17/11 / 23 · 174	One of your fans liked one of your Page posts in the last seven days.	The friends of your fans who liked your Page posts.
App Used/ Game Played	Lauryn Hale played Glory of Rome / Glory of Rome · Play	Someone used your App or played your Game at least twice or for at least 10 minutes in the last month.	The friends of the people who used your App or played your Game.
App Share	Hayes Metzger is supporting the UCSF Benioff Children's Hospital Double win. / Eventbrite – Tech-Crunch and Crunch-Gear present TRON: Legacy in 3-D (San Francisco) Eventbrite / 4 Get Tickets	Someone shared a story from your App in the last seven days.	The friends of the people who shared a story from your App.
Check-In	Lisa Carey Second time today — at Starbucks with Philip Zigoris. / Starbucks · Like / 1 1	Someone checked in and/or claimed a deal at one of your claimed Places in the last seven days using Facebook Places.	The friends of the people who checked in or claimed a Deal.
Domain Share	Mike Fretto Great cause / Autism Thing Dark T-shirt on CafePress.com www.cafepress.com / 1 Share	Someone liked a piece of content on your website using the Like button, shared a piece of content from your website using the Share button, or pasted a link to your website in his status update in the last seven days.	The friends of the people who liked or shared content from your site.

Facebook's demonstration of how advertisers on their site can take advantage of social proof to place adverts in the news feed by piggybacking on your friend's posts

Now, Facebook has launched a similar feature called Sponsored Stories. If friends use the name of a company or product in a post that they make, or "Like" a company elsewhere on the web, this feature shows the logo or other advertising visuals for that company or product attached to the friends' posts, called out in the right column among other ads, in the ticker, and more recently in the news feed. The main difference in functionality and presentation this second time is that the feature works much more like a social proof than a broad spam.

The more similar the subjects of the social proof are to you, the more likely you are to respond favorably. That's why the social media implementations work so well —the social proof is provided by people within your network. However, even a weak form of social proof can be sufficient to tip the balance. You may have noticed online advertisements for car insurance, work-from-home schemes, or mortgages that highlight how someone in your neighborhood has saved money, earned millions, or otherwise improved their life. Obviously all they are doing is geolocating your IP address, but the end result is a marginally more convincing advertisement.

Even weak forms of social proof can be effective. Advertisers wouldn't pay the extra money to customize advertisements based on the approximate location of your Internet connection unless there was some payback for them.

Will users call you out for using social proof? No. Most individuals—even when told about social proof—claim that other people's behavior doesn't influence their own. So they don't believe that they will fall for these tricks even while they are falling for them.

How to make it personal

» Prime users to do what you want by showing how other people have already done that thing.

» Make sure that these "other people" share characteristics with your users so that users identify with them as much as possible. Using someone's friends or contact list has additional influential power.

» If it's likely to benefit you, show what other people did in a similar situation. Case study white papers, Amazon.com's "people who viewed this also viewed these" and "n percent ended up buying…" widgets are good examples.

» Encourage Likes and +1s, comments, retweets, and responses to your social media activity. The social proof provided by a large number of recommendations can be highly convincing.

» Social proof works best if the social group used as the proof closely matches the current user. Use your users' profile information to craft a story that matches their needs well.

 ## Gain public commitment to a decision

Make a user's decision public and they will feel more inclined to carry through with the action and defend the decision.

New year's resolutions are hard to keep: 22 percent of people fail after one week, 40 percent after one month, and 81 percent after two years. Quitting smoking, reducing alcohol consumption, and losing weight are all hard to do.

Although the only tried-and-true method to lose 10 pounds in 48 hours is food poisoning, companies like Weight Watchers know that the social element—regular meetings where you "weigh in" and share your progress with others—are big drivers for successful weight loss and long-term weight maintenance. The key here is the shared commitment that you make to reach your goal. By meeting with and sharing encouragement with others in a similar position, it becomes easier to stick to your plans.

Getting that commitment is one thing. Sharing it with others is even more powerful. Now the user faces social reprobation if they don't follow through. This could be as simple as adding the user's name to a wall of commitments, or e-mailing the referrer of the user to say they've signed up. Commitment to a goal is much more concrete if the commitment is written down.

Many sites and apps exist to assist you with your efforts. One big motivational technique that several of the sites use is to replicate the social element by making your goals public. This way, people in your social network can see your planned and actual workouts, and leave encouraging comments for you. Runkeeper, Fitocracy, Fleetly, and MapMyRun/MapMyRide all have publicly accessible pages for each user and optional sharing via other social media such as Facebook and Twitter.

The GymPact site and iPhone app allow you to set goals ("pacts"), put money ("stakes") against them, and then check in to the location to verify that you attended. People on average miss 10 percent of their commitment days. When this happens, they have stakes deducted from their account. That money goes to reward people who did attend. (gympact.com)

HabitForge, 21habit, and GymPact take a different tack: A third party (the site or app) holds you to your commitment. 21habit and GymPact even include a financial incentive. With 21habit you pay the site up front, and then on each day that you complete your activity you get to reclaim your day's dollar. Skip a day, and your money goes to charity. Even though this might at first seem like a straight contract between the individual and the site, the act of telling the site (and subsequently being reminded on a daily basis) makes the activity external—public, rather than internal—private.

How to gain public commitment

» Persuade your users to give you access to post to their social media accounts. You probably don't have to be deceptive: If you have done a good job of selling the product or service, then it should be easy to explain how a public commitment can make the user more likely to follow through.

» Create an environment such as a forum where users can form groups with a shared commitment to performing an activity that you care about. Peer pressure can keep the group more committed.

» Display a simple metric of "success" that shows at a glance whether users are progressing toward their stated goals. This metric should be easily interpretable by users and by their extended social network. Allow users to "share" this metric as a widget on other sites to gather even more public commitment.

» Combine public commitment with an affiliate program. This gives users more motivation to share because they make money from the process of expressing their commitment.

Change opinions by emphasizing general similarities

People don't like to change opinions and will ignore counterfactual information. Instead, show them how similar your desired position is to their current opinion.

Changing your opinion on something involves admitting that you were wrong. The more public your initial statements, the more pride you must swallow in moving to the new perspective.

This is so deeply ingrained that we even have a tendency to search out and interpret information in a way that confirms our current beliefs. More interestingly, after we find sufficient information, we stop. We don't tend to seek out information that might prove us wrong. This is known as *confirmation bias.*

Clever sites that need to sell people on an idea that involves making them change their minds do it by giving users selective information that confirms their preconceptions while also supporting the concepts that the site wants to get across.

This is easier to achieve than you may think. Stephen Colbert hosts a late-night comedy show in the persona of an outraged Republican, while actually satirizing right-wing policies. Or maybe I only think he does. According to a study run by researchers at Ohio State University, viewers with right-wing tendencies still find the show funny. "Conservatives were more likely to report that Colbert only pretends to be joking and genuinely meant what he said, while liberals were more likely to report that Colbert used satire and was not serious when offering political statements."

Colbert's response when asked about his political leanings was "I have no problems with Republicans, just with Republican policies." By creating parodies of these Republican policies, Colbert could be seen as using Republican-held beliefs to change Republicans' perceptions.

Stephen Colbert: Funny to both sides of the political divide, despite parodying
Republican philosophies (Photo: Joel Jefferies from Comedy Central site)

Online, there are few better examples of changing people's opinions by
expressing similarities than DivaCup. This company discusses a generally
taboo topic (menstruation) and changes women's minds about abandoning
traditional practices (tampons and pads) and trying something that at first
glance seems like it couldn't work (an insertable silicone cup). It achieves this
by first co-opting the audience into agreeing that yes, they have experienced

the issues that the site lists, and then going on to show how the DivaCup solution is similar-to-but-better-than what the audience is currently doing. This then allows them to emphasize the positive elements of the product that people couldn't disagree with wanting (clean, hygienic, comfortable, green, and so on).

DivaCup's "have you ever..." section gets women thinking about situations that are similar to their lives. (divacup.com)

How to emphasize similarities

» Don't try to persuade people that they should change. Instead, show them how they are already doing elements of what you want them to do.

» Emphasize the positive and the similar elements rather than requiring them to think about the negative and the unfamiliar aspects.

» Talk in general terms that can be interpreted positively by any user. "Family values" is a positive term to everyone who hears it, regardless of how they interpret it.

» Talk about aspirations. "Yes, I do want to lose weight/find a partner/make tons of money/…"—people feel motivated to achieve their aspirations even if they never actually work toward them.

Use images of certification and endorsement

Membership of third-party certification schemes is cheap in comparison to the conversions it can produce. Or just create your own certification, promise, or guarantee.

In 2002, I was a user researcher at Microsoft, working on the newly announced Trustworthy Computing initiative. I was testing user comprehension of security features that would subsequently make their way into Windows XP and Windows Vista. Some of the prototypes that we used for our studies needed a trust certification logo. The designer, Angela, made up a credible-looking logo just so that we had something on the screen for the usability tests. Much to our surprise, users expressed great trust in the fake logo despite never having seen it before and never having heard of the (imaginary) certifying company.

In 2006, John Lazarchik, VP of eCommerce at Petco.com heard that a third-party security icon, when used on a home page, could improve the rate of conversion from browsers to buyers. The team ran some tests that involved displaying a security logo on the home page and on subsequent pages of the Petco.com site. Using 50–50 split A/B testing, Petco found that it could increase conversions by 1.76 percent just by adding the icon at the bottom right of the page, way below the fold. Moving the icon to the top left just below the search box gave an 8.83 percent increase in conversions. This is a massive jump in sales for a tiny piece of screen real estate—much smaller than the space taken up by an advertisement.

What makes us trust these logos? All take the form of an endorsement. The endorsement is a type of social proof, even if it originates from the site itself.

Why is it that users express trust in a logo for an imaginary company? What is it about a certification image that reassures them sufficiently to be more likely to spend money on a site? Luckily, it's all about perception rather than reality. B.J. Fogg, founder of the Stanford Persuasive Technology Lab, lists four elements to website credibility. They are: *presumed credibility* (assumptions made by the user), *surface credibility* (first impressions of the site), *reputed credibility* (third-party endorsements), and *earned credibility* (built over time).

Trust logos fall into two of these credibility categories. Surface credibility is provided in part by a professional looking certification image with words such as "guarantee" or "certified" on it. For images provided by third parties, the certification is an endorsement of the site, which is a type of reputed credibility.

Obviously these certification images are often little more than paid endorsements—getting someone else to sing the site's praises or just showing membership of an arbitration service like the Better Business Bureau (BBB). However, even paying for someone else's positive remarks sounds more credible than the site's own commentary.

It turns out that although they work well to increase the perception of trust, neither of these elements are necessarily good indicators of Fogg's fourth credibility category: earned credibility. Ben Edelman, a Harvard economics researcher, discovered that typically the sites displaying trust certifications are actually significantly less trustworthy than those that forego certification. Using MacAfee's SiteAdvisor tool to compare almost 1,000 TRUSTe certified sites with more than 500,000 non-certified websites, Edelman discovered that "TRUSTe-certified sites are more than twice as likely to be untrustworthy as uncertified sites."

However, perception seems to be more important than reality in this situation. Petco no longer uses the "Hacker Safe" logo from 2006, but they have replaced that security certification with two new "trustmarks": a McAfee antivirus message at top right and a Bizrate "customer certified" icon at bottom right. These certificates both theoretically denote earned credibility (the Bizrate icon is only available to sites with a certain level of customer satisfaction), but the aim is probably still financial. The McAfee antivirus site boasts that sites displaying its "SECURE trustmark have seen an average 12% increase in sales conversions."

Although it may not mean much in real terms, certification raises the credibility of the site marginally above that of its competitors in the eyes of visitors. In an environment in which users are unsure who they can trust, they'll take whatever they can find. That marginal level of additional reassurance may be all it takes to sway someone toward using the certified site instead of other similar destinations.

How to use certification

» Find certification authorities that you can sign up for. Options might be the Better Business Bureau, SSL certificates via your site host or domain registrar, TRUSTe certification of your privacy policy, and ratings and review companies such as Bizrate, antivirus companies, or industry accreditation programs.

» Be sure that your certification image addresses your users' concerns. Are they most worried about viruses? Your returns policy? Their credit card number's security? Talk to this fear in the certificate you display.

» Place the certification images wisely. Only use them at places during the interaction where users are likely to be looking for additional reassurance. Using them on every page might make them blend into the background too much and wastes space that could be used for other purposes.

» Consider making up your own certificate, perhaps to advertise your site's guarantee. The guarantee doesn't have to be anything special, but having a logo makes it look impressive.

Closure: The appeal of completeness and desire for order

How would you describe the following image?

   Most people would immediately say "A circle," despite the fact that there is a distinct gap in the shape, and it's actually more like a rotated capital "C" than a circle. It seems that our brains are designed in a way that favors clean, unambiguous outcomes, so we often describe items that are more ambiguous using these unambiguous terms.

In psychology, this is known as *closure*: people's "Desire for a firm solution rather than enduring ambiguity." The feeling of ambiguity or uncertainty puts people on edge. It is only when they have reached their goal or found a solution that people can feel comfortable setting the thing aside. The feeling of completeness that accompanies closure puts people at ease. Oftentimes people will deceive themselves by mentally "completing the circle" in order to reach this state of happiness rather than remaining in ambiguity.

This desire also manifests itself as a social pressure. Pride is predicated on being orderly and complete rather than sloppy and half-finished. There are ways to leverage closure online. They mainly focus on encouraging people to strive for completeness by achieving certain subgoals or collecting items until they have a full set.

Help people complete a set

The compulsion to collect, to be complete, drives people to action. Give people some initial items "free," then set them to work completing the set.

Foursquare is a location-based social media site that allows people to "check in" at locations to unlock badges. Checking in at the same location on a frequent basis may be enough to make an individual the "mayor" of that place. Although it could be seen as a game, the compulsion to keep collecting badges and to remain as the mayor of a location definitely don't harm sales at the retail locations, restaurants, and cafes that people check in to.

Codecademy does a similar thing in a learning environment. The online learning site teaches visitors to write JavaScript code. Again, it uses achievements in the form of points and badges to first encourage visitors to register, and then to encourage registered users to continue completing coding exercises and assignments. As part of Code Year (an initiative to encourage more people to become code-literate in 2012), almost 400,000 people took part in a weekly coding challenge.

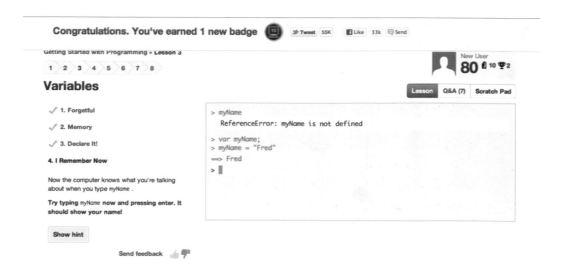

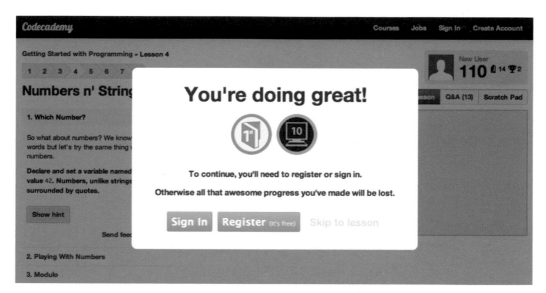

Codecademy.com encourages you to learn to program by awarding points and unlocking achievement badges (top). By showing you what you've already earned in your first session (bottom) they can encourage a sense of ownership that makes you more likely to register with the site, even though the badges have no real "value."

Sites that rely on user-generated content also need mechanisms for encouraging contributions. Question askers will come to a site that actively answers questions; the trick is to reward the answer providers. Reward comes in the form of "points" for answering questions.

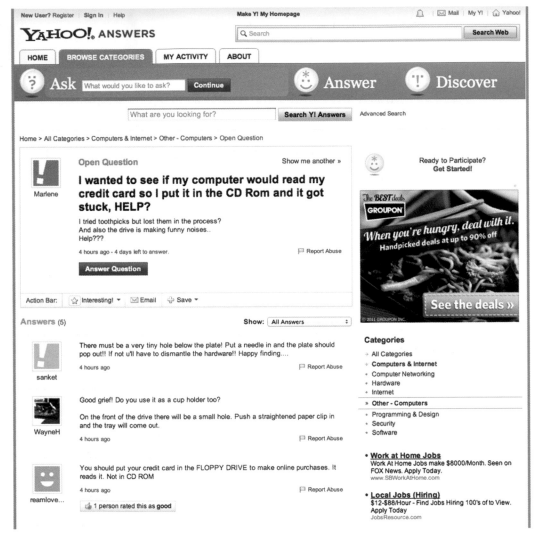

Yahoo! Answers is a crowdsourced knowledge base, which relies on user contributions to create both the questions and the answers. (answers.yahoo.com)

Sites like Yahoo! Answers have found that the reward doesn't even have to be financial. Some people will participate just for the status they achieve by providing the best answer to questions.

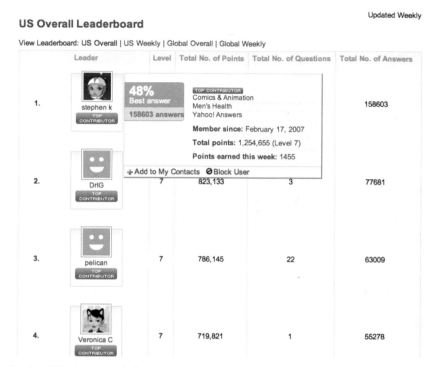

Stephen K had answered almost 160,000 questions in just under five years. That is almost four questions per hour, every hour, every day, over that period. There is no physical redemption for these points. They are merely a status symbol. (answers.yahoo.com)

Obviously, online games such as *World of Warcraft* also encourage closure through leveling up and collection of in-game items, but the real trick lies in turning nongame tasks into a type of game (often referred to as *gamification*).

Cow Clicker is the ultimate abstraction of this mechanism to its basic elements. Ian Bogost, a professor at Georgia Tech, created the *Cow Clicker* game within Facebook as a form of social commentary on gamification, the social gaming genre (of which he is not a fan) and the reward culture that it engenders.

You get a cow. You can click it. In six hours, you can click it again. Clicking earns you clicks. You can buy custom "premium" cows through micropayments (the *Cow Clicker* currency is called "Mooney"), and you can buy your way out of the time delay by spending mooney. You can publish feed stories about clicking your cow, and you can click friends' cow clicks in their feed stories. *Cow Clicker* is a Facebook game distilled to its essence.

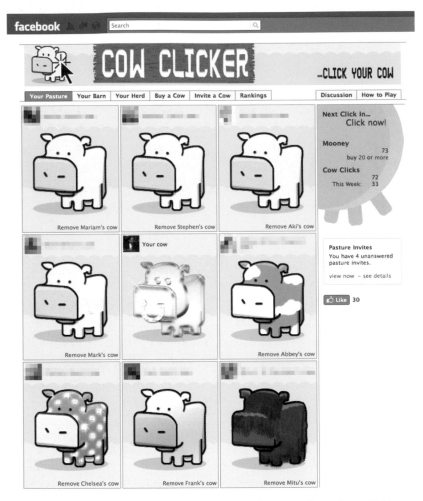

Cow Clicker: The game in which you click cows, send status updates about clicking cows, and buy new cows to click on using Mooney. The nine empty spaces around your cow are filled with friends' cows through pasture invites (viral awareness raising). The lack of purpose is the game's purpose. (Image from bogost.com)

If this doesn't make much sense to you, you probably aren't a *Farmville*, *Castleville*, or *Cityville* fan. These games, all living inside Facebook and all created by one company, Zynga, combined to produce 12 percent of Facebook's revenue in 2011. That's $445 million funded entirely by Facebook users clicking on things.

Obviously these games have slightly more content than *Cow Clicker*, but to Ian Bogost's point, they are fundamentally designed to get users to click on things, and to worry about those things sufficiently that they come back and click some more, time and time again.

An added twist is that users can reduce their level of worry (about whether their crops need watering, their cows need milking, and so on) by paying for in-game items to make their lives easier. Earning points to buy these items is theoretically possible in-game (with LOTS of clicks) but is much more easily achieved by buying points (see also the pattern "Move from money to tokens," in the chapter on Greed) or completing "offers" that give points in exchange for purchasing items from advertisers' sites.

How to help people complete a set

» Give people some achievements early in their interaction so that they get used to the concept.

» Show them the empty slots that they need to fill with more achievements.

» Provide levels of membership, with achievements to gain extra points, and potentially more benefits to reaching each level. Benefits may include the ability to do more of something that you want people to do anyway, such as moderate a forum.

» Turn it into a game, or at least give ways to game the interface. You can earn bonus points for making it look like the "gaming" is in some way illicit and thus create groups committed to maximizing their potential gains (such as the online coupon communities).

» Give users ways to progress through paying rather than through working for it. Examples are using Mooney in the *Cow Clicker* game, or the secondary market in *World of Warcraft* where you can buy anything from gold to pre-experienced game characters.

Pander to people's desire for order

Capitalize on people's compulsion to be tidy. Make them "tidy up" by giving you the information you want or completing the tasks you require.

Dan Lockton studies how design in the physical world can encourage certain behaviors. He demonstrates how desire for order can be used to make people perform tasks in the physical world. The following pictures show a light switch in its on position (left) and off position (right). Users of the switch can only achieve closure by turning off the light, thereby saving energy.

This light switch just cries out to be "aligned," which then turns off the associated light. It was created to demonstrate easy ways in which people can be encouraged to save power. It is part of the AWARE project, by Loove Broms and Karin Ehrnberger at the Interactive Institute in Stockholm.

Social networking sites such as LinkedIn need your data to create the connections that make a useful network. However, it normally takes a bit of convincing to get users to do something as personal as sharing an address book. To add encouragement, LinkedIn uses language that makes it clear that you are currently in a disorderly state. Claiming "your profile is 25% complete" creates enough disharmony to convince people to hand over their e-mail address book, add more connections, and start recommending others in the network.

25% profile completeness

Profile Completion Tips (Why do this?)

- Add a position (+15%)
- Add your education (+15%)
- Add a picture (+5%)
- Add your summary (+5%)
- Add your specialties (+5%)
- Ask for a recommendation (+5%)

See Who You Already Know on LinkedIn

Searching your email contacts is the easiest way to find people you already know on LinkedIn. Learn More

Your email:

Email password:

Continue

We will not store your password or email anyone without your permission.

Do you use Outlook, Apple Mail or another email application?
Import your desktop email contacts »

LinkedIn profile completeness—why WOULDN'T I give them access to my e-mail so that I can be 100 percent complete?

Making it clear that you have a small number of connections in comparison to other individuals provides the motivation to start "collecting" more contacts. If you think this is silly, explain the existence of sites such as TopLinked.com, which provide a way to quickly grow your social networks (through "open networking"), for the small recurring fee of $10/month. This turns social networking from a useful linking of like-minded individuals into a lowest common denominator competition fuelled by pride.

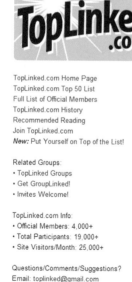

TopLinked.com Home Page
TopLinked.com Top 50 List
Full List of Official Members
TopLinked.com History
Recommended Reading
Join TopLinked.com
New: Put Yourself on Top of the List!

Related Groups:
• TopLinked Groups
• Get GroupLinked!
• Invites Welcome!

TopLinked.com Info:
• Official Members: 4,000+
• Total Participants: 19,000+
• Site Visitors/Month: 25,000+

Questions/Comments/Suggestions?
Email: toplinked@gmail.com

The TopLinked 50

The Top 50 most connected people out of 29 million+ LinkedIn members!
(only active TopLinked.com Members are linked*)

- **Click here to** *Power Check/Connect* -
(The quick and easy way to connect with the TopLinked.com Top 50!)

Rank	Name (linked to profile)	Connections
1	Ron Bates	40,000+
2	Kenneth Warner Weinberg	40,000+
3	Andrew 'Flip' Filipowski	40,000+
4	Wei Guan	30,000+
5	Steven Burda	30,000+
6	Jan Mulder	25,000+
7	Marc Freedman	25,000+
8	William (Bill) Howell	25,000+
9	Malcolm Lawrence	25,000+
10	Pier Paolo Mucelli	25,000+
11	Peter R. Luiks	25,000+
12	Scott Sullivan	25,000+
13	Jan Karel Kleijn	25,000+
14	Marjan Bolmeijer	25,000+
15	Barack Obama**	20,000+
16	Christian Mayaud	20,000+
17	John L. Evans	20,000+
18	Shally Steckerl	20,000+
19	Adam S. Levy	20,000+
20	Octavio Pitaluga Neto	20,000+

TopLinked.com encourages "open networking," appealing to contact collectors everywhere.

TopLinked used to run a high-score table listing the LinkedIn members with the most connections. Back in 2008, several celebrities were near the top of the list.

> *Yes, #15 on this list of the "TopLinked people on all of LinkedIn" is the real senator and possible future President of the United States of America, Barack Obama! He has not officially signed up as a TopLinked.com Member (probably because he is currently rather busy running for office), but, as his campaign message is about inclusiveness and bringing people together, we know we can continue to count on him to be welcoming of TopLinked.com people who wish to help him further expand his LinkedIn network. . . . The real key question though is whether he can make it to the Top Spot on this list! :-)*

TOPLINKED.COM, 2008

This again appealed to users' competitive nature but was completely counter to LinkedIn's mission to create a "professional network of trusted contacts." LinkedIn claims that "Connecting to someone on LinkedIn implies that you know them well" and that makes business sense. LinkedIn makes its money from analyzing the connected nature of individuals to determine their traits and target advertising. If the connections are random, there is no money to be made. It also makes money from upselling users on premium features such as wider searches (beyond third-level connections) and the ability to send "InMails" to people outside their network. Again, if an individual has a massive network, this reduces the need for these services. Steven Burda, a highly linked individual, claims he can reach 97 percent of LinkedIn members via his third-level connections.

When LinkedIn changed users' profiles to show a generic label of "500+ Connections" rather than a true figure, TopLinked could no longer maintain its leader board. Instead, it had the clever idea to allow people to buy Top Supporter points (again on a monthly recurring subscription). The person who purchases the most Top Supporter Points each month gets to the top of the Top Supporter List.

This Top Supporter List has no credibility outside the TopLinked site. It no longer reflects the member's position within the LinkedIn community or has any relationship to their actual number of contacts. However, it is still a list, and there is still a way for people to get themselves to the top of the list, by purchasing more Top Supporter Points. Surprisingly, that is all that it takes for people to want to take part.

Recruiters and salespeople seem to figure frequently in the TopLinked Top Supporter List. Open networking may be a way to scrape more names to spam with job openings, but it's a shotgun approach that values quantity over quality and so appeals to the bottom feeders in the industry. Sad as it is to feel that you need to pay to have friends, especially if most of those friends are as freaky as you are, there are obviously people out there who are prepared to fork over cash for this type of completeness.

How to leverage desire for order

» Show users the disorder associated with their account. Give them easy ways to resolve the disorder into harmony.

» Create a sense of progression by providing a set of logical steps toward order.

» Show gaps where data is missing—if possible make these gaps public to shame users into completing the empty pieces.

» Reward tidiness. Give users more access, power, points, or whatever other unit of currency you use as they complete more of the actions you want.

Manipulating pride to change beliefs

Society has an ambivalent attitude to pride. As we mentioned in the introduction there are different levels of pride. Pride in our appearance or in our abilities (self-esteem) is acceptable, so long as it doesn't lead to vanity. But too much pride causes people to enter into hubris, where they become stuck in their ways, sure their current practices and beliefs are right.

Trying to change the decisions that led people to their current state is hard. Any new concept that you introduce that differs from their existing knowledge will create cognitive dissonance. People don't like being forced to consider two competing ideas because that keeps them out of the state of closure that they desire. It doesn't help that the people who most feel a need for closure tend to also have attitudes associated with dogmatism, a need for order, and conservatism.

So people will have a tendency to ignore or rationalize away the newly introduced concept. Resolving the dissonance this way allows them to carry on with their beliefs, however strange this makes their reasons seem to others.

Getting stuck in a certain mindset—inertia—causes people to act in certain ways that you can either seek to leverage or to overcome.

To leverage the inertia, you can provide supporting reasons to prevent buyers' remorse, and to help remove any trace of cognitive dissonance. Hearing the same message repeated many times from different sources or seeing many other people behaving the same way (social proof) gives added weight to someone's decision. This is especially true if friends or members of the same group provide the social proof. The social proof provides credibility, which is especially useful to help people justify infrequent or unfamiliar purchases.

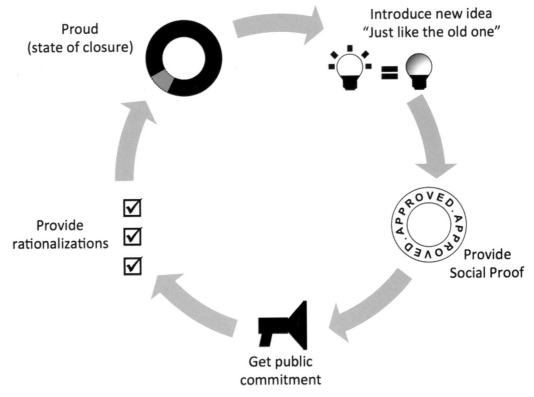

Complete the loop by first introducing change in a subtle way, and then helping people justify their new behaviors. Once they get to the point of publicly admitting their new stance, you can set that behavior and create closure once again.

Social proof is also useful when you want to start overcoming inertia and get people to make a change. Because the need for closure is associated with conservatism, a good appeal is through subtle changes in behavior led by example. For instance you can show how someone's friends are doing this new thing, and demonstrate how the new thing is similar to the old way they currently use. Highlighting the general similarities between two views helps to ease people across to the new perspective.

It is important to provide confidence that your proposed new way of doing things is acceptable. Appealing to people's need for order by using images of certification provides credibility that is itself a form of social proof.

If you can get people to make a public commitment to the new approach, it means they can no longer back down. The public commitment might set off more cognitive dissonance, but now, because they have openly aligned themselves with the new approach, the dissonant belief that will be expelled is the old one.

At this point, the individual will start to rationalize their new behaviors. Now you are back in the position of wanting to leverage inertia again. You can assist by providing reasons that allow the individual to keep their self-esteem intact, and by showing social proof for the new behaviors. The individual whose mindset you just changed will be a willing participant in this process. They will tend to be selective in what data they look for and believe. Because they are now trying to remove cognitive dissonance in favor of the new idea that you introduced, they will seek out reviews, certification, and other social proof that supports that viewpoint in order to reach closure once again.

Sloth

We excuse our sloth under the pretext of difficulty.

QUINTILIAN

THESE DAYS, THE WORD SLOTH describes laziness, but laziness is the outcome rather than the source of sloth. Sloth is actually avoidance of work or a "don't care" feeling. In earlier times, when the work being avoided was God's work, this was seen as a major sin.

Thinking of sloth as avoiding work or not caring about outcomes gives us a useful perspective; namely that people are not motivated to do more than the absolute minimum work to achieve their online aims. You could call this "lazy," but that isn't necessarily true. Instead, customers demand easy-to-use sites and software. We have been trained to look for cues that help us move forward in our tasks with the minimum of effort, and we'll often abandon sites that make us work too hard.

It doesn't take much additional design work to create an interface where the path that requires the minimum of user effort is the one that is most profitable for the developer.

Desire lines: From A to B with as few barriers as possible

You see desire lines in everyday life. Look at the landscaping around a university campus or in the parking lot of a shopping mall. If the landscaping happens to form a barrier between individuals and their destination, they will jump over it or forge a way through it.

This section of Richmond Park in London has five "official" paths. Numerous desire lines provide faster access between features. (image © 2012 Bluesky, DigitalGlobe, GeoEye, Getmapping plc, Infoterra Lts & Bluesky, The GeoInformation Group. Map data © 2012 Google)

Sure, the first couple of people must expend a little extra effort to push past the shrubbery, but soon the constant foot traffic wears a smooth trail. These informal paths, worn through the follies of the landscape architects, are known as *desire lines*. The lines follow users' perceived path of least resistance between their current location and their desired goal.

Designers have been co-opting this natural inclination for some time. The (re)design of Central Park in New York and of the University of Oregon campus both relied on observing existing desire lines that people had worn into the ground, and then building proper paths at those locations.

The easiest way to get people to your desired outcome is to ensure it follows the path of least resistance. Desire lines show us that path.

Path of least resistance

Ensure that your desired end result is on the easiest path through the process. Hide disclaimers in locations away from this path.

Why would freecreditreport.com go to the trouble to tell visitors to its home page about one of its competitors? It turns out it was forced to. Its business practices involved collecting credit card details as part of the sign-up process, and then after providing one free credit report, users would see monthly charges of $14.95 to their card.

In this image, captured in 2008, freecreditreport.com points out on its homepage that it is not the true "free" credit report site (which is annualcreditreport.com). However, its chosen location is perfect from a desire line perspective.

In 2005 the FTC filed suit against the site, alleging deceptive marketing practices. It later collected more than $1.2 million in settlements. As part of the settlement, freecreditreport.com had to put a disclaimer on its home page. That could have been bad for business, except that freecreditreport.com knew what it was doing when it redesigned its homepage to include the disclaimer.

The trick it used was to combine an understanding of where users' eyes naturally fall, and distracting designs that pull attention and create a desire to follow its preferred path. Left to their own devices, most users in Western societies scan content-rich web pages in an F-pattern. They start by reading across the top of the page, and then scan down the left edge making forays into the content whenever their eyes are attracted by (for instance) headings, paragraphs, or pictures. In application dialogs and calls to action, users tend to work from top left to bottom right, and the top-right and bottom-left corners are known as *fallow areas*. However, you can distract users from this typical flow by placing desirable objects (large, bright buttons, for example) in other locations on the page.

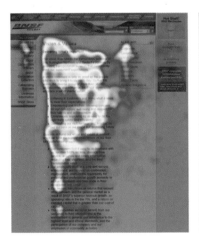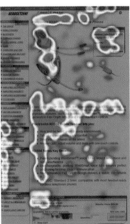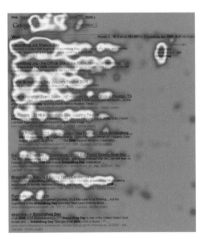

The F-pattern shows up in heat maps of users' gazes on text heavy pages. In these images, red shows where people looked the most, blue where they looked the least. (Image courtesy of Jakob Nielsen, Nielsen Norman Group, nngroup.com/articles/f-shaped-pattern-reading-web-content/)

Freecreditreport.com may as well have placed an empty gray box in the disclaimer area. The text is designed to disappear. It is low contrast, in a visual dead spot, and surrounded by much more attractive targets. This puts it far away from any desire lines. Compare that section of the page with the bright orange "call to action" button and the high-contrast panel describing the benefits of the service.

In a subsequent version of the freecreditreport.com home page, the disclosure information moved to a location above the logo. This space is normally reserved for banner advertisements, which people have learned to subconsciously filter out. This company truly understands the principle of desire lines.

Its use of desire lines didn't stop there, however. Even subsequent to the 2005 fines, freecreditreport.com was still using subscription forms that, although probably within the letter of the law, were somewhat dubious from a design perspective. It cleverly hid the information about recurring fees by placing it directly below and in the same font as the privacy policy. Theoretically, there are warnings that money will be removed from your account, but with a good understanding of user behavior, the site managed to turn its users blind to the consequences of their actions. After all, who reads privacy policies?

Mike Dean, the chief marketing officer for the Experian consumer direct division, which runs freecreditreport.com said, "We've always been a very aggressive marketer. It absolutely is the free credit report. It's not the one by the government, which is why we put the link on our front page of the landing site, and it is a free report. It's really a test drive for people to understand what's in that report because a report can be very complex."

Now if it had only spent as much time redesigning the report to make it less complex as it did designing the site to make it so effortless to avoid reading unpleasant information. …

Sufficient numbers of the general public were still taken in by this revised design that the government stepped in again. As part of the Credit CARD Act of 2009, marketers advertising free credit reporting services on television and radio were forced to include prominent disclosures about trial offers and also provide prominent links referring potential customers to the government's annualcreditreport.com website and toll free number.

Did this resolve the issue? Hardly. The sites all still exist. Now, however, rather than offering you a free credit report, they offer you a free credit score. Did you catch the difference? Apparently that is sufficient to bypass the legislation. Anyone requiring a credit report can still obtain one from these sites (including freecreditreport.com), only now the report costs $1, so that it isn't technically "free" and thus again skirts the legislation. And now that it offers scores rather than reports, freecreditreport.com has completely removed the disclosure language from its website. Oh, and it successfully lobbied the FTC to allow advertisements for its services on the government's "official" credit report site, which has turned out to be particularly lucrative because 14 precent of consumers apparently proceeded to buy services from companies like freecreditreport.com after viewing these ads.

How to design for the path of least resistance

» Design and test desire lines on your web pages and promotional e-mails. Ensure that users' eyes are drawn to the items you want them to see, and away from items you'd rather they didn't see.

» Move any mandatory disclosures far away from the path of least resistance.

» Use low-contrast text in "dead" areas of the screen (top right, bottom left) to hide information. Alternatively, make it look like an advertisement so that people skip over it without reading it.

» Label buttons with dynamic calls to action to encourage users to move forward without reading too much on the screen.

» Make buttons large and colorful to attract attention toward moving forward rather than reading the current page.

» Hide content by placing it below the action buttons on the page. When users find the action button, they're ready to move on.

Reduced options and smart defaults smooth the decision process

It's no surprise that people stick to their known habits and products even in the face of evidence that other options would be better for them. In most Western societies, a trip to the supermarket can quickly turn into a rapid-fire quiz show. Do you want your tuna in brine, spring water, or oil? Was that olive oil or vegetable oil? Skipjack, albacore, yellowfin, or white? Steak or chunks? Dolphin-friendly for just another couple of pennies? What about sardines or salmon instead? It's easier just to grab the brand you used last time and run.

And it's not just the food aisles. There were 352 distinct types of toothpaste on offer in U.S. supermarkets in January 2011, with 69 of these introduced in 2010. With all this choice, they run the risk of scaring people off. Research suggests that the issue here is that people confuse the large number of options with importance. This then leads to spending more time trying to make a decision than the decision actually merits.

Companies want people to make decisions while they are in the store or on the site rather than postponing them, or worse still, choosing to make the decision elsewhere. So what do they do?

Provide fewer options

The more items, the more likelihood of procrastination.

Barry Schwartz suggests in his book *The Paradox of Choice* that choice paralyzes us and makes us dissatisfied. The more choices we have available for us, the higher our expectations become. The higher our expectations, the more likely we are to be disappointed when the outcome isn't exactly what we want. In contrast, if the only choice is "take it or leave it," we'll be happy that we even had that option.

In an experiment where participants had to choose chocolates to sample, Sheena Iyengar and Mark Lepper found that even though participants enjoyed the choice process more with 30 chocolates than with 6, they felt more responsible for the choice, and later proved more dissatisfied and regretful of the choices they made. The participants were subsequently considerably less likely to choose chocolates rather than money as compensation. And that's just for chocolates. This "choice overload" gets much worse when there are financial or personally significant long-term outcomes at stake.

Schwartz suggests that people fall into two groups when making decisions. *Maximizers* need to be confident that every decision they make is the best. They'll compare every option and worry even after their purchase that they maybe didn't get the best deal. *Satisficers* understand that above a certain quality or aesthetic threshold almost any of the choices available to them would be sufficient. Their strategy is to choose the first option that meets their requirements and then move on with their lives quickly without having to search for too long.

Sites that present options need to deal with both types of people. The maximizers must feel like they got the best deal, whereas the satisficers need fast access to an option that sufficiently meets their expectations.

The simplest solution is to cut down the number of choices available. Reducing the number of options lowers the time necessary for comparison and leaves people feeling better about their decisions. However, maximizers like knowing that they chose from all the available options, so just presenting three alternatives may not be sufficient. The problem here is that they may look to other sellers for more choices. So the trick is to demonstrate that you have sufficient options to keep the maximizers happy but also provide tools that allow both the maximizers and the satisficers to find the options they want quickly.

The three techniques you can use (alone or in combination) are to present many compatible choices, to use a recommendation engine or filter, and to offer a best choice guarantee. Brands that offer greater variety of compatible (that is, focused and internally consistent) options are perceived as having greater commitment and expertise in the category, which, in turn, enhances their perceived quality and purchase likelihood.

When you want to increase the perceived importance of making the decision, allow users to choose between multiple similar options (all with positive outcomes for you). The longer they spend in this illusion of choosing, the more importance they will attribute to the resulting decision (and the more they'll be wedded to it).

But be careful. The composition of the items must be consistent; for example, present variations of gourmet chocolates rather than showing both gourmet and cheap chocolate bars. The comparison must also be aligned—for instance varying cocoa percentage or offering many flavors but not varying simultaneously along both dimensions. It's a trade-off because offering more choices leads to a more difficult and frustrating decision process but a potentially higher perception of brand quality.

One of the key places that multiple compatible options are useful is in configurators such as when choosing options for a new car. Here, it's important that the company be seen to have flexible alternatives that allow customers to obtain just the vehicle they want, but it's also important not to overwhelm potential buyers. These configurators reduce the load on customers by presenting options in groups (drivetrain, body, interior) and by also offering packages that combine many options into a single trim level, ideal for the satisficers.

To reduce the confusion caused by the number of options while still retaining the perception of quality, many sites employ recommendation engines or filters. Recommendation engines provide a small set of options based on either comparison with prior behavior or on answers to a set of preference questions.

Netflix uses a recommendation engine to suggest new movies based on ones that customers have already watched. Its business is so dependent upon this functionality that it recently offered a one million dollar prize to anyone who could increase the accuracy of the engine by more than 10 percent. Currently, 75 percent of movies watched on Netflix come from a recommendation made by the site.

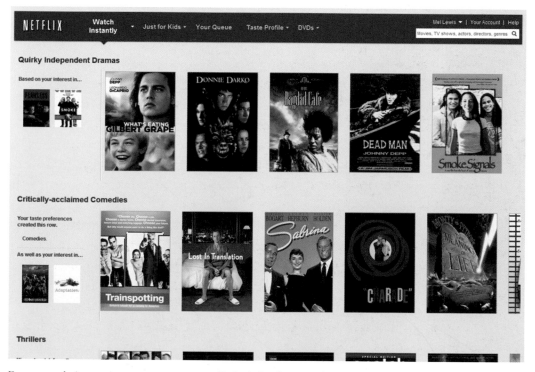

Recommendation engines are a great way to limit choice from an otherwise overwhelming quantity of items. (Netflix.com)

Filters rely less on preference algorithms and more on on-screen choices. Customers refine a product search by choosing successive properties of the product they are looking for—size, color, style, and brand—until they have narrowed the set down to a manageable group. Because individuals are responsible for each successive decision, they should still feel invested in the outcome but not overwhelmed by the number of items they've discarded during the process.

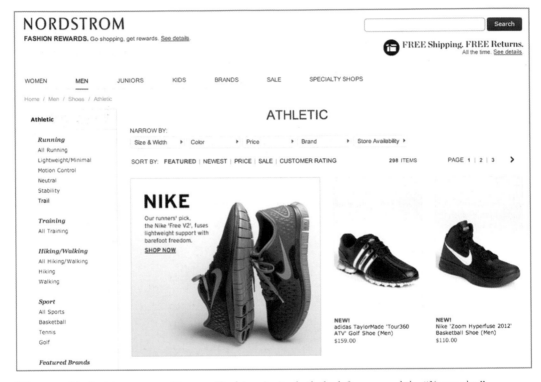

Filters provide decision support. Here, on Nordstrom's site, both the left menu and the "Narrow by:" functionality provide filters to reduce the number of choices. (Nordstrom.com)

The best-choice guarantee reassures customers that whatever decision they make, it's guaranteed that they got the best possible deal. Travel sites, rental car companies, and hotels use this technique primarily to persuade customers to shop at their corporate site rather than through third parties.

The best-choice guarantee has the side benefit of comforting both maximizers and satisficers. Maximizers now know that even if they were to find a better deal elsewhere, this site would match the price. Satisficers can narrow their search to just this site, confident that it contains suitable options comparable to ones they'd find elsewhere.

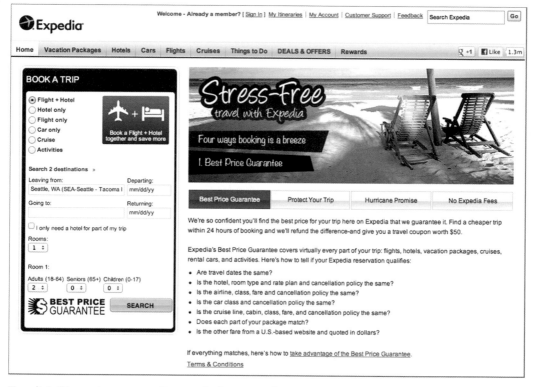

Expedia's "Best price guarantee" reassuringly prevents buyer's remorse for maximizers while simultaneously telling satisficers that they've found a suitable place to buy. (Expedia.com)

A combination of filters, recommendations, and guarantees can convince even the most hard-core maximizer that they've performed all the necessary research. That same set of functionality will allow a satisficer to quickly slice through the many different options and find one that they feel suits their needs.

How to design for fewer options

» If you want users to make a quick decision about your services, don't give them too many options. More choices lead to more procrastination.

» Conversely, if you want to increase the perceived importance of a decision, or if customization is important, ensure that the only choices available to users are between multiple compatible options within narrow boundaries.

» If you have a larger number of items, use a recommendation engine or filters to quickly bring the number down to a manageable set.

» If you can't easily reduce the number of available items, speed people to a decision by reassuring them with a best-choice guarantee.

 ## Pre-pick your preferred option

Prime people so that they are open to accepting the choice you highlight.

Psychologists have known for a long time that if they show you specific words or pictures beforehand, you'll find it easier to recall those items or related ones in a later test, even after you have consciously forgotten the specific words. This effect is called *priming*.

This is one reason why you see so much brand-related advertising. Rather than specifically telling you to buy a certain thing, the adverts build a picture of a brand associated with a specific location (say a bar), emotion (perhaps happiness), or occasion (for instance a celebration). The next time you are in a bar for someone's birthday party, all that brand priming comes straight back from your subconscious brain and hits you. Now you aren't going to get a rum and coke; you're going to get a Bacardi and Coca-Cola. You're not going to buy a beer; you're going to buy a Budweiser.

Websites exploit this same effect by helping people "recognize" one of the options as acceptable, by priming with suitable words or concepts beforehand. Priming can take several forms. It can be as subtle as brand-related marketing or as blatant as a recommendation.

The more subtle approach works by showing potential customers evidence of people being successful after choosing the preferred option. This way, because they've seen the same recommendation elsewhere before they make the decision, then social proof will kick in, convincing them that this is the correct choice.

Another way to prime is to draw people in with a proposition such as best value or highest quality, and then label the preferred option as the one that provides the value or quality. This works well on targeted marketing campaigns because anyone who clicks through to the site from a specific advertisement can be pretty much guaranteed to have been interested in the initial proposition. Now, by matching the label on the preferred option to the proposition they reacted to, people will be directed to the choice that you want them to make.

The proposition that led to this page focused on protecting your family, so the choices are presented in terms of family security. (Norton.com)

A slightly harder but equally rewarding type of priming requires undertaking research to understand people's motivations, and then using terms that fulfill those motivations. If we're motivated to save, we'll want the cheapest option; if we're motivated to keep ourselves to ourselves, we'll want the one that promises to keep us private.

A more blatant but effective form of priming happens within the list of options. Adding a word such as "recommended" or "preferred" can either rely on social proof (most people do this) or authority (we say you should do this). When Microsoft wanted more people to enable automatic updates within Windows XP (with good intentions; it helped prevent virus proliferation) it relied on its authority as the creator of the operating system to recommend a course of action during the installation process. The priming in this instance happens beforehand to set the scene or build authority. Unless people feel like they have been given enough information to make a decision, or enough information to trust the site to make the decision for them, they won't be ready to accept a recommended option.

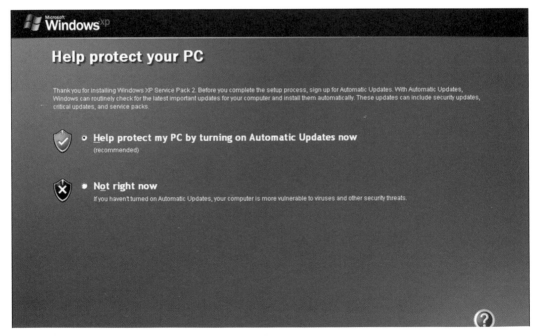

The choice to enable automatic updates in Windows XP Service Pack 2 pre-chooses the preferred option. This was probably the first widespread use of the term "recommended" next to an option to reinforce the choice.

Sites also default the selection to the option that they would prefer you to pick. Defaulting to a certain option relies in part on sloth (it takes more work to change the option than to leave it) and in part on the recognition brought about by the prior priming.

How to design for preferred options

» Convince people that you have given them sufficient information to make a decision by priming them so that the options you present seem familiar rather than strange.

» Ensure your recommendations look credible by priming with supporting information or demonstrations of your authority on that topic.

» Put the action that you want people to perform as the default. As long as you've built up sufficient credibility, they'll do what you want.

Make options hard to find or understand

Place opt-outs out of the way and obfuscate.

How many End User License Agreements have you read? How many Privacy Statements? How many Terms of Use documents? Unless you're currently wearing a tin-foil hat, I suspect the number is small. In all my years of observing usability studies, I can probably count on the fingers of one hand the number of people who purposefully read these documents during the course of their interactions with software and websites. Instead, most people notice that there's a link that says "privacy policy" and just click the Next button. It doesn't matter that the privacy policy could actually say, "You have no privacy," the assumption is that if the site is volunteering to share that information with you, it must be OK.

One reason that people quickly click past the license agreement, terms of use, privacy policy, and all the other formal-sounding agreements is because they are displayed at a time when people are trying to perform a different task (the one the software or site is designed to do), so they just swat any interrupting dialog out of the way. Another reason is that the text is boring and hardly intelligible.

One company, PC Pitstop, even hid a customer offer in the End User License Agreement for its Optimize product. It took 4 months and 3,000 downloads before anyone noticed it and contacted them to claim the reward.

This isn't to say that users are unconcerned about privacy, just that given the choice between reading several pages of legalese or trusting that the company won't do anything terrible with your data, they resolve the cognitive dissonance (see the chapter on Pride) and give in to sloth by leaning toward trusting the company.

Of course, that trust isn't always earned. Between 2007 and 2009, several U.S. Internet service providers (ISPs) installed ad-serving technology produced by a company called NebuAd that could inject advertisements into their customers' web pages. At about the same time, users in Europe experienced ads served by a similar technology called Phorm. Typically, this technology (which used deep-packet inspection to collect and forward user behavior information to NebuAd's servers) was introduced to users via a change in the privacy policy buried on the ISP's corporate web pages and was opt-out (therefore on by default). One ISP, Embarq, when questioned by the U.S. Government's House Energy and Commerce Committee, said that it had a 0.06 percent opt-out rate.

Customers could easily be forgiven for not checking updates to their ISP's terms of service because they probably consider Internet access to be just another utility like electricity or water. They probably visit the ISP's site rarely, if ever. However, it seems that people are just as lax when it comes to the products they use every day.

Facebook launched in 2004 with the concept that only your friends get access to the personal information you post. Over the years, this philosophy has changed, with Facebook's founder, Mark Zuckerberg, claiming in a 2010 interview that the new social norm is openness, not privacy. "We view it as our role in the system to constantly be innovating and be updating what our system is to reflect what the current social norms are. … [We asked ourselves] what would we do if we were starting the company now and we decided that these would be the social norms now and we just went for it."

The path of least resistance through Facebook's privacy options is to never visit the privacy settings page, and instead just accept these defaults. But that leads to some interesting "openness" issues. The default overall privacy setting makes information available to everyone; ads default to social ads; third-party advertising is allowed; third-party websites get data about you to allow instant personaliza-tion; and your timeline is visible in public searches.

That's a lot of information being shared with a lot of people—which would be fine if the sharing was intentional and easily managed. But here, again, sloth is working in Facebook's favor. Although 71 percent of 18–29-year-old social network users say they've changed privacy settings, only 55 percent aged 50–64 have moved from the defaults. Only 44 percent of young adult Internet users say they've taken steps to limit how much personal information is available about them online, and that figure reduces to 25 percent of users who are aged 50–64.

In Facebook's defense, getting privacy right is hard. As Mark Zuckerberg says, "The paradox is that people share their phone number in the telephone book but want to keep it private online." The interesting disingenuity in that statement is that there's a difference between public information and public*ized* information. Marketers must know either someone's name or their address to retrieve their phone number from the book, but on Facebook they get name, address, friends list, phone number, photos, Likes, and many other pieces of information delivered to them all wrapped up with a neat little bow.

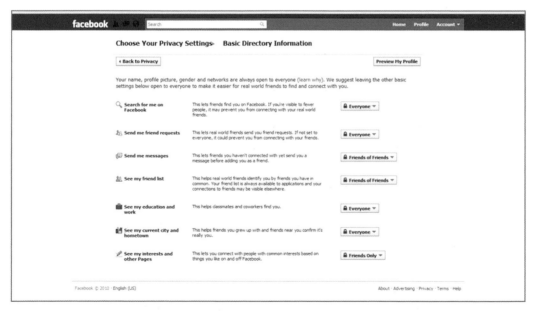

Facebook's privacy options obfuscate the issues at hand. By giving a glib and acceptable reason why people would want to share, it glosses over the actual items shared. (facebook.com)

What else can you expect when users are the product, not the customer, for Facebook? Facebook survives by sharing user data with companies so that they can better target adverts to those individuals. The more private people's lives are, the less sharing could take place, and so the less valuable would be the perception of personalized advertisements.

Facebook claims that the new social norm is openness, but it seems what's actually happening is that Facebook is relying on sloth to move people to that new social norm through changes to defaults that few will understand and fewer will bother to change.

How to design for opt-out obfuscation

» Remove any talk of opt-out activities from actual transactional points. Instead create a separate location (a "privacy center") where you can obscure the true activities with general statements.

» If you are caught doing bad things with user data, apologize profusely and then add more check boxes, explanations, and options to your privacy center, so it's even harder to divine the correct settings.

» Obfuscate. Make it too effortful to actually understand the points in the privacy statement by hiding them in legalese and convoluted options. As long as you have sufficient user trust (or sufficient utility) users will assume that you can't be doing anything too bad with their data.

Negative options: Don't not sign up!

Sign people up by default and make it harder for them to unsign than to continue down your preferred path. Use desire lines to hide the sign-up in plain sight.

However good we get at spotting the marketing opt-in check boxes on registration forms, it seems we still must read them extremely carefully. Is the box pre-checked? Is it offering to opt us in or to opt us out? Is the second box, which talks about sharing details with third parties, also prechecked? And is that one opt-in or opt-out?

The company's goal is to get you to start receiving its e-mails because inertia (sloth) means that you're less likely to make the effort to unsubscribe after you're signed up. This is the basis of negative options: Sign people up to receive something until they specifically choose to stop receiving it.

Login Information

E-mail:

Retype e-mail:

Password:

Your password must be at least 6 characters and it is not case sensitive.

Re-type Password:

E-mail Address
Your e-mail address will be used to login to the system.

I would like to receive Hotel Chocolat offers via email.   ☑

We sometimes allow other carefully selected advertisers to use our postal mailing list. Please tick this box if you would prefer not to receive their material.   ☐

I would like my recipients to receive Hotel Chocolat offers via email.
(If you would prefer not to be contacted by us with special offers using the information you have provided please contact us)   ☐

If you have opted not to receive our marketing communications you will still receive email communications that are essential to our services. This may include information about our services and your interactions with us.

Once you have filled in your details, click Register

Register ▸

Three innocuous-looking check boxes that can have major repercussions on the future size of your e-mail inbox and that of the people you send gifts to. Read carefully: Which boxes need to be checked, and which unchecked, to not receive any e-mails? (hotelchocolat.com)

A study by Steven Bellman and his colleagues found that simply using a negative option doubled opt-in rates. Phrasing an option as "Notify me about more surveys" with the check box unchecked (people must take an action to get the additional surveys) led to a 48 percent uptake. Changing the text to "Do NOT notify me about any more surveys" while still leaving the check box unchecked (people need not take any action to get the additional surveys) produced an astounding 96 percent uptake. Of course, as Bellman notes, not all of the individuals who opted in (or rather didn't *not* opt in) in the second example are actually good prospects, but the apparent consent rate is incredibly impressive.

Negative options, which are also called *advance consent marketing* by the people doing the marketing, are the foundation of book-by-mail or DVD-by-mail clubs.

Harry Scherman founded the Book-of-the-Month Club in 1926 using the concept of negative options. Despite many subsequent changes in the marketplace, this and similar clubs still survive, having moved their recruitment process online.

The process works like this: You choose an initial set of books at a reduced price as an introductory offer when you join the club. Membership of the club means that you are then sent books on a regular basis. With Book of the Month club (bomcclub.com) the editor's featured selection is sent and billed automatically unless you overcome inertia sufficiently to remember to send in a reply card, call, or navigate its website each month to decline the offer. There is a minimum annual purchase quantity, so after a while even sending in the reply card is not sufficient to stop the books from arriving. The billed price of the books is also often much higher than the comparable store price.

This is the basic premise of *negative option billing*. You are signed up to receive something unless you specifically act to prevent it from being sent. There are four main types of negative option processes:

>> *Prenotification negative options* provide periodic notice of the next item, which consumers subsequently receive if they take no action. This is the typical book club setup.

>> *Continuity negative options* are a type of subscription in which consumers receive the item on a regular schedule until they cancel.

>> *Auto renewal negative options* require purchase of a set of installments (for instance, a magazine every month for 1 year) but then automatically charge for the next set of installments unless canceled.

>> *Free-to-pay or nominal fee-to-pay negative options* use a free or cheap trial offer period coupled with subsequent payments unless consumers cancel before the trial period expires.

The irony of the term advance consent marketing is that although the sites that use it claim to have gained consent, it's not clear that their customers actually knew they were giving consent.

The Federal Trade Commission (FTC) held a hearing in 2009 to gather comments about negative option or advance consent marketing from the industry and from consumer groups. As part of the report, they note:

> The panelists revealed that many online consumers exhibit certain characteristics, including inattention, unwarranted confidence, exuberance, and a desire for immediate gratification, which make them less likely to see and read disclosures. Panelists further explained that, as result of these online characteristics, consumers become "click-happy" and quickly navigate through webpages, without paying much attention because they believe nothing will go wrong and want to complete the transaction as rapidly as possible. As a result, consumers often do not read or understand the terms of the agreements they accept.

NEGATIVE OPTIONS: A REPORT BY THE STAFF OF THE FTC'S DIVISION OF ENFORCEMENT

This is sloth at work. Consumers don't feel like they should put extra effort into reading and understanding every term and condition on the site, so they take the path of least resistance and trust that the site wouldn't do anything "bad" to them.

Of course, not all blame rests with the companies. If the deal looks too good to be true, it probably is. But finding out that it's false can be hard. An ongoing class action lawsuit against Bookspan (the company behind Book of the Month club) claims that:

> Nowhere on the face of the 25 pages of the Clubs' multi-step registration process does it disclose any the following:
>
> (1) that there is a purchase requirement;
>
> (2) the timeframe in which those purchases must take place
>
> (3) the cost per item to fulfill the purchase requirement;
>
> (4) the penalties for failing to fulfill any purchase requirement;
>
> (5) that "featured selections" will be automatically sent on a periodic basis;
>
> (6) that affirmative action will be required to stop the shipments and prevent a consumer from being charged;

and (7) the actual cost of any "featured selections."

… a consumers' purported assent to the Membership Agreement occurs on a page prior to and separate from the credit card submission page, an intentional design meant to decrease the number of prospective consumers who will actually attempt to read the Membership Agreement.

CLASS ACTION COMPLAINT FILING, MARTHA CORNETT V. DIRECT BRANDS INC. AND BOOKSPAN

And it gets even better. As if registering people in one negative option club weren't enough, in 2005, Scholastic received a $710,000 fine for violating the FTC's Negative Option rules when the small print of its club membership agreement automatically enrolled people in a second club after they became members of the first one.

Even that relatively brazen ploy seems tame in comparison to the discount clubs. These are companies who claim to offer free shipping across many sites, cash back, or other similar benefits, in return for club membership. If you've never heard of these clubs, you're not alone. Their recruitment method is to work with online retailers to incorporate the negative option agreement into the flow of signup or checkout as part of a customer offer. The offer then appears to be coming from the site itself—an entity you obviously trust because you've just done business with it.

Desire lines can span several web pages. If users expect a process such as checking out on an e-commerce site to follow a certain pattern, then they will keep clicking through (doing and reading the minimum possible on each screen) until they reach the final step.

Discount club companies take advantage of this effect to tag their sales pitch on to the end of the process using "highly aggressive sales tactics to charge millions of American consumers for services the consumers do not want and do not understand they have purchased" according to the Senate Commerce Committee, who investigated these tactics.

The system works like this: Just after checkout at many popular e-commerce sites (buy.com, expedia.com, Orbitz, US Airways), users are presented with an offer to get cash back on the purchase just by entering an e-mail address and hitting a "Yes" or "Continue" button. The choice of button text is deliberate, making the offer seem like a continuation of or necessary step in the checkout process.

What isn't clear is that the discount comes through membership of a club, and that the companies running these clubs (such as Affinion, Vertrue, or Webloyalty) have access to the "card on file" record held by the retailers they partner with, so that innocuous e-mail address is accompanied by the user's full billing details in a process known as *data pass*.

An internal Vertrue customer feedback document found that 43 percent of visitors to its "membership center" were trying "to find out about the charge on my credit card that I did not recognize." Another 44 percent had come "to cancel the program." A single person showed up "to find out more about my membership benefits."

The desire line works by removing the speed bump of re-entering credit card details. During senate hearings, Webloyalty was quite open about the impact of requiring consumers to re-enter credit card information: "With data collection on the page you can expect at least a 70 percent decrease in conversion."

And there you have it: The desire line would be broken by reminding users that there is a financial impact to their actions. After being trained for so long to expect to enter credit card details if a financial transaction is occurring, "streamlining" the process ends up confusing users and creating profit for the discount clubs and their e-commerce partners.

As the commerce committee noted,

> *Once they had acquired consumers' billing information and deceptively enrolled consumers in their negative option membership clubs, Affinion, Vetrue, and Webloyalty made money as long as consumers took no action. The three companies charged consumers month after month for services that consumers did not use and did not understand they had purchased. When consumers finally realized that the three companies were charging them, Affinion, Vertrue, and Webloyalty withheld important information about the charges from consumers and made it as difficult as possible for consumers to get their money back.*
>
> SENATE COMMITTEE HEARING ON AGGRESSIVE SALES TACTICS ON THE
> INTERNET AND THEIR IMPACT ON AMERICAN CONSUMERS

A typical interstitial "offer" during checkout, inserted into CafePress.com's site by FreeShipping.com. Interestingly, of 34,262,674 members who were promised automatic cash gifts or other incentives, the Senate Committee found that only 3 percent actually received the promised enrollment benefit.

By sliding the agreement into an otherwise familiar process, and by using the same style of wording that the process normally uses, it is possible to get users to agree to things that they would never normally countenance.

A key part of the success of the discount club enrollment process is that it relies on the concept of negative options: Much like book or CD club membership, consumers are charged unless they take an action. In the case of the book club, that action would be to cancel or return the book that has been sent. In the case of the online discount club, it's hard to know exactly what the negative option is, short of calling to cancel membership, which as the Senate Committee noted was not an easy option.

Opting out of a negative option scheme can be hard. First, consumers must notice that they are part of it to start with. As you've seen, that doesn't necessarily happen at enrollment time. In the discount club example, most customers' first indication that they were club members came when they examined their credit card bills.

After they've noticed, customers must find a way to unsubscribe. The book clubs have penalties if members try to leave before their commitment period finishes. The discount clubs find ways of penalizing people who try to call their helpdesk by having long wait times and staff who are more concerned with selling additional benefits than canceling existing ones. Often, the telephone helpdesks direct customers to a paper form that they must fill out to complete the cancellation process, declaring that they need a customer's signature to close the account, even though none was apparently needed to open it.

These tactics are designed to wear consumers down. The harder it is to cancel the membership, the more people's slothful behavior will kick in. A large proportion of people will fail to follow through with these demands. Perhaps the regulators should insist that opting out take as few clicks from the homepage as the process of opting in, using links or buttons equally as prominent.

How to design for negative options

» Choose your type of negative option and design around it:

  » **Prenotification**: Draw people in with reduced-price offers, and then recoup your money over the minimum subscription period.

  » **Continuity**: Stress the benefits of regular updates and the lower relative cost compared to the nonsubscription rate.

  » **Auto-renewal**: Emphasize the savings that customers will obtain over the course of the subscription; de-emphasize that you'll be charging them for the next subscription automatically.

  » **Free-to-pay**: Offer a free trial period, but capture credit card information anyway. Believable reasons for gathering card information may be to verify an account, to charge a nominal fee, or to pay for a separate transaction. Many customers will forget they have signed up by the time the trial period is over.

» Integrate your signup requests within flows that users complete in a semi-automatic manner such as registration or checkout.

» Use button labels like "Continue" or "Yes" to associate the negative option offer with the flow that it is integrated into.

» Offer subsequent opt-out of the service, but require users to perform a difficult task (completing and mailing in a paper form, for instance) to opt out. This leads to large cancellation abandonment rates.

Sloth: Is it worth the effort?

It is human nature to want the greatest outcome for the least amount of work. Once we internalize some useful behaviors we tend to re-use them constantly, even if they aren't necessarily the best fit for the task we're performing. Clicking "next" without reading all the text on the screen normally serves us well. That's why we are sometimes surprised to subsequently find out that we signed up for more than we'd bargained for. The normal behavior failed us when a savvy marketer slid their proposition onto the fallow areas of the page away from the desire line.

But it isn't just straight-out deception that leads us to unintentional choices. Our sloth also leads us to accept default options either because we can't be bothered to change them, or when we have run out of decision-making energy.

In the United States, many employers offer personal retirement savings plans (401[k] plans) for their employees. Sign-up is typically optional, and once started, employees can choose how much to contribute. Those employers who automatically enrolled new employees saw higher rates of contribution than when staff had to make the personal effort to enroll. In both instances, many staff couldn't be bothered to change the default state. This has major implications for the future financial health of the country because participation in personal retirement plans reduces the burden on Social Security. Interestingly, many of the automatically enrolled staff kept both the default contribution level and fund allocation, which shows that it makes sense to set the default option to the behavior that you want to encourage.

If making even one decision is hard, consider the effect of making multiple decisions. After making a series of decisions, people tire of the process and start to accept the default option more frequently. The effect is stronger when the first decisions that people must make are the ones with the most options. It seems that we have limited reserves of decision-making potential, and once those have been depleted we just can't make more evaluations. We end up either giving in to temptation or accepting the default suggestion.

We also use the most convenient method to complete our tasks, and tend to stop as soon as we get acceptable results. Companies can hide a lot of information on a site, quite confident that we won't seek it out because it's obfuscated inside a Terms of Service document or obscured by euphemisms in a "privacy center."

Often it's easier just to keep doing what we've always done than to make a change, even if that change would save us time, money or the hassle of a spam-filled inbox.

So yes, it is worth the bother for companies to design with customers' sloth in mind. Manipulating desire lines, recommending defaults, obfuscating important information, and carefully wording negative options can all lead to higher levels of compliance.

Gluttony

Too soon, too expensively, too much, too eagerly, too daintily.

St. Thomas Aquinas, *Summa Theologica*, 1274

GLUTTONY OCCURS WHEN WE over-consume to the point of extrava-gance or waste. Historically gluttony was seen as a major sin (it distracted people from their religious observances), but today it's almost as if gluttony is expected in Western culture. We demonstrate our wealth by showing an overabundance of "stuff."

Companies encourage this overabundance by making us feel like we deserve to be rewarded and by escalating our level of commitment beyond what we first intended, drawing us in from early engagement through to full-on compliance. Sites also make us fearful of missing out—scarcity, exclusivity, and loss aversion play on the fears behind gluttony.

Deserving our rewards

We are easily fooled into gluttony. Just having healthy options available on menus or among the selections from a vending machine is sometimes enough to make our brains think we've satisfied our health and nutrition goals, and therefore have permission to choose less honorable options.

The average restaurant meal in the United States is four times larger now than it was in the 1950s, yet we might still be fitting into the same size clothes as we always have—not because we've stayed slim, but because our clothes have grown. Not in the sense of Betabrand's gluttony pants, which have three waist-line buttons labeled *piglet*, *sow*, and *boar* "to accommodate waistline expansion during feeding time," but because what was a size 14 dress in the 1970s is not the same size garment today. *The Economist* found that women's size 14 (UK) clothes are about 3 inches larger in the hips than they were in 1970, thus about the equivalent of a 1970s size 18. Men's clothes also lie: A recent *Esquire* investigation found that some brands of 36-inch trousers actually measured as much as 41 inches.

The one thing this expansion does is makes us feel good about ourselves—we can still fit into the same size clothes as we did years ago, and so we feel flattered and thus more likely to buy from the companies that accommodate us.

CHOOSE SIZE & BUY ~~$90~~ $60

The Facts

Caramel Cotton Canvas Pants with Glutton Print Liner

HOW DO THEY FIT?
Straight legged, relaxed fit. Not baggy. These pants fit true to size. In case of overeating, extra buttons let you expand the waist and give your distended stomach extra room.

WHAT IF MY INSEAM IS 30" OR 34"?
We're a small business, so we offer only a couple of lengths right now. Fortunately, any tailor can hem our pants to a great fit.

HOW DO I CARE FOR THEM?
They're prewashed. Wash in cold water, tumble dry on low heat.

Waistband + pockets feature graphics depicting the life cycle of a glutton.

A trio of ivory buttons (lovingly named Piglet, Sow, + Boar) indicate precisely how far your waistline has expanded with each meal.

soft caramel canvas

burgundy colored cotton liner

✱ Each pair comes with its own napkin!

Betabrand's Gluttony Pants: "The first trousers equipped with their own napkin." (betabrand.com)

Gluttony is about conspicuous consumption, about finding bargains regardless of whether the bargain item was a necessary purchase, and about a feeling that we deserve what we purchase.

From a persuasion perspective, gluttony is actually an easy way to draw people in. With the apparent lack of embarrassment about gluttony in current Western culture, all that is required is to make people think, "I've earned it; I deserve it."

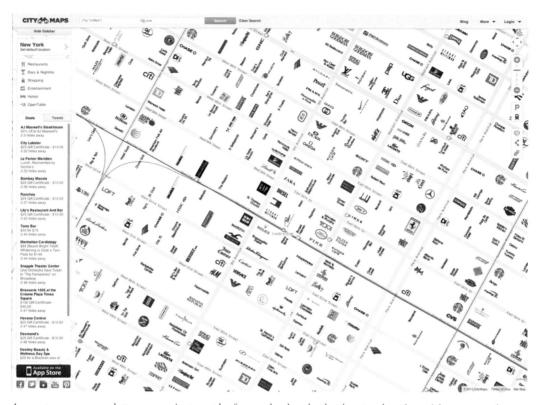

A map to encourage gluttony—navigate not by famous landmarks, but by store locations. (citymaps.com)

Make customers work for a reward

People put more value on a reward that is not available to everyone.

Canadian Tire is a retail and automotive service company with more than 480 stores across Canada. In 1961 it introduced Canadian Tire Money as a fuel purchase loyalty program, giving customers Canadian Tire "bank notes" as a reward, at a rate of 5 percent of the fuel purchase price.

Over time the reward proportion has fallen to 0.4 percent of purchase price, but even this relatively meager return hasn't stopped customers from saving the notes, even for inordinate lengths of time. It took one Edmonton man 15 years to save enough rewards to purchase a ride-on lawnmower. The mower was priced at $1,053, which required Canadian Tire money equivalent to spending $263,250, or $17,550 per year, at the store.

Canadian Tire money is also often accepted at other locations in the country. The folk singer Corin Raymond collected donations of the currency to pay for $3,500 of recording studio time for his album *Paper Nickels*, which includes a song with the refrain "Don't spend it honey, not the Canadian Tire money, we've saved it so long."

Corin Raymond used Canadian Tire money donated by thousands of individuals to finance album production. Many of the bank notes in this image are 5 cent, 10 cent, or 25 cent denominations. (dontspendithoney.com)

It appears that despite the seemingly tiny savings that Canadian Tire and other similar discount schemes provide, they attract fervent audiences. The question is, why?

Seth Priebatsch, a gamification expert who runs the company SCVNGR, suggests that just handing a coupon to customers means that they will assign a value to it equal to its redemption value. However, if they have to unlock, win, or otherwise work for that coupon, then there is an additional emotional impact that translates into additional perceived value for the individual.

Purchasing items to save tiny denomination Canadian Tire "bank notes" toward a challenging and seemingly unattainable goal fits nicely into this category.

The most value to the business is when the user perceives that there is more personal value than the face value of the coupon. A hard-won $1 discount may be worth disproportionately more in terms of loyalty than handing out $5 vouchers to everyone who enters the store.

The best perceived value occurs when the barrier to getting the discount is set at the correct height so that the right number of customers decide it's worth the effort or risk to participate. It's likely to be the most ardent (hopefully this equates to the most valuable too) customers who are prepared to jump through the most hoops.

How to create extra reward value

» To make customers value even a small reward, make them work for it, either by collecting items over time or by performing a task to get the reward.

» Increase the perceived value of the reward by making it harder to achieve, but keep it sufficiently attainable so that the right number of customers will act.

» Use language such as "winning" or "award" rather than "coupon" to make it clear that effort was involved in attaining the prize.

Consider a small reward rather than a big one

Customers will be forced to create justifications, which increase the perceived value of the reward.

Amazon.com's Mechanical Turk is an online marketplace where individuals get paid to perform small tasks that computers aren't good at, such as making preference choices, composing descriptive sentences, searching for an item in an image, transcribing audio, or extracting meaning from phrases. These tasks are called Human Intelligence Tasks or HITs.

Anyone can set up a HIT, using Amazon.com's platform to advertise and host the tasks, and anyone can work on HITs; although, some require workers to take a simple test first, or to meet certain demographic criteria. Amazon.com takes a 10 percent commission for running the site.

The HITs are normally broken down into small chunks, and individuals who complete them ("providers") get paid for their time. But the rate of pay isn't exactly high. Finding the e-mail address for a given individual might pay 3 cents/person. Copying and pasting the most relevant search result for a given keyword could pay 12 cents/keyword. The highest paying gigs, requiring real skills, provide approximately $40 for transcribing a 2-hour voice recording.

Analyzing the self-reported earnings on a couple of the popular provider forums suggests that committed individuals will make approximately 10 cents per HIT, and earn approximately $3.80 per hour full-time equivalent if they are U.S.-based and therefore can access all the HITs. That is just slightly more than half the federal minimum wage.

But despite this low payout, providers (who tend to refer to themselves as Turkers) keep coming back. One commenter, posting on Turkernation.com says, "I am spending way too much time on turking, kinda like when I used to play WoW. Do you guys find it addictive? The payout is like a score, and as you get qualifications, it's like getting levels. It's like I'm playing a game."

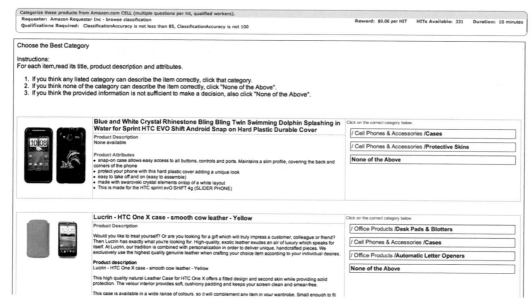

Amazon.com's Mechanical Turk—in this HIT, you'll earn six cents for checking the classification of a set of products on the site.

Why do people commit so much time to something that—even for experienced Turkers—pays out so little? For some people, there are good reasons: unemployment, ability to work from home in micro-shifts between other tasks such as child minding, or the ability to work from work—either students during dull lectures, or others at their regular workplace using their work Internet access.

For other people, the reasons are much less solid. They revolve around setting goals to reduce debt, to have "toy fund" money for frivolous expenditures, and simply being entertained: "Why not get paid for sitting at the computer, which I would be doing anyway?"

Lots of these reasons appear to be justifications that attempt to remove the *cognitive dissonance* of doing something that isn't actually particularly "worthwhile" in financial terms. And that fits in nicely with some findings from way back in 1959 when Leon Festinger and James Carlsmith found that in situations where there is cognitive dissonance between effort and return, people will be forced to create justifications for working so hard for a small reward, thus increasing their perceived value of the reward. Giving a larger reward just fits into their expectations and so doesn't create dissonance that needs to be resolved.

Festinger and Carlsmith ran an experiment where people conducted a boring and repetitive task for a period of time. After the study, they gave participants either $1 or $20 in 1959 money in return for lying to the next participant about how interesting the study was. When subsequently asked about their own experiences of the study, participants who had been paid only $1 to tell the lie rated it as more interesting than participants who had been paid $20, despite both telling the same lie to subsequent participants.

It seems that participants who were paid $20 to say how great the study was found it easier to justify their lying (they were paid well to lie) than students who were paid only $1. That meant that the people in the $1 situation had to rationalize the boring task in their minds and believe it was actually interesting to overcome the cognitive dissonance of lying about it.

As Festinger said, "If a person is induced to do or say something which is contrary to his private opinion, there will be a tendency for him to change his opinion so as to bring it into correspondence with what he has done or said. The larger the pressure used to elicit the overt behavior … the weaker will be the… tendency."

So a small reward (or the threat of mild punishment) forces the participants to create their own justifications for their actions, whereas a large reward (or large threat) provides an external reason. Counterintuitively, if Turkers were paid any more, they may start comparing the work to other potential work they could be doing and start seeing it less like entertainment and more like a badly paying chore.

How to motivate with small rewards

» Provide just a small reward to make people create their own reasons for participating. They will come to believe and defend those reasons as a way to resolve cognitive dissonance.

» It might help to also subtly provide a couple of sample justifications that people could use to help accept this small reward.

Hide the math

People don't like doing sums, and so if you show them answers rather than the workings, they'll be inclined to believe you—even if the answers are only partial.

You too could win an iPad for only 30 cents if only you were bidding on this auction site! (dealdash.com)

You have probably seen the adverts—iPads (or whatever other gadget is hot right now) being sold for ridiculously cheap prices. The chapter on Lust covers the motivating factors that make people want shiny devices like these, but this is a good place to consider the gluttonous element of the transaction—why somebody would feel that they can actually get a $500 piece of hardware for under $5.

One site lists nearly 40 companies working in the online penny auction or "entertainment auction" space. Take arrowoutlet.com as an example; although sites such as flutteroo.com, bidstick.com, swoopo.com, and many others employ similar strategies.

First, you buy a package of "bids" at 50 cents each. Bids allow you to enter auctions for items. Auctions are timed, but each bid extends the closing time by a set amount (normally 15 seconds). The winner is the last bidder when the timer runs out. Obviously then, there is an element of excitement (winning something), urgency (the ticking clock), and competition (other bidders). All this conspires to mask some simple accounting issues.

Studying the selling price for one item (iPad 2 16Gb Wi-Fi) over the course of one week in 2011, the average selling price was $120. To be clear, that means the winner of the auction can now buy the item for $120. This does not account for the number of bids that they spent to win.

Now, because each bid raises the price of the item by 1 cent, you know that there were 12,000 bids on average per iPad. 12,000 x $0.50 = $6000. $6000 + $120 = $6120.

Apple's own site sells the same model for $499, so the revenue per iPad to arrowoutlet.com is $5621. It needn't even hold stock of the item because it can drop-ship it directly from Apple. The sites often claim to lose money on a large proportion of their auctions. However, there is no need to feel sorry for them. Apparently the losses are more than compensated for by the 1100 percent profit on high-ticket high-desirability items such as iPads.

Ned Augenblick at Berkeley used an algorithm to capture the statistics for 166,000 auctions and found that auction revenues typically exceed 150 percent of the value of the item being auctioned, as long as the site has a sufficiently high number of bidders for each active auction so that the war of attrition continues for long enough to bid the price up. Auctions for direct cash payments return an average profit margin of 104 percent—the site makes a dollar in profit for every dollar they auction!

It's easy to argue that the winner still got a bargain—the cost for the iPad was $120 plus the winner's share of the bids. However, most auctions end with two people bidding against each other for some time (the sites even have bid-o-matic robots that can automate this process for you), so the winner most often provides a disproportionate number of the bids. And then there are the auctions that the bidder doesn't win. It's possible to sink a lot of bids into an item and then "lose" to somebody else. Because each bid costs you money regardless of whether you eventually win the product, total expenditure on the site can easily be more than the retail value of the products you end up "winning."

A couple of interlinked psychological and economic principles are at work here: *irrational escalation of commitment* and the *sunk cost fallacy* (a form of loss aversion).

You place a couple of bids on an auction in its later stages, and now you are in the game. Soon you realize that your 50-cent bids are raising the price by only 1 cent each time. You've spent quite a bit of money and bidding is still quite active, extending the time of the auction. But you made the decision to start bidding, and losing now would be costly, so you feel like you have to continue. Maybe you just want to win—to beat the other bidders who you're competing against. You figure they're in just as deep as you are. This reluctance to admit past mistakes and need to justify prior behavior is irrational escalation of commitment.

At some point, you end up in a position where your sunk cost (the amount you've spent in 50-cent bids) when added to the purchase price of the item will exceed the actual value of the item. The cost has now outweighed any future benefit, but irrational escalation of commitment keeps you going because you feel you can still win and recoup some of your losses. You basically continue to bid because of how much you've already bid. This is the sunk cost fallacy.

Augenblick collected data from six different penny auction sites and showed that auctions are less likely to end, and bidders are less likely to leave an auction as they make more bids. Both behaviors are indicative of sunk cost fallacy behavior, and both drive up the cost of the auctioned item.

In the case of these penny auctions, irrational escalation of commitment is thankfully short-lived for most bidders. Augenblick found that 75 percent of bidders left the site before placing 50 bids, and 86 percent stopped before placing 100 bids. However, that did leave a hardcore set of active bidders, most of whom struggled to break even, let alone to make a profit. On one site, Swoopo, the most experienced 11 percent of bidders contributed more than 50 percent of the site's profit.

Of course, none of the penny auction sites spell it out exactly like this. It is important for the auction sites to maximize the number of bidders per auction, and the best way to do that is to get customers excited about the low purchase price for each item, tell them how to win the opportunity to buy it, and then sell them a chunk of bids to play with. Even their tutorials are designed to provide step-by-step instructions for placing bids rather than an explanation of the underlying process. And this is on purpose. Any mention of the sums would dampen bidders' enthusiasm before they had sufficiently escalated their commitment.

How to hide the math

» Make the arithmetic associated with your product hard to perform.

» If possible, add confounding factors such as urgency, excitement, or competition so that users focus on these rather than the math.

» Use familiar terminology, but make the words mean something slightly different. For instance, in traditional auctions bids cost nothing unless you are the winner, whereas in penny auctions, bids cost money the moment they are placed.

» Automate the process of spending money wherever possible so that it slips out of awareness for people.

» Provide tutorials that explain how easy the process is without pointing out the implications.

» Use tokens to remove the sense of spending real money (see more on this in the chapter on Greed).

» Make a clear statement about the value of the item being auctioned/sold, but neglect to mention associated costs.

» Keep people interested until they reach the point of irrational commitment by having sufficient cost sunk in the item. From then on, psychology will do your work for you.

 ## Show the problems

Mention weaknesses before customers find out. They'll trust you more.

The original Volkswagen beetle was sold via a long series of self-deprecating advertisements. The honesty and humor in each ad made people more open to the strengths that followed.

You'd lose.

The racy-looking car in the picture would have trouble beating a Volkswagen.

Because it is a Volkswagen. Inside.

Outside it's a Karmann Ghia.

A Karmann Ghia isn't really a racing car. Though it is custom-built like one.

Its lines are too sculptured for mass production.

The front fender, for instance, has to be formed in three sections.

Each section is welded together. Then ground down, filed and sanded. All by hand.

But beneath that wanton exterior beats a heart of Volkswagen.

Same engine, same chassis, same transmission. Which means same reliability, same economy, same service.

We know a Ghia can't do much at the Sebring road races.

But it can cruise at 72, corner like a sports car, and hold the road like one.

And it might comfort you to know, you'd be driving the best-made loser on the track.

The Karmann Ghia looked like a sports car, but was just a Volkswagen Beetle underneath. This advert reinforces the sporty looks while simultaneously making fun of it. The flip side that draws you in is the practicality and fuel economy of the vehicle. (Ad agency: Doyle, Dane and Bernbach, 1964)

Although it's tempting to hide flaws, it is often beneficial to mention weaknesses or issues with your product or service before customers find out. They'll subsequently trust you more because you have shown that you have the integrity to be open and honest with them.

We are wired to reciprocate, and so when someone has already apparently demonstrated that they are trustworthy, we reciprocate by trusting them in return.

Just be sure to follow the weaknesses up by mentioning strengths that customers can use to justify continuing to do business with you. The positive reasons should be related to the weakness. In other words, if the weakness were cost, follow up with talk of economy ("This LED light bulb costs more to buy, but it lasts 10 times longer, so you'll make your money back and more over the life of the product"), rather than talk of the quality of the light, which is an unrelated topic.

Without a basic level of mutual trust, commerce would never happen. The vendors must trust that they'll be paid, and the customers must trust that they'll receive the goods. Rising above the default by demonstrating that the trust was earned is a way to cement the relationship.

That raises a more ethically challenging question, "Is it worth CREATING a trust incident to recover from?"

You could argue that manufacturing and then recovering well from a trust issue is a way to create more trust. Machiavelli saw this as a legitimate tactic.

> *Without doubt princes become great when they overcome the difficulties and obstacles by which they are confronted, and therefore fortune, especially when she desires to make a new prince great, who has a greater necessity to earn renown than an hereditary one, causes enemies to arise and form designs against him, in order that he may have the opportunity of overcoming them, and by them to mount higher, as by a ladder which his enemies have raised.* **For this reason many consider that a wise prince, when he has the opportunity, ought with craft to foster some animosity against himself, so that, having crushed it, his renown may rise higher.**
>
> MACHIAVELLI, *THE PRINCE*, CH. 20, PT. 4

Nowadays there are probably several cheaper strategies than resorting to manufacturing a trust incident. The Online Trust Alliance reports that data breach incidents cost U.S. companies $318 per customer in 2010. That much money could probably buy a lot of trust.

Recently however it appears that many organizations haven't had to purposefully create these incidents, as they've been happening to them unbidden. "Fortune causes enemies to arise…" and all that.

The typical path appears to be to first hide the problem, then deny it, then understate it, and finally admit it but do little to reassure customers. Although hiding the issue may seem like the ideal evil route, it's actually the stupid solution.

Graham Dietz and Nicole Gillespie, writing for the Institute of Business Ethics, say "An organisation can demonstrate its trustworthiness through the technical competence of its operations, products and services (ability), as well as through its positive motives and concern for its multiple stakeholders (benevolence), and honesty and fairness in its dealings with others (integrity)."

A smart organization would exploit the situation caused by a trust incident by owning the issue and turning it into a positive trust experience (ability) so that customers feel better disposed toward the company in the future (integrity), having proof that the company is prepared to take care of them (benevolence).

First, look at a company that has become the poster child for letting events get ahead of them: Sony Corp.

Between April 17 and April 19, 2011, somebody broke into the servers hosting the Sony PlayStation Network and stole details of 77 million customer accounts, including information such as name, address, birth date, e-mail addresses, and login passwords, and potentially credit card information including billing address and security question answers.

Sony initially closed down the network and displayed "undergoing maintenance" screens to users. Although it subsequently appeared that it was working hard behind the scenes to find out exactly what had happened and what data was involved, it took until April 26th—more than a week later— to admit that personal details may have been compromised. At that point, Sony did not do much to placate angry users, instead just pointing people to the three U.S. credit reporting agencies and federally available ID Theft information. It was only after significant pressure from Congress that Sony decided to offer ID theft insurance to all users for 12 months—a distinct lack of benevolence.

Twenty-three long and low-communication days later, Sony brought the service back online, and pointed users to a password reset page to re-enable their online accounts. Adding insult to injury, this page soon had to be taken down because it turned out to be exploitable; you could reset someone else's password just by knowing his e-mail address and date of birth. This didn't do much to improve customers' perception of Sony's capability or concern for its customers.

Although Kazuo Hirai, chief of Sony Corp.'s PlayStation video game unit, said, "I see my work as first making sure Sony can regain the trust from our users," and Sony offered "welcome back" freebies such as complimentary game downloads and 30 days of free service, user reaction was not positive. The lack of communication and the seeming reluctance to "do the right thing" for customers seriously hurt Sony's reputation in the gaming world. Actions such as changing the terms and conditions document for the PlayStation Network to limit users' legal rights if the same thing happens in the future suggest that Sony is still taking a defensive rather than proactive approach to user trust, further damaging any concept of its integrity.

In contrast, consider the case of the University of Michigan Health System, a group of hospitals that, when they identified a medical error, pre-emptively reached out to affected patients and their families, communicating openly and honestly about the issue and its ramifications. This is in direct contrast to the majority of healthcare providers, that seem to work on a principle of "deny and defend" when faced with an adverse event.

Contrary to popular assumptions, the University of Michigan Health System found that rather than reaching out being seen as an admission of guilt and an invitation for more lawsuits, this pre-emptive approach halved the number of claims, reduced the claim resolution time from 20 to 8 months on average, and halved the cost of compensation awards.

It seems that many patients who file malpractice lawsuits do so mainly to understand what happened and why, and through a need to prevent the same incident from happening to others in the future—or to use Dietz and Gillespie's language, they are motivated by integrity. By acknowledging errors and apologizing, the healthcare provider removed the primary motivation for legal action. When legal action was undertaken against the University of Michigan Health System, 71 percent of the plaintiffs' lawyers settled for less than it anticipated, and 57 percent said they chose not to pursue cases they would have pursued before the program was in place.

A similar program at the Veterans Affairs (VA) Medical Center in Lexington, Kentucky, led to average malpractice payouts of $14,500 per case. That compares favorably to payout rates at other VA facilities, which averaged $413,000 for malpractice judgments, $98,000 for pretrial settlements, and $248,000 for in-trial settlements. Despite having more claims overall, probably as a result of improved patient awareness, the Lexington VA hospital still had the eighth lowest total claims payments among all VA hospitals. As a sign of the financial and moral value of this approach, these full disclosure policies have now been adopted at all 35 VA hospitals in the United States, as well as several other private healthcare institutions in the United States, Canada, and Australia.

So, show the problems. Turn issues into positive trust incidents. Counterintuitively, this may cost you less in financial terms while also giving you much more moral currency with your audience.

How to build trust from problems

» See weaknesses as an opportunity to build trust rather than as something to be hidden away. It's better that you manage the message around the weakness rather than leaving it to people external to the company who will shape it to their own advantage.

» Be open and honest. It's hard to over-communicate, especially in times of crisis.

» If you find yourself in a trust incident, think how you will demonstrate your technical competence (ability), concern (benevolence), and fairness (integrity).

  » **Ability**: Have a pre-prepared plan and policy for how you'll handle trust incidents. Acknowledge that a trust incident will cost you money, but that it's also an opportunity to manage losses and demonstrate aptitude.

  » **Integrity**: Stick to facts, not speculation. Even if the fact is, "We don't know the answer yet," it's important to remain accountable rather than having to backtrack later.

  » **Benevolence**: Demonstrate that you have given affected people more than was expected in terms of apologies and recompense.

Escalating commitment: foot-in-the-door, door-in-the-face

Reciprocity describes people's behavior when they are given something. It is in our nature to feel more charitable toward the gift giver, and therefore more likely to do something for them in return—in other words, to reciprocate.

At some point in the past you may have received "free" address labels from a charity, or "yours to keep whatever you decide" samples from a company. This is a calculated investment. The charity or company knows that on average, recipients will be more likely to give or spend if they are reciprocating for a gift that was given to them. In fact, it's worth researching charities before contributing to them. At least one charity hit the news recently for using more than 80 percent of its donations in marketing costs, primarily through sending out gifts to new potential donors.

Two old tricks to create reciprocity started in the real world and have found their way online despite being somewhat tied to physical events. Both were originally practiced by door-to-door salesmen, hence the names foot-in-the-door and door-in-the-face.

Foot-in-the-door

Gain commitment to a small thing to convince about a big thing.

When people see the value (or at least the lack of harm) in agreeing to a small favor, they will be more likely to commit to a larger one.

This sales technique has been used for centuries. Door-to-door salesmen would ask the owner of a house if they could at least come in to demonstrate their product, perhaps in the process leaving the owner with a cleaner floor or windows. Door-to-door fundraisers might first ask residents to sign a petition, and after the resident complied with that small request, the fundraiser would later come back and ask them to make a donation. Studies show that more people donate after agreeing to the initial petition request than if they are just asked for money.

In the online world, participants in one study were more likely to fill in a survey sent through e-mail if they had previously responded to a much smaller question sent by the same individual.

On the web, asking for an initial small favor might mean asking for only the bare minimum of information that you need to set up a relationship with someone. This could be a ZIP code to allow personalization, or an e-mail address to save information for later.

In these situations, asking for more information would most likely be a turn-off for users of the site. Not having a deep relationship with the site, and not understanding its value to them, they would refuse to give particularly detailed information and would instead leave.

Icelandair uses a variation on foot-in-the-door by "giving" you a song to listen to in the hope that you'll then reciprocate by taking the time to provide feedback. (icelandair.com site from a post-flight satisfaction e-mail)

By instead letting visitors see the large gains they get for providing just a small piece of information, the site has placed a foot-in-the-door, so that the door won't be shut again. Now, when the site asks for a deeper level of involvement from its visitors, they will have seen the benefits and will be ready to reciprocate. Having already given a small piece of information will smooth their journey to full engagement with the site.

The step from no relationship to a simple relationship is much larger than any subsequent steps. After there's an initial agreement, it's easier to change the boundaries of the agreement because it would be cognitively dissonant for customers to go against what they first agreed to. Best compliance happens if customers think they're committing to a worthy cause, or if they've already pictured themselves positively as part of the group you've invited them into.

How to use foot-in-the-door

» Make it easy for visitors to share a small piece of information with you, such as asking for a ZIP code to customize a weather forecast or calculate local sales taxes. This reduces the barrier to later sharing larger pieces of information.

» Escalate commitment gradually so that each individual step seems reasonable, and by the end, you'll have a level of commitment that would have seemed totally unreasonable at the beginning.

» If some time has passed between asking for the initial information and a subsequent larger request, remind users that they already gave you the small favor. This will put them back in giving mode and make it harder for them to decline.

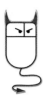

Door-in-the-face

Ask for a big thing, expecting to be turned down. Then ask for a small thing immediately afterward. Guilt at turning you down makes people more likely to agree to the small thing.

Reciprocation can also be used to guilt people into doing something for you. The urge to reciprocate is so strong that even if a request is blatantly unreasonable, individuals being asked will want to show that they are still compassionate and will therefore often be quite happy to perform a smaller task instead, as a form of apology for not agreeing to the larger request.

So, after expecting to have the door slammed in your face by asking for something audacious, knock again and this time ask for something much more reasonable—or at least reasonable compared to your first request. Now that you have set an anchor point, the smaller request will seem quite tame and achievable in comparison.

Robert Cialdini and his colleagues first described the setup required for successful door-in-the-face interactions in 1975. They ran an experiment where students at a university were approached in the hallways and asked to volunteer to council juvenile delinquents for 2 hours a week over a 2-year period. This is obviously a major commitment and was turned down by everyone who was approached. The requester would then ask whether they would be prepared to chaperone these same individuals on a 1-day zoo trip. Fifty percent of the time, the answer was yes. In comparison, when Cialdini's team asked for the smaller favor without first presenting the larger request, the compliance rate was only 16.7 percent.

Cialdini emphasizes that it's important to make the individual feel like they are making a reciprocal concession. There must be a large difference between the overly ambitious condition and the second more reasonable condition, and only a yes/no option for each condition. This is important because it's necessary for individuals to first refuse the large request so that they feel obliged to reciprocate when they notice how much smaller the second request is, and the only way to do so is to say, "yes."

It's also important that the same person makes both the overambitious and the smaller requests, because otherwise the individual won't feel the need to reciprocate with a concession of his own. To maximize compliance, the second request must also be a smaller version of the first one rather than new request.

Online examples are slightly harder to find because if the initial request is seen as just plain crazy, the back button is just one click away. The way to combat this is to show that you know it's awkward and unusual to ask for the big thing, but to still ask for it anyway. By making it clear you understand the discomfort, customers will be less likely to use it as an excuse.

Door-in-the-face techniques can work in virtual worlds with avatars asking first for an unreasonable and then a more reasonable request, but what about on websites, where one of the key variables—the consistency of the individual making the request—is no longer visible?

The most apparent use of door-in-the-face is to get purchasers to register their information with a site. By presenting a sign-up form at the beginning of the process, but allowing site visitors to skip that registration process, it might make those same individuals more likely to agree to "saving" their shipping details (ostensibly the same information) at the end of the checkout process.

More subtle applications require a longer task flow, such as the one LegalZoom has to help business owners fill in the forms required to set up a business. Although it advertises the cost of an LLC filing as "from $99," there are plenty of upsell opportunities within the flow. One is where LegalZoom offers to act as the company's registered agent, for an annual fee of $160 (sensibly charged at a later date to avoid *sticker shock*). If you decide to forego this service, the next page of the form offers a notification service that reminds you of state compliance dates, for just $69/year.

Door-in-the-face works because you control the anchor—the initial unreasonable request—and so you control the level of contrast between that and the reasonable request that follows it. People aren't good at making absolute decisions, but they can be quite good at making comparative decisions. In comparison to the unreasonable request, the reasonable request is relatively small. It's also possible that people feel that by backing down, you have made a compromise on their behalf. As such, they now feel compelled to reciprocate for your compromise by agreeing to the smaller request.

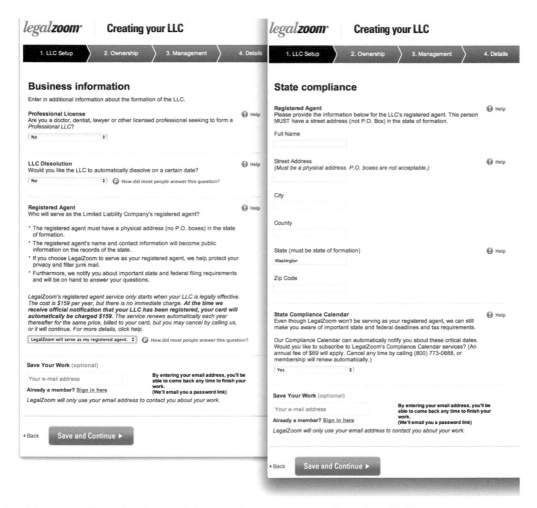

LegalZoom.com offers online forms to help create business entities. It first offers a high-cost service option (left), but if that's refused, on the next page it offers one that requires hardly any work on its behalf for a much more "reasonable" annual rate (right).

How to use door-in-the-face

» Ask for a big commitment first, and then request a smaller thing if people refuse.

(continues)

(continued)

» Make it clear that you know it's unusual/uncomfortable to ask for the big thing. By acknowledging this, you make it harder for people to refuse the smaller thing based on discomfort.

» Invoke reciprocity by showing that you've made a compromise in asking for the smaller thing.

» Make sure that you provide a clear funnel into the door-in-the-face process. When you present the unreasonable request, provide a No Thanks button that draws people in to the presentation of the reasonable request.

» Just occasionally people will actually agree to your initial unreasonable request. Be sure that this doesn't catch you off guard, and that you have a way for people to actually sign up for your large request.

» Guilt most affects in-group members, so make it clear how much like your visitors you are (and what positive traits they have) as you make your request.

Present hard decisions only after investment

Ensure that users are hooked before you ask them to give you "valuable" information or perform hard tasks. Better to give something away free than lose the future value.

Sites used to require up-front registration before even letting users in to see or test out a service. Now, few use that model and instead are more likely to balance the need for up-front information with the need to show the product off through use.

This concept of delaying the request until it is in context has its roots in theories of reciprocity. Users feel obliged to respond (reciprocate) when given something. Even if the gift is small (such as free entry to a site), they will respond with valuable (to advertisers) personal information.

Users aren't necessarily unreasonable in their value assessments; for example, they will give City, State, ZIP, Age, Gender (CSZAG) information to get access to a service that they want to use, reasoning that the obligatory ads that they will see would at least have some relevance. Also, not surprisingly, there is little requirement on users to make this data accurate as it is unlikely to impact service provision. For the longest time, the Hotmail e-mail service had an inordinate number of users who claimed to live in the Beverly Hills area. (Cultural reference: ZIP code 90210 was etched in many people's minds thanks to a long running TV soap series.)

More unique and accurate information normally requires a higher value service in response. For instance, numbers (date of birth, phone number, house number, Social Security number, and credit card number) tend to have more perceived value to people than non-numerical data, probably because they are better identifiers or allow financial transactions to occur.

Posterous, a blog creation site, takes this concept to the extreme; you just e-mail content and it shows up as a blog in your name on its site. The company still asks for all the same information that other social media sites request, but it delays the request until it is in context: when users want to access more complex site functionality, or to keep some content private.

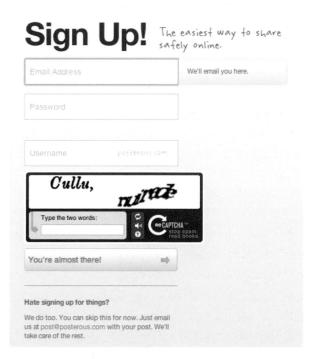

Posterous.com understands you don't always want to give any information. Instead, at the bottom of the form it tells you that you can just e-mail content and it'll start a blog for you. It subsequently deepens the relationship with you after you commit to using the platform.

This approach is especially important for services that require a network of users to function. WebEx's online conference product does this well. New users can try out the service with absolutely no commitment if an existing user invites them. It's only when they want to initiate a call that they need to sign up. They have to provide only the minimum of information until they want to do something more complex.

A corollary of this is not asking people to create accounts at your e-commerce site until after they've finished the checkout process. Here, it's easy to remind them that they already trust you (they just bought something from you) and that they have already given you all their information. All they need to do to make it easier to check out next time is create a password. Whereas registration would have been seen as a burden, they are now willing to give you permission to store all their information as a service.

Leaving these questions until the user is invested means that they're both more likely to trust the site and also more willing to give true information because they have spent time and effort to create the content they've added.

How to save big decisions until after investment

» Gather the minimum amount of information necessary to furnish the service.

» Prompt for additional information when visitors start using additional services. Justify the information request with reference to the additional value that users will get from the service.

» Always try to tie the requests to a reciprocal agreement (give me X so that I can give you Y) to ensure that the data is accurate rather than fake.

» If you've gathered information as part of a checkout or other process, offer to store it for later. That sounds like a time-saver rather than a burden or imposition.

» If you can't provide enough value to elicit reciprocity, try the door-in-the-face strategy: Ask for a lot of information, and then settle for much less.

Invoking gluttony with scarcity and loss aversion

Imagine you are given a $1 bill. You hold it in your hand. Now you have the option to keep the money or to gamble it on a coin-toss where you can either win $2.50 or lose the dollar entirely. What do you do?

If you're like most people, even when this task is repeated 20 times, you'll still only gamble your $1 on 11 or 12 of the rounds. And if you do lose your $1 in one round, you'll be much less likely to gamble in the next round. As the rounds progress, you'll be less likely to gamble at all.

Now the thing is, it actually makes sense to gamble on every round. On average, each round where you gamble will net you $1.25 because you will win the coin toss one-half of the time.

So why don't you follow this rational course? It seems that your emotions can get in the way of making logical decisions. This is especially true when the logical decision involves giving up something that you already have. In fact, it takes individuals who have brain damage that causes problems in processing emotions to perform more "sensibly" in this test.

Even though there is the potential to earn more money, there is also the potential to lose what you are already holding in your hand. The fear of losing what you already have (your *loss aversion*) is sometimes as much as twice as powerful as your desire to benefit from a potential gain.

Another powerful fear-based motivator is scarcity. By either creating a scarce thing (a title, award, or membership) or selling a scarce thing (where demand is greater than supply), you can count on people's fear of missing out to ensure that they attribute more value to the item than it is actually worth.

The Tom Sawyer effect

Scarcity breeds desire: "In order to make a man or a boy covet a thing, it is only necessary to make the thing difficult to attain."

Tom Sawyer got other kids to work for him because he convinced them that it was a scarce event ("Does a boy get a chance to whitewash a fence every day?")

only open to select individuals with sufficient skill ("I reckon there ain't one boy in a thousand, maybe two thousand, that can do it the way it's got to be done") and where demand was greater than supply ("If he hadn't run out of whitewash he would have bankrupted every boy in the village"). Tom pushed all the right buttons that turn scarcity into desire.

You can use these elements of scarcity—infrequency, exclusivity, and competition—to appeal to people's natural gluttonous tendencies.

Often it is sufficient to manufacture the feeling of scarcity without actually limiting supplies. For instance, the sentence "If operators are busy, please try again" has much more social proof than the sentence "Operators are standing by to take your calls" because it implies high demand for the item being sold.

You can also create scarcity by limiting the time that something is available. The Humble Bundle games offers bring a set of well-liked independent computer games together into a pay-what-you-like deal, but only for a 2-week period.

Even though the games have normally been released for some time before the bundle is introduced, the fact that they are offered together at a low price (you pay what you want), with bonus extras, and with a proportion of proceeds going to charity, makes them a great deal.

Even if you hadn't been planning on purchasing all the games, or if you had already purchased one of them at full price, this limited-time offer provides a good incentive to get the whole bundle while the games are cheaper than they would otherwise be. This is a form of loss aversion that applies even before people have the product in hand. Paying full price for one of the games is now a "loss" in comparison to purchasing it as part of this bundle.

The addition of bonus extras such as the game soundtracks and "making of" documentaries provide exclusivity. Often the bundle is the only time that these items are made available.

The Humble Bundle includes the added element of competition because to get the bonus extras that come with the bundle, purchasers must pay more than the current average price. This means that as more people purchase the bundle, the average price rises. Thus, it pays to be one of the first if you want a bargain.

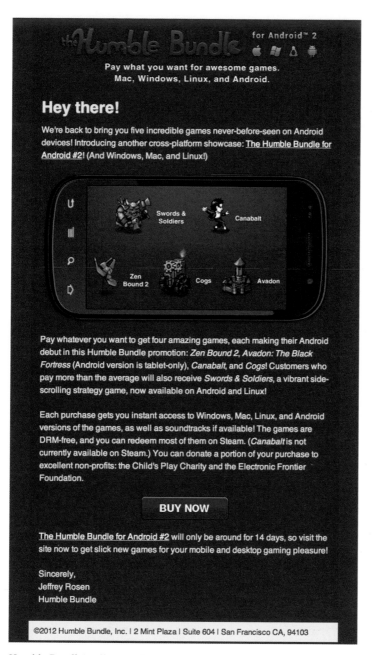

Humble Bundle's offers invoke scarcity by being a limited time offer and *competition* by gradually increasing the price required to unlock the *exclusive* bonus extras. (humblebundle.com)

How to use the Tom Sawyer effect

» Include the three elements of scarcity to ensure people want your product:

  » **Infrequency:** Make it clear that the offer or event is only available for a limited time.

  » **Exclusivity:** Promote items that only certain people will qualify for (even if the qualification criteria are as loose as "has a pulse").

  » **Competition:** Show that there are others who are also interested in the scarce resource.

Instill doubt to prevent cancellations

If customers want to cancel, instill doubt by tapping into loss aversion.

In 1990, John Gummer, the Agriculture Minister for the UK Government, needed to keep people eating beef. Public fears about mad cow disease had increased after several types of beef offal were banned in the UK. Sales of beef products were falling.

His solution was to instill doubt in the minds of people who thought that beef was bad. His method was to feed a beef burger to his 4-year-old daughter, Cordelia, at a well-publicized media event held at a boat show in his constituency. After all, who could believe that beef was unsafe if a public figure with direct responsibility for public food safety was prepared to feed it to a 4-year-old girl?

The real master-stroke was to use burgers, a form of beef that almost everyone could identify with and would be unhappy to give up (nearly 50 billion are eaten annually in the United States—three per person per week). Showing Cordelia enjoying her burger triggered loss aversion and simultaneously reinforced that beef was safe.

This was near the beginning of the bovine spongiform encephalopathy (BSE) scare that would later lead to 4.4 million cows in the UK being slaughtered and more than 200 human deaths from a variant of Creutzfeld-Jakob disease caused by eating meat from cows that had contracted BSE.

John Gummer "enjoying" a burger with his daughter, Cordelia. Who could possibly doubt his intentions? © *Press Association*

It later turned out that Mr. Gummer knew of the dangers but was scared of the economic outcome if the news spread. He was thus prepared to risk his daughter's health for political gain. This act didn't seem to hurt his political career, as he is now a life peer in the House of Lords. However, he did leave a legacy because now when other politicians try similar PR tactics in the UK, it's described as "doing a Gummer."

You too can instill doubt to prevent people from canceling subscriptions or memberships. You simply need to tap in to the natural loss aversion that people will feel when they are reminded of what they have in their hands and what they'll lose as a result of their actions.

One way to do this is to start people's membership with a certain level of service included free of charge. Subsequent fear of losing this "free" level of service means they'll pay more to keep it than they would have paid to obtain it in the first place.

Obviously, after people start using a service, they also create data and artifacts (photos, documents, contacts, and so on) that are tied to the service. Any time that customers attempt to cancel their membership can also reinforce just what they'll lose. Even when companies such as Google offer migration of data so that there's less to lose, there's still a lot tied up in social capital (friends and colleagues with whom the data is shared) that can't necessarily be replicated elsewhere. Instilling doubt in these situations simply involves pointing out what people might lose by closing their account or migrating their data. Trying to deactivate your Facebook account brings up a series of photos from friends' accounts that show you with those friends. Each has the caption "so-and-so will miss you" and invites you to send them a message. Obviously sending them a message takes you away from the deactivation page and back into the loving embrace of the site.

Companies don't need to reserve this tactic just for serious situations such as account closure. They can instill doubt to get people to choose an option that they prefer. Again, Google is a master of this. In Google Voice, for instance, choosing particular settings leads to a prompt designed specifically to instill doubt in customers' minds. The option is still available, but because Google (rightfully) doesn't recommend it, it makes users think twice and feel bad for selecting this option over the "safer" alternatives.

Google Voice settings can have unexpected side effects. This dialog instills doubt by presenting a scary scenario to make users think twice before choosing the risky option.

All of these situations work by framing the doubt in terms of what people may *lose* by choosing the *undesired* option. Although that's a double negative, it has more power than reminding people of what they might *gain* by choosing the *desired* option. People feel loss more powerfully than gain, so it's easier to manipulate them through doubt about negative outcomes. The magic of loss aversion will do all the rest.

How to instill doubt

» Loss aversion is strongest when people have recently experienced the benefits of the product or service. If customers are canceling after a period of inactivity, find a way to convince them to use the product again (for instance by offering a free month of service, or access to a premium feature) so that they will feel the loss more keenly.

» At select points in your product, remind users of what they might lose by not choosing your preferred option. Be subtle, but remember to phrase in terms of loss.

» Save fear tactics for high-stakes interactions. People don't like being scared on a regular basis, and the effect is diminished with over-use.

» On cancellation forms, invoke loss aversion by asking, "Which of these features will you miss the most?" This may be sufficient to pull customers back from the brink, and it's still useful information to know regardless of the outcome.

Impatience leads to compliance

Put a time constraint on a task and then offer to help users through it.

Fear of losing out disproportionately influences people's value judgments. Forcing people to act fast also changes the way they make decisions. They tend to become more conservative, preferring less risky options and paying more attention to negative information.

Putting those two facts together creates a powerful force that companies like Ticketmaster have learned how to harness.

Ticketmaster gives customers a limited amount of time to make a purchase. This is ostensibly to prevent individuals from "holding" tickets for a show without actually paying for them. It has the additional effect of creating an environment where customers are forced to act quickly to secure the tickets they want, especially when Ticketmaster has a virtual monopoly on ticket sales for many venues.

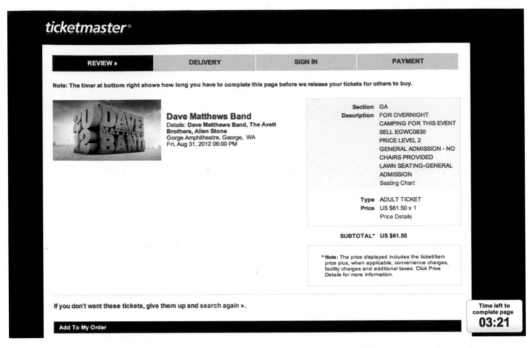

The Ticketmaster interface induces panic because it is timed. Coupled with loss aversion, this makes it easy for Ticketmaster to get customers to agree to things they otherwise may not. (ticketmaster.com)

The time constraint induces a kind of panic. Fear of losing out on the tickets leads people to try and complete the process as quickly as possible. They are therefore less likely to pay attention to details, and more likely to do whatever it takes to get through the process unhindered.

Each page in the checkout process has a highly visible countdown timer. This serves as a constant reminder that the tickets could "disappear" if you don't act fast. Acting fast means skipping over apparently inconsequential information and acting to reduce risk where possible. The outcome of this type of urgency is that customers will be less likely to change default selections (the highest price tickets), more likely to choose fast and secure shipping options (at a higher cost) and less likely to question the additional "convenience fees" that are added by the company.

An interesting side effect of adding time constraints is that it enhances people's commitment to completing challenges, but only for low-complexity tasks.

Giving people task-completion aids that let them follow rules by rote increases their performance on these time-constrained tasks.

This makes you wonder what would happen if Ticketmaster started offering a robo-booking option—just choose "best seat" or "cheapest seat" and let the site do the rest (for a fee). This feature might be especially attractive for people who had been caught out by the time-constraint issues previously.

How to ensure compliance through impatience

» Place a time constraint on a task to push people toward less-risky options and to accept the default selections.

» Add a task-completion aid that does not require analytical thinking. It should list simple rules for people to follow to complete the task.

» Offer to bypass the time-constrained task by providing an automated output with the default settings. You may even charge more for this "convenience."

Self-control: Gluttony's nemesis

Gluttony is a failure of self-control. Once we have made a small lapse, a larger one becomes much easier. A small nibble of chocolate while on a diet doesn't satisfy our craving. Instead it makes subsequent bingeing much more likely. Similarly, when companies try to persuade individuals to do something, a small immediate concession can lead to a much larger one later. Self-control tends to break down when we focus more on emotional impulses than on rational thought. We know rationally that we shouldn't eat the chocolate, but emotionally it just feels so good.

Psychological research into *self-regulation failure* suggests that there are several ways in which people misuse or fail to use their self-control.

First, over-optimism leads people to miscalculate their likelihood of success, so they continue with tasks long after they should have quit. Making people work for a reward is one way for companies to take advantage of this. Once customers have attributed a personal value to a reward, they will work harder for it than they rationally should. The same is true when companies provide seemingly tiny rewards. The value justifications that people create in their own minds lead them to false assumptions about the ultimate value of the payout they will receive. Perhaps the simplest self-regulation failure caused by false assumptions is people's inability or unwillingness to do some simple sums when faced with what appears to be a fabulous bargain in penny auctions. Here, even though people know the deal must be too good to be true, they will continue anyway in the over-optimistic hope that there will be a pleasant outcome.

Self-regulation failure also happens because we sometimes think we can control things that really aren't under our control. This is true for both companies and consumers. When a company is hacked it is by definition not in control of the situation, yet many act as if they still are. Failure to behave honestly and show the true problems can create real trust issues. Customers are definitely not in control when they are drawn in with the lure of scarcity, especially when there is a deadline for acquiring the scarce thing. By manipulating availability, exclusivity and competition companies make consumers panic. That emotional response suppresses rational thought and so removes self-control.

The third area of self-regulation failure comes from focusing on the emotional outcome rather than the cause of the problem. This can lead to impulsive behavior, which people subsequently regret and which in turn leads to a worse emotional outcome. One example of this is reciprocating when we logically shouldn't. Foot-in-the-door and door-in-the-face techniques rely on people's emotional feeling of commitment, leading them to reciprocate even when they know that they would never agree to perform that same task outside the implicit contract that has just been created.

There is however some hope. People who are made to think about the payoffs of self-control are less likely to subsequently lose control. A real-life example of this is the apparent calming effect that social media have had on unruly spring break behavior. Typically, spring break is a time for college students to unwind and have fun. Traditionally that has tended to involve large quantities of alcohol and alcohol-induced behavior. However, anecdotal reports suggest that since the advent of sites such as Facebook, which document every moment of people's lives, spring breakers have tended to become better behaved, aware that photos of their behavior will be posted online for friends, family, and future employers to see.

Anger

Anger as soon as fed is dead—
'Tis starving makes it fat.

EMILY DICKINSON

ANGER IS FEAR WITH A FOCUS: an understanding of what caused the fear and often also the capacity to resolve the fear by acting to remove it.

It's an active emotion; people want to deal with the cause of their anger in ways they don't with other emotions. This happens on an intellectual and also a physical level, with biological changes as a result of feeling anger. However, just because people have the capacity to deal with the anger doesn't mean they necessarily will. Anger often leads to brooding and plotting. Dante called it "love of justice perverted to revenge and spite." That, in a nutshell, is what turns it from a virtue into a vice.

What causes anger? Typically, anger is caused by a negative event that someone or something else is responsible for. If we were responsible we would experience shame or guilt instead. If the cause were unknown, we would experience fear or anxiety. But if we have a target cause of the negative event, we feel anger.

Anger has different effects on judgment and decision making than do other negative emotions. Anger influences how we perceive, reason, and choose. Its effects spill over from the initial cause to other things we're doing, affecting how we respond to situations that have no bearing on the thing that initially made us angry.

Anger can be a difficult emotion to harness. When we look back on instances when we were angry, we tend to think of them as unpleasant and unrewarding. However, while we are in the angry state, prior to resolution, the feelings we experience can be pleasant and even rewarding. In the right contexts, anger can be a highly motivating force.

Avoiding anger

When there's a possibility that a company's actions will create an angry response, there are two possible reactions. The company can either embrace the anger and try to shape it to its own ends or alternatively can try to minimize the anger by diffusing or displacing it.

As previously mentioned, anger without a definite cause becomes anxiety, and anger with a self-created cause becomes guilt, so one way of displacing anger is to shift the blame to someone else or back to the customer. This doesn't necessarily provide resolution, but it does change the target from an external to an internal source. One problem with this approach is that blaming customers isn't necessarily a good way to gain repeat business—especially blaming angry customers.

Instead, it's better to attempt to avoid the anger in the first place. Here, we discuss three patterns that can enable companies to get what they want without creating anger in their customer base.

Use humor to deflect anger

If you mess up in a small way, convey your apology with humor to defuse the situation. However, for bigger issues or if you anticipate an angry response, use a calming and respectful tone instead.

Relax all the muscles in your face. Now, tighten the muscles above your eyes that bring your eyebrows toward your upper eyelids and at the same time tighten the muscle that attaches your cheekbones to the corners of your lips (otherwise known as "smiling"). Are you feeling happier? Paul Ekman found that even getting people to consciously form their facial muscles into a certain expression could trigger the physical sensations of the corresponding emotion.

Using humor online can be challenging at the best of times because it is so easy to misread, but if you are sure the message is clear, it might be worth using a technique that gets a little grin out of somebody to help prevent them from becoming truly angry.

One thing that's almost guaranteed to infuriate people online is when the service they are trying to use is unavailable. For a while in 2011, Tumblr.com used fan art created by Matthew Inman (TheOatmeal.com) on its server error page after a grassroots campaign by Inman's blog readers. Tumblr is an image-based blogging platform. Because it isn't likely to be seen as a mission-critical service, a humorous error page is likely to diffuse any anger before it starts.

Tumbeasts loose in the server room can cause no end of problems. (Tumblr.com 503 message created by Matthew Inman, theoatmeal.com) © *Matthew Inman, The Oatmeal. (theoatmeal.com) CC BY 3.0*

It's worth pointing out that the tone of your humor is also important. Cartoons depicting hostile humor (one character putting down another character, for instance) could actually contribute to rather than reduce anger and aggression.

There are sites and situations where using humor would not be appropriate. Mozy is an online backup service. It uses a light-hearted and somewhat humorous tone across its site, potentially in an attempt to make backing up data seem less daunting. However, applying this to its error page is probably not a good idea. The result of an error on a data backup site is more serious than on a photo blog. Unfortunately, a couple of Mozy's error messages start with a humorous tone saying, "Whoops!" Considering that at the point when they see this information people are already likely to be a little angry or upset, this approach is more likely to fuel anger than alleviate it.

Mozy.com makes its business from backing up customers' data. How would you feel if you were in Mozy's server room and heard somebody say, "Whoops!"?

The context of customers' interaction with Mozy means that if they see an error on the system, they are more likely to be angry and need to have that anger addressed by providing ways to solve their problem rather than resorting to deflection, which would be more appropriate for a lighter-hearted or entertainment-driven product.

Humor also won't cover persistent errors. Twitter's equivalent to the tumbeasts is its Fail Whale image. Unfortunately, in Twitter's early days the Fail Whale appeared so frequently that the visual gag lost its humorous aspect. That, coupled with Twitter's move from novelty to more serious communication platform, meant that humor became a less suitable style of response.

How to prevent anger with humor

» Use humor to reduce the potential for anger, but not to deal with existing anger.

» The humor you use should be whimsical rather than containing hostile or aggressive themes, such as one person putting down another person, because these can increase aggressive feelings.

» Jokes are only funny once. Ensure that people aren't going to see the humorous content too many times; otherwise, its effect will wear off and may even backfire.

» If you know that users are likely to be angry at the time they see your response, consider a placatory approach instead of a humorous approach. Apply the punch-in-the-face test: Ask yourself whether using humor would get you hit if you were face to face with your user at this point.

Avoid overt anger with a slippery slope

Start small, and avoid a backlash by making several small sequential changes rather than one large one. If individual changes are sufficiently inoffensive, people won't become irate enough to revolt.

Netflix wants to get out of the physical DVD rental business by converting all its users to online streaming customers. Although both businesses are profitable, it costs Netflix a lot more to service the mail order DVDs than to let users stream digitized content over the Internet. As of October 2011, Netflix streaming accounted for almost one-third of downstream Internet bandwidth in North America. That is more than all HTTP (website) traffic combined.

In July 2011, Netflix announced a price increase from $10 to $16/month for the combination streaming-and-physical service in an attempt to make the $8 streaming-only option seem more appealing. The price change alone caused a measurable issue: Approximately 1 million of the company's 25 million subscribers canceled within the same business quarter that the changes went into effect.

This price increase was quickly followed in September 2011 by the announcement of a split into two separate companies: Netflix for online streaming rentals and Qwikster for physical DVD rentals by mail—each priced at $8/month. This was just too much change for both consumers and for the press. As Jason Gilbert at the *Huffington Post* wrote:

> *In its month of existence, Qwikster did nothing but foster ill will toward Netflix. The assumed purpose of the split—to enable Netflix to focus its resources and energy on acquiring streaming content and to phase out the less profitable, less popular DVD-by-mail service—was never well articulated. Qwikster was pitched, in a blog post and accompanying video, as a way to offer users more convenience, though the entire concept of Qwikster seemed anything but: Netflix was all but forcing its 12 million customers with joint streaming-DVD accounts to create two accounts, at two different domain names, with two credit card statements and two different sets of ratings and preferences, all on a new website run by a guy who couldn't even spell the word "quick" correctly.*

To its credit, Netflix realized (helped in part no doubt by plunging stock prices) that it messed up. Reed Hastings, the CEO, said, "There is a difference between moving quickly—which Netflix has done very well for years—and moving too fast, which is what we did in this case." It canceled the break-up plans and made a short, sweet announcement to its customers.

Although it's clear that Netflix' plans failed for several reasons, increasing both the financial and the physical burden on customers, even it admitted that it introduced changes too quickly.

People hate change. They love consistency. The posh name for this is *status quo bias*: the tendency to like things to stay relatively the same, and to perceive any change from the current situation as a loss. *Loss aversion* leads people to over-estimate the potential losses from a change and under-estimate the potential gains. They also tend to over-value their current situation (the *endowment effect*). The combinatory outcome of these behaviors is to stick with their current option. People will also stick with their current option if they feel that they have less information about their potential choices. Making people more knowledgeable about or even just giving them increased exposure to their other choices can reduce status quo bias.

NETFLIX   Your Account | Help

Dear Mel,

It is clear that for many of our members two websites would make things more difficult, so we are going to keep Netflix as one place to go for streaming and DVDs.

This means no change: one website, one account, one password...in other words, no Qwikster.

While the July price change was necessary, we are now done with price changes.

We're constantly improving our streaming selection. We've recently added hundreds of movies from Paramount, Sony, Universal, Fox, Warner Bros., Lionsgate, MGM and Miramax. Plus, in the last couple of weeks alone, we've added over 3,500 TV episodes from ABC, NBC, FOX, CBS, USA, E!, Nickelodeon, Disney Channel, ABC Family, Discovery Channel, TLC, SyFy, A&E, History, and PBS.

We value you as a member, and we are committed to making Netflix the best place to get your movies & TV shows.

Respectfully,

The Netflix Team

Netflix' admission that its plans went too far. An apology without apologizing. (e-mail from Netflix)

This is all, of course, predicated on the new choices being truly as good as or better than the current option. If the new choices would make people worse off, as in the case of the Netflix scenario in which customers would have had to administer two separate accounts, a yearning for the status quo is not necessarily an irrational bias.

Another way to introduce change is to do so incrementally. There is an anecdote that says if you place a frog in hot water, it does its best to hop straight out. However, if you place it in cold water and then heat the water slowly enough, the frog won't attempt to jump out. Although this is apparently not true, the description is still apt as a metaphor for certain human behavior. If you make changes slowly enough, users won't notice.

Google makes frequent low-key changes to its Gmail e-mail service. Although users probably don't notice most of the changes, comparing the interface from just a few years back with the interface of today can show a surprising number of differences. On the odd occasions that it needs to make large scale changes (such as during its 2011 interface consolidation), or changes to noticeable elements (such as its compose experience changes in 2012), Google offers an opportunity to preview the new layout and a chance to revert. Billing the preview as a sneak peek gives it a feeling of exclusivity. Metrics on how many users choose to become early adopters and how many of those subsequently revert to the old way undoubtedly give Google an early indicator as to how successful a change might be and enables it to test different change messaging options.

Even if customers do notice, smaller changes may invoke an outcry when the move is first enforced, but after a relatively short period of adjustment, users will typically begin to accept the new way of doing things. After a while they may even forget that there was a previous (different) way of doing things. Facebook has taken advantage of this on several occasions to implement major interface additions, confident that after a short time period people will forget their petitions and activism and just stop complaining.

The Oatmeal   http://theoatmeal.com

Major Facebook interface changes in 2010 led to uproar and petitions. Two months later, the changes were completely forgotten.
© *Matthew Inman, The Oatmeal*. (theoatmeal.com)

How to use the slippery slope

» Measure the impact of the change before you make it. Offer a preview of the change and then an option to revert. Measuring the number of reversions lets you know how likely the change is to be accepted by your general user base.

» Reassure customers that the thing you want them to do is much like what they're already doing, and that it won't require much of a change to their existing routines, habits, or workflows. This can help bypass status quo bias in getting people to agree with the new plan.

» Familiarize customers with the change over a period of time so that when it happens it isn't actually "new" any more.

» Message to customers that change is unfortunately necessary, but give them an option to "stick with what they have now" with only the changes that are necessary for technical reasons. If the changes are subtle enough, the messaging tactic will overcome status quo bias.

» Make changes in small increments. You may even need to create interim states to move customers from where they are today to where you want them to be.

» If you must make a big change, get customer feedback beforehand to ensure that you don't break too many of your customers' assumptions. Even if your new site is more efficient or feature-rich, you need to ensure that users can still perform their existing tasks.

» Claim that changes were made in response to customer requests. Even consider having a publicly accessible list of feature requests that you can link to as evidence.

» Pay more attention to the tone of subsequent complaints than to the volume. There may be some truth in the issues that customers describe.

» As an alternative to the slippery slope, if you hold a virtual monopoly, you can try just implementing the change anyway. Your mileage may vary. Facebook has confirmed its unassailable position in this way a couple of times already. Netflix tried and found that its position was not so unassailable as it had imagined.

Use metaphysical arguments to beat opponents

When appeals to rational thought fail, side-step logic and use metaphysical constructs in your arguments. Claim to have something that science can't explain.

It's hard to have serious debates about topics such as intelligent design versus natural selection because one side of the conversation stems from religious conviction and the other stems from scientific observation. For every scientific argument in favor of evolution, someone in favor of a creationist approach can give a faith-based response. The incompatibility of these two modes of thought is almost guaranteed to create an angry environment.

The reason that scientific arguments fail in this situation is because the opponents have moved the argument into the realm of the metaphysical (*meta* meaning *beyond*). Now, the discussion centers more on what you believe than upon what is demonstrable using the methods of science.

It appears that people often choose to discount scientific data if it conflicts with their beliefs, even if they still perceive themselves as generally pro-science. They rationalize this dissonance by claiming that the contentious area can't be described well by science. Geoffrey Munro at Towson University calls this "scientific impotence." In these situations, people who disagree with the findings might find it hard to discount the source of the information or the study's methodology, so instead they tend to claim that the topic is too complicated for science to understand. In other words, they are making a claim for a metaphysical (lack of) explanation. If this type of justification is happening in the heads of otherwise science-minded individuals, it's happening everywhere.

It's also not a level playing field. People resorting to metaphysical arguments have a wider range of tools available to them than those who stick to science. Arguments for a particular pseudoscientific idea may try to reverse the burden of proof so that skeptics must prove the thing false; claim that things that haven't been proven false must be true; use vague claims that are untestable or obscure; or appeal to emotions rather than logic, for instance by stating that there is a conspiracy against the idea.

Anthony Pratkanis, professor of psychology at UC Santa Cruz and an expert on persuasion and propaganda, lists nine things that are used to sell pseudoscience that go beyond the types of claims that scientists can safely make about their work:

1. **Create a phantom:** An unavailable goal that looks real and possible but in reality always remains at least one more step away.

2. **Set a rationalization trap:** Get people committed. Then, rather than evaluating merits they will instead seek to prove how they are right.

3. **Manufacture source credibility and sincerity:** Create someone believable as the authority figure making the claims.

4. **Establish a granfalloon:** The term is appropriated from the author Kurt Vonnegut and means "a proud and meaningless association of human beings" who share rituals and symbols, jargon and beliefs, goals, feelings, specialized information, and enemies.

5. **Use self-generated persuasion:** By asking people to "sell" the concept, they get more personally convinced of its merits.

6. **Construct vivid appeals:** A graphically described single incident can trump logical arguments.

7. **Use pre-persuasion:** Frame the argument in terms that make the competition look bad (the FDA wants to remove your freedom to choose our treatment), use differentiation (we have a special technique that sets us apart from the frauds in this field), set expectations (for instance through labeling), and specify the decision criteria (set your own guidelines for what is acceptable evidence).

8. **Frequently use heuristics and commonplaces:** These are rules, norms, and beliefs that are widely accepted. For instance "What is natural is good" and "If it costs more, it must be more valuable" can both be attached to a premium health food product to give it credibility. Because of their general acceptance, these statements will not often be questioned.

9. **Attack opponents through innuendo and character assassination:** Make them out to be biased, bad scientists who will probably shortly be investigated for their obvious wrongdoings.

Using metaphysical claims such as these correctly can invoke feelings similar to religion. That's not surprising because these are indeed some of the same techniques used by religious organizations. A 2011 BBC documentary on "Superbrands" found that an MRI scan of an Apple fanatic suggested that Apple was actually stimulating the same parts of the brain as religious imagery does in people of faith. Kirsten Bell, an anthropologist at the University of British Columbia moved from studying religions in South Korea to the culture of biomedical research, but while reporting on an Apple product launch for TechNewsDaily, she noted the direct comparisons such as sacred symbols (the Apple logo), a keynote address from a revered leader, and a crowd of willing acolytes (the press). This reinforces earlier research by Pui-Yan Lam at Washington State University who found that Mac devotees' relationship with their technology bordered on the spiritual.

Bell does admit that there isn't a direct comparison because religion is aimed at explaining the meaning of life, whereas technology probably doesn't have such lofty goals. Still, religious fervor among your customer base can obviously be useful, especially if customers feel like they are supporting the underdog, as Apple was for many years before its recent ascendancy. Customers' anger allows them to label any criticism as "envy" from those who have "inferior" products.

Just for fun, unpack some of Pratkanis' techniques from the Apple perspective:

1. **Create a phantom.** Every new Apple product release seems to add just enough new functionality or sex appeal to highlight the deficiencies in your current version. Perhaps Apple needs to make customers feel the religion so that they will continue upgrading. "This *next* iPhone will be the last one I ever need." …until the next one is released.

2. **Set a rationalization trap.** The newer influx of Apple users may have diluted the original fervor of Mac devotees, but it's still possible to see rationalization at work just by starting a discussion of the relative value-per-dollar of Apple computers versus generic PCs.

3. **Manufacture source credibility and sincerity.** Steve Jobs, the now-deceased father of Apple, has been replaced by head designer Jony Ive as the spiritual leader of the Apple clan.

4. **Establish a granfalloon.** Enter any Apple store to see ritual, symbolism, and feelings at work creating a feeling of belonging for the in-group of Apple users. Door greeters might as well be saying, "Welcome home."

5. **Use self-generated persuasion.** Apple fans are the company's best salespeople. Hype and limited initial availability lead to total strangers asking early adopters how they like their new toy. It's unlikely these avid fans are going to say, "I hate it!"

6. **Construct vivid appeals.** New products are demonstrated on-stage using a few select applications that show off the key elements of the product in an emotionally compelling manner (editing vacation photos, planning an exciting event, and so on).

7. **Use pre-persuasion.** Apple often shies away from direct technical comparison with competitors. Indeed, CEO Tim Cook said, "[Product specifications] are the things tech companies invent because they can't provide a great experience." Instead, the company bypasses this rational comparison. Apple marketing normally makes performance comparisons only to previous versions of the same Apple product, and instead redirects by providing aesthetic and emotional (metaphysical) comparisons to competitor products.

8. **Frequently use heuristics and commonplaces.** Some of the widely accepted statements that Apple has adopted include "Quality is never cheap," "You are paying for good design," "It's easy to use," and "Think different."

9. **Attack opponents.** This is one technique that Apple doesn't tend to openly employ. Despite Jobs' promise to "go to thermonuclear war" on Android, Apple's marketing rarely even mentions competitors. Instead it talks sadly about how the rest of the industry just doesn't "get it" the same way that Apple does.

If you are an Apple product user, I apologize if you felt anger at any of my characterizations in the preceding list. However, that emotional response is worth analyzing. After all, if it were only the technology at stake, why would we bother to move beyond a strict logical comparison? And no hate mail, thanks—I wrote this book on an iMac.

"Every iKeynote ever" courtesy of The Doghouse Diaries © *The Doghouse Diaries.*
(thedoghousediaries.com/?p=2628)

How to use metaphysical arguments

» Rather than relying on rational arguments, create a relatively unassailable position by introducing "evidence" that can't be disproved scientifically. Arguments that make an emotional or spiritual appeal, or claim to have something "unexplained by science" cannot be directly confronted by scientific facts alone.

» Put the burden on others to "disprove" your claims. So long as your claims are sufficiently broad or generic, you can reframe the issue even if compelling negative evidence is presented.

» Find a charismatic and believable spokesperson to repeat your broad and generic claims. It helps if that spokesperson has credibility, even if it's only in a slightly related field. ("I'm not a doctor, but I play one on TV.")

» Recruit customers to be salespeople. This can both convince those customers that the product is worth selling and also force them to justify their own use of the product.

» Enhance customers' sense of belonging by giving them a sense of identity, and somewhere to hang out and reinforce each other's belief in what they are buying. Creating an "us versus the world" ambience will draw customers closer to each other and to defending your product.

» Create a couple of clear and emotionally appealing case studies rather than relying on pages of facts.

» If you do have lots of facts, show them. It will help polarize your audience. The people who already were against you will become more so, but the people who believed in you will become firmer adherents.

» If all else fails, complain about "the establishment" and how "traditional" ways of evaluating products are hurting your wonderful new idea.

Embracing anger

On January 12, 2011, a lady walking down a street in Coventry, England, stopped briefly to pet a cat, and then proceeded to pick it up, dump it in a trashcan and close the lid. The cat, Lola, spent the night in the trashcan before being found the next day by its owners.

What the lady probably didn't anticipate was that Lola's owners had a surveillance camera mounted on the outside of their house. Understandably confused, they posted a clip of the incident online. The Internet went to work, and within a few hours the anonymous lady who had dumped the cat was identified as Mary Bale, a bank teller who worked in nearby Rugby and lived just down the road from Lola's owners. Along with details of where she lived, the Internet sleuths also posted links to her Facebook profile, her place of work, and her boss' phone number. As a result of the threats she subsequently received, Bale was given a police guard for her own protection.

Mary Bale and Lola (youtube.com video)

The "outing" was performed by a group who thrives on anonymity—members of the /b/ (random) board of the 4chan community. 4chan is closely linked with Anonymous, the group that is behind many high-visibility online retribution attacks. Although much of the content on /b/ will "melt your brain" according to Gawker.com's Nick Douglas, /b/ members seem to have a soft spot for cats. They are responsible for the Lolcat meme and had previously interceded to ensure the welfare of Dusty, another cat who was seen being abused in a YouTube video. 4chan and Anonymous found a way to channel the anger of individuals within the community into coordinated action.

Mary Bale commented after the event, "I did it as a joke because I thought it would be funny. I think everyone is overreacting a bit." It is unlikely that she ever expected to be identified. Her expectation of anonymity may indeed have contributed to her actions. It's probable too that the somewhat inevitable angry backlash against her, both her identification by 4chan members and the subsequent Internet wide condemnation, which included several death threats, was amplified somewhat by the commenters' ability to remain anonymous.

As Bale demonstrated, when the burden of taking responsibility for their actions is removed, people often do things that they otherwise wouldn't. That can be beneficial, such as when an anonymous donor steps in to provide finances for a struggling charity, or potentially harmful, such as when anonymous commenters bully people online. The trick to embracing anger is to find ways of channeling it toward the ends you seek.

Use anonymity to encourage repressed behaviors

People will do more when they're anonymous than when they're identifiable.

Normally, physical social structures prevent people from actually demonstrating hate and anger. However, protest marches can soon turn into riots because the anonymity of being in a large crowd and the feeling of being part of a group that reinforces your attitudes are both states that encourage behavior that individuals wouldn't normally engage in. This behavior can be either positive or negative.

Interestingly, the "deindividuating" effect of anonymity and group membership is true both of the protesters and of the group policing the event. Philip Zimbardo performed one of the key psychological studies that investigated this effect. Called the Stanford prison study, Zimbardo randomly assigned 24 individuals to be either prisoners or guards in a cell block constructed at Stanford University's psychology department. The study was designed to last 2 weeks but had to be stopped after only 6 days because the participants had taken on their roles a little too well. The prisoner group had started to act in a passive and depressed manner, whereas the guard group had begun to exhibit overly controlling and even sadistic behavior toward the prisoners.

The same factors are at play online. If you can create an anonymous group of individuals with similar interests but different opinions, just sit back and watch the flame wars start! This phenomenon has been documented frequently enough that it has led to *Godwin's law*, coined by Mike Godwin in 1990, which states, "As an online discussion grows longer, the probability of a comparison involving Nazis or Hitler approaches one."

John Suler, professor of psychology at Rider University, names six factors that contribute to what he calls the online disinhibition effect:

>> **You don't know me:** Being anonymous provides a sense of protection.

» **You can't see me:** Someone's online embodiment is different than that person's true self.

» **See you later:** Online conversations are asynchronous. There is nobody to instantly disapprove of what is said.

» **It's all in my head:** It's easier to assign negative traits to people you don't interact with face to face.

» **It's just a game:** Some people see the online environment as a kind of game where normal rules don't apply.

» **We're equals:** The reluctance someone might feel to speak his mind to an authority figure is removed when it's not clear who is or is not an authority figure.

Anonymity cuts both ways. People posting anonymously or in a forum feel confident that their online insults won't affect their real-life relationships. They are safe to "troll." But social networks also introduce a layer of pseudo-anonymity between the poster and the reader, so that posters don't always think as clearly as they should about what they post. People post comments about their boss or about skipping work that get them fired. Students post comments about their teachers that get them suspended. It could just be stupidity, but it's likely also that the audience was anonymous to these individuals, so they didn't think about the consequences of what they were doing. Had they been standing in a room with all the people who could read their post, they probably wouldn't have written it.

The middle ground is pseudo-anonymity. Pseudonyms are names that help identify the same person across multiple interactions (multiple forum posts, for instance) but do not disclose who that individual is in the real world.

Google kicked up a lot of controversy when 1 month after the launch of the Google+ social network it suddenly started requiring people to use their real names to sign up. The uproar created by the subsequent removal of pseudonymous accounts led to what has been termed the *Nymwars*. Although Google wasn't the first to believe that requiring a real name would reduce abusive behavior (game company Blizzard did the same thing with its RealID; Facebook has always required real names or brand verification), Google's crackdown on accounts that used pseudonyms, stage names, and well-known nicknames provoked sufficient backlash to get the Electronic Frontier Foundation involved.

The EFF argued that pseudonyms enable many individuals to participate in online communities without fear of discrimination or reprisal. This might sound much like the situation that enables anonymous trolls to thrive, but as the EFF notes, the words "to protect unpopular individuals from retaliation" are enshrined in the first amendment to the U.S. Constitution. The protection can be used for good or for evil.

Pseudonymous participation in forums is different in several ways from anonymous participation. Disqus.com, a commenting platform used to handle discussions on more than 1 million websites, analyzed the quantity and quality of comments from anonymous, pseudonymous, and named individuals. They defined quality as the number of "likes" and/or replies each type of comment gathered, as opposed to the number of flags, spam markers, and deletes that commenter received. Anonymous users provided the lowest quality comments, but it was pseudonymous rather than named users who provided the highest quality comments. Overall 61 percent of the pseudonymous comments were seen as positive, whereas 51 percent of those from people using their real names and only 34 percent of the anonymous comments possessed the positive quality attributes.

Online disinhibition doesn't always take place. When the conversations are synchronous (removing Suler's third factor from the equation), people tend to talk the same online as offline and tend to talk the same way over time. Antonios Garas and his colleagues at ETH Zurich found that online real-time chats also seem to be emotionally balanced and generally positive. The authors suggest that this is because chatters return to the chat rooms regularly, to meet users they may already "know," even if all of them are still pseudonymous.

Clear online rules of engagement (removing Suler's fifth factor) can also help. In a metastudy of deindividuation research (the "acting as part of a crowd" effect), Tom Postmes and Russel Spears found that when individuals were in this deindividuated state, although they acted less according to their normal personal rules, they were more sensitive to situational norms: the cues that people get from their environment that tell them what behavior would be appropriate at that time and place. So, if the group's normal behavior were to engage in flame wars, that's what people would do. If the group norm were to help new members find their feet, that's what people would do. In other words, making it clear what the group norms are helps set the tone of the online communication.

A couple of useful sites can exist only online because of the level of anonymity they offer. Glassdoor.com and tellyourbossanything.com both work by enabling anonymous contributions. In both situations, using their real names could get posters into trouble, so posters may feel too inhibited to say what they actually felt. These sites enable a type of communication that would otherwise not happen.

Glassdoor.com aggregates employee reviews of their companies, salary information, and interview questions that are frequently used with external candidates. Although the site requires Facebook or an e-mail address to sign in, it posts each review anonymously as "Current Employee" or "Former Employee," thus allowing individuals to be more open in their analysis. As a result, Glassdoor.com has become a source of relatively honest if not completely independent reviews that can help jobseekers decide whether they want to join a particular organization.

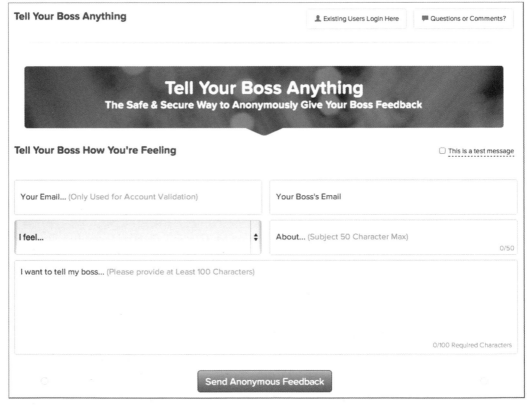

It's not possible to tell your boss everything you'd like to face to face, so an anonymizing service like tellyourbossanything.com can help employees feel more valued and managers receive better (or at least more honest) feedback.

Tellyourbossanything.com enables managers to get feedback from their employees through an anonymous survey, or enables employees to initiate the conversation by telling their boss how they feel. The site is actually a subset of (and marketing tool for) happiily.com, which provides a way of tracking employee sentiment over time. As a free anonymizing tool, it's an easy way for groups to remove the effects of authority, Suler's sixth factor.

Overall, although anonymity can have negative consequences, it also has the capability to uncover issues that are too personal or emotional to discuss when the participants are identifiable. People dealing with gender or sexuality issues, disabilities that they prefer to keep private, and questions on topics that are taboo in their local environment all benefit from anonymity. Pseudonymous behavior can still be civil while allowing sharing of information and feelings that would otherwise be hidden.

How to use anonymity

» Help visitors feel that they have the pseudo-anonymity of being in a like-minded group. This allows them to "deindividuate" and take on the values of the group. Adopting those values allows them to do things that they might not otherwise countenance.

» Manipulate Suler's six factors of online disinhibition to create a suitably sustainable environment:

» Use pseudo-anonymity rather than straight anonymity so that contributors can be recognized across sessions (Suler's "You don't know me" and "You can't see me" factors).

» Allow some indication of real-life attributes (achievements, location, skills, and so on) to provide a link to the real world (Suler's "It's all in my head" and "We're equals" factors).

» Provide synchronous communication to limit out-of-bounds behavior (Suler's "See you later" factor).

» State the rules. Say what is allowed, and what will get people thrown out. Follow through with post deletions and bans (Suler's "It's just a game" factor).

» Balance the online disinhibition that can follow complete anonymity with the protection offered by pseudo-anonymity.

Give people permission

If an authority figure tells people to do something, it removes individual responsibility.

In his now-infamous psychological study, Stanley Milgram told participants that they were helping him with experiments into memory and learning. Participants played the role of "teacher," and their task was to administer electric shocks to a "learner" if they gave wrong answers, starting at 15 volts and rising in 15-volt steps to 450 volts. Before the session started, participants were given a sample shock to demonstrate the low end of what the learner would receive for wrong answers.

What the participants didn't know was that the "learner" was an actor following a script who made purposeful mistakes in his answers so that the participant was required to give him a shock. The "learner" never actually received the shocks, despite acting like he had. The voltages were labeled on the electric shock box, which also made noises appropriate to each voltage when activated. Although the "learner" was in a different room, participants could still hear him, so the effects of their actions were obvious. Milgram or one of his co-experimenters was in the room with the participants and instructed them to continue if they voiced concerns.

Sixty percent of participants went all the way to 450 volts, even after hearing screams, pleading, or an ominous silence from the "learner." Many were obviously uncomfortable continuing to this level, showing physical and mental signs of distress, but most still bowed to the wishes of the authority figure.

Milgram's reason for running the experiment was primarily that he wanted to disprove the defense used after the Second World War by German officers accused of war crimes. These men claimed that they were "just following orders." Before undertaking the study, Milgram and those he consulted were sure that no more than 1 percent of individuals would proceed to the highest level of shock.

The results surprised everyone. As Milgram wrote later, looking back on the study "Many of the subjects, at the level of stated opinion, feel quite as strongly as any of us about the moral requirement of refraining from action against a helpless victim. … This has little, if anything, to do with their actual behavior under the pressure of circumstances." That "pressure of circumstances" is the authority figure telling them what to do. "The subject entrusts the broader tasks of setting goals and assessing morality to the experimental authority he is serving."

The experiment was not a one-off event. It has been repeated multiple times in different countries with many variations, and typically sees 61 to 66 percent of participants reaching voltages that would be fatal if truly administered to the "learner."

It turns out that individuals can "morally disengage" when an authority figure requires them to act. This moral disengagement takes several forms. For instance, someone might attempt to reframe morally ambiguous acts as being morally justified ("It's for their own good"), might mentally minimize the effects of their actions ("It didn't cause lasting harm"), might blame their victim ("They had it coming to them"), or simply claim that their superiors were the responsible ones ("I was just following orders"). Moral disengagement is also easier if a group collectively engages in the activity because then moral responsibility is diffused among the individuals.

Part of the disengagement happens simply because of the authority wielded by the person giving the command, and part happens because of the additional justifications that the individual either is given by the authority figure or makes up for himself. So when an authority figure provides us with the excuses we need, what more permission could we need to act?

Much of the advertising we see around us uses this authority permission effect. That is especially true in the field of prescription drug advertising. WebMD.com is a trusted online source of medical information, and its advertisers use WebMD's authority to help sell their products by association with the authoritative, advice-giving site. WebMD devotes whole sections of its site to sponsored content, where the sponsor has complete editorial control. Without reading the small print, it's hard to know where the authoritative voice of the site ends and the advertorial content starts.

Sea-Tac airport gives you permission to buy a Frappucino from Starbucks rather than drinking free water from a water fountain. Go on, you deserve it.

The permission-giving doesn't stop there. Within the sponsor's content there are several helpful guides that, for instance, teach people the euphemistic terms for certain conditions, provide justifications for taking specific medication, compare their medication favorably to other outcomes, and play down side effects by hiding them in small print. This authoritative permission-giving can be helpful in raising general awareness, but when it's sponsored by an individual product, you have to wonder at the motives behind the awareness-raising and permission-giving.

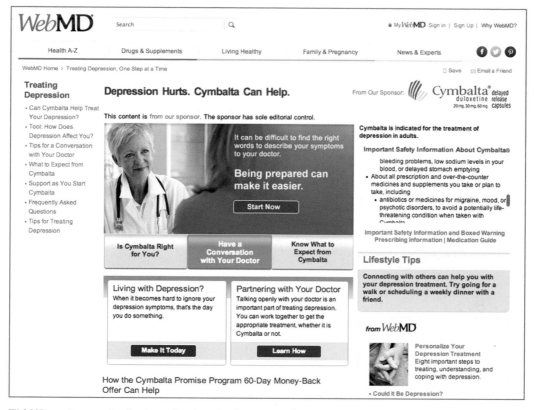

WebMD.com's aura of authority makes it easier for sponsored content to give people permission.

Thankfully, reverse-engineering this effect allows it to be used for good instead of evil. Authority figures can tell people to take positive actions. They can avoid displacement and diffusion of responsibility by ensuring that individuals remain personally accountable.

Regardless of the motivations behind its actions, Anheuser Busch (the makers of Budweiser and other alcoholic beverages) use authority and responsibility as the key factors in its "Responsible Drinker" campaign. Its main website contains content from the Budweiser sponsored NASCAR driver Kevin Harvick, who talks about the importance of having a designated driver when out drinking. In this context as a professional race car driver, Harvick is seen as a voice of authority. This page links to Anheuser Busch's microsite, NationOfResponsibleDrinkers.com, which encourages individuals to take responsibility by signing a pledge to drink responsibly and then post the pledge to their Facebook page. This public display of personal responsibility makes it harder for individuals to later morally disengage.

How to use authority to give people permission

» Create an authoritative stance, either by association with people who truly have authority or by using the trappings and language of authoritative people.

» Give people permission by providing them with reasons to do the thing they otherwise might not. Typically those reasons fall into one of the following categories:

   » **Moral justification**: *We're fighting a ruthless oppressor.*

   » **Euphemistic labeling**: Civilian deaths during war are called *collateral damage.*

   » **Advantageous comparison**: *We're killing lots of people in this country so that they don't turn into communists, which would be worse.*

   » **Displacement of responsibility**: *I was just following orders.*

   » **Diffusion of responsibility**: *Everyone else was doing the same thing;* or *I only played a small part.*

   » **Distortion of consequences**: *There was no real harm.*

» Give people a small role to play so that they don't feel entirely responsible. For instance, carrying out only one part of a procedure may allow people to morally disengage, even if they'd refuse to perform the whole procedure.

» To purposefully withhold permission, use an authority figure to make individuals take responsibility for an action. For instance, by following a race car driver's lead and signing up to be responsible drivers, people accept that they no longer have permission to drink alcohol.

Scare people (if you have the solution)

Make people afraid, and then show them how to remove that fear using your product.

Happiness rarely triggers commerce. Unhappiness often does.

Purchases are triggered by dissatisfaction with the way things are. We purchase when we have a need, a desire, an itch to scratch. We want to change our condition, our surroundings, our state of mind. We buy because we are dissatisfied.

And this dissatisfaction is often created by the advertising that offers to remedy it.

ROY H. WILLIAMS

When did static cling between the clothes in a tumble dryer become a problem? You have a magical machine that dries your clothes in less than half an hour and yet you worry that sometimes a couple of items may get stuck together.

Static-removing conditioning liquids and sheets are a solution to a manufactured problem. There is a marginal inconvenience; there is no "problem." Fabric conditioner is actually mainly made of grease (the same thing you were trying to remove from your clothes). It just smells nicer than the grease that was on there before.

This is an example of a manufactured problem to which solutions can be sold. Others include Listerine mouthwash, which popularized the obscure medical term *halitosis* to invoke fear of bad breath; and Lifebuoy soap, which made the term B.O. (body odor) famous in order to sell a solution.

The social psychologists Anthony Pratkanis and Elliot Aronson suggest, "All other things being equal, the more frightened a person is by a communication, the more likely he or she is to take positive preventive action."

Fear is a great motivator, but fear without resolution is too hard for people to deal with, so they find ways to block out the fear-inducing stimuli. The audience must feel that they have the power to deal with the fear and make it go away. A successful appeal requires showing how your product or service can remove that fear. Often the path to removing the fear is through anger.

Think for instance about how right-wing radio talk show hosts stir up their audience. First, there is the cocky self-assuredness while introducing a topic that leaves no doubt in listeners' minds that they are right, and the simplification of the problem into an us-versus-them battle that pitches the righteous listener against some evil liberal or foreign plot.

Next come two neat tricks: complimenting the listener on being too smart to believe the lies, and revealing the big secret about what's actually happening. This reveal is delivered with enough bluster to create not just fear, but anger. At this point the audience is demanding that someone take action, and it's just up to the host to tell them what needs to be done.

This is, of course, the traditional conspiracy theory formula with an added sprinkling of incitement to riot added in. Making people fearful or angry enough and providing a sensible-sounding solution can ensure that at least some of them take action.

Why do people fall for this type of fear-mongering? Research into prejudice by Gordon Hodson and Michael Busseri suggests that people who have difficulty grasping the complexity of the world might tend toward prejudice and conservatism because they find it too hard to interact with people not like themselves and because they like the structure and simplicity provided by socially conservative ideologies. In addition, Hodson and Busseri showed a correlation between poor critical-reasoning skills, prejudice, and acceptance of right-wing authoritarianism.

Hodson suggests that an appeal to feelings rather than thoughts might be effective for individuals who find it too difficult cognitively to take the perspective of others. Of course, Hodson is suggesting that we create positive feelings. The talk show hosts seem to have already demonstrated that this works for negative feelings.

Fear is used overtly in the selling of several types of product. Product categories such as vitamins (fear of ill-health), child safety (think of the children!) and home security (fear of strangers) tend to be high on potential drama so that they can then show that they have solutions that will remove the need for fear.

The Truth About Area 51 and The NSA

It's pretty obvious that Area 51 is playing host to one of FEMA's detention facilities. Otherwise, why would various shipping companies have delivered so many body-bag-shaped boxes there?

Over the years, the Vatican has built a secret property empire using millions donated from the NSA. You know where the NSA got those millions? Area 51.

If you listen to radio waves coming from the constellation of Orion, you will be shocked to hear what sounds like routine transmissions from the NSA -- but why are they coming FROM outer space?

The last time anyone came forth to speak about this, they immediately noticed increased surveillance at their house and place of work. Suspicious, right?

If you think BP is what they claim, think again: in 2008, the night before the government bailout, the NSA accepted over $150 million in donations from BP.

Now that you know the truth, save your family and friends. Let them know the truth.

Sources:

1. Donnelly, John J., Jeffrey B. Ulmer, and Margaret A. Liu. "DNA vaccines."Life sciences 60.3 (1996): 163-172.
2. Eckstein, Harry. "Pressure group politics." Academic Medicine 35.11 (1960): 1069.
3. Derkzen, Petra, Alex Franklin, and Bettina Bock. "Examining power struggles as a signifier of successful partnership working: A case study of partnership dynamics." Journal of Rural Studies 24.4 (2008): 458-466.

Verifiedfacts.org is a wonderful site that provides an almost endless supply of randomly generated conspiracies on demand. Each describes a precedent, an us-versus-them elite, someone determined to unveil the truth, an expert who backs the suspicion, and an imminent threat to deal with.

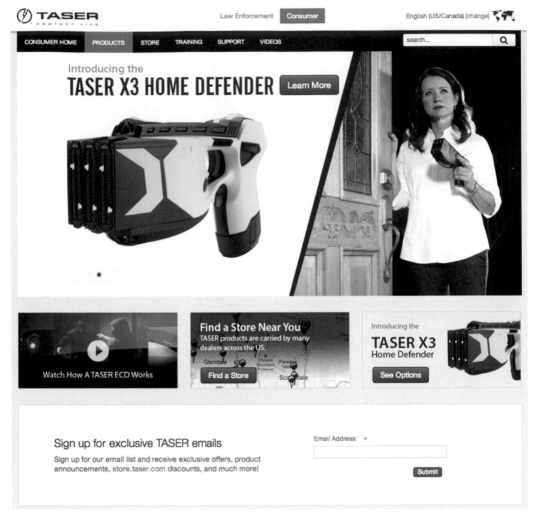

TASER International, Inc. manufactures conducted electrical weapons to "incapacitate dangerous, combative, or high-risk subjects who pose a risk to law enforcement officers, innocent citizens, or themselves." TASER claims to provide solutions that "Protect Life, Protect Truth, and Protect Family." (taser.com)

An example of this is the marketing for TASER "nonlethal" electric shock guns. These are marketed to police forces in terms of number of lives saved, the assumption being mainly that suspects would have been shot with guns if

Tasers weren't available. But obviously that's not a suitably fear-inducing tactic to encourage civilian purchases, so instead TASER resorts to videos of masked intruders to reinforce the threat and images of people answering their front doors brandishing the weapon to emphasize the solution.

The tactic apparently works. TASER has sold more than 255,000 weapons to private individuals since 1994, accounting for approximately 5 percent to 6 percent of its annual business, worth upward of $4.6 million per year.

How to scare people

» Ensure you have all three ingredients: the anger-inducing threat, a convincing recommendation for dealing with that anger, and an action that people can take right now.

  » Make it clear who the enemy is and how unlike the audience this enemy behaves. *The French don't believe that we should go to war against Iraq. What kind of American allies are they?*

  » Show what this enemy is doing. Make it clear how bad this thing is. Potentially project to a future state in which the bad thing has occurred in a highly inflated way, and how bad this situation would be for the audience. *How can we possibly maintain world peace unless we fight Iraq? Everyone knows it has weapons of mass destruction. America(n interests) could be at risk! Think of the children!*

  » Show how the audience can prevent the enemy from winning by taking an action. The action should, if possible, require minimum effort and be instantly achievable and gratifying. *Stick it to the French. Only eat at places that have relabeled French Fries as Freedom Fries.*

Pour les Français: Je m'excuse pour les folies d'un petit groupe de mes compatriotes. Je sais que les «Frites Français» sont vraiment belges.

Using anger safely in your products

There's a lot in life to be angry about. Sturgeon's law states "90% of everything is crap." That's a lot of stuff to wade through to find the good things. We're very likely to end up with one of the bad things at some point, and that will make us upset and potentially angry.

In their paper "Portrait of the angry decision maker," Jennifer Lerner and Larissa Tiedens note that anger is one of the most frequently experienced emotions. It is also, they say, one that disproportionately infuses other events in our lives. It can make people indiscriminately optimistic about their chances of success, careless in their thought, and eager to act.

That's great news for companies trying to persuade somebody to make a purchase, but there obviously is also a downside. If the company is the target of that anger, it can expect irrational mass reactions that go way beyond what identifiable individuals would perform on their own. The power of the anonymous group can have chilling effects.

Anger is an emotional reaction to unwelcome news. The choices are to prevent the reaction or to use it as a tool for social persuasion. If you plan on intentionally working people into a rage, you also must channel that anger by telling them how to fix the issue.

It's been suggested that humor and anger are incompatible responses, so if you can get people to experience humor, it will at least temporarily remove their angry thoughts. Better yet might be to avoid the anger all together by introducing potentially anger-inducing changes piece by piece. Taken as a whole, those changes could cause an uprising. Seen individually they are merely annoying, if they invoke any reaction at all.

Angry people aren't necessarily rational. Actually, angry people tend to rely on pre-existing conclusions rather than applying analytical thought. Companies make use of this by appealing to people's emotional state through the use of metaphysical arguments. As you've seen, the result is "scientific impotence" because metaphysics trumps physics. In other words, companies don't even need to make a rational argument. If they can harness a strong emotion such as anger, they can appeal purely to people's emotions and still get their way.

Sometimes, amplifying anger can work for a company rather than against it. People who feel that they are either anonymous or that someone else will accept responsibility for their actions will do things that they would never normally countenance. So long as the company can channel that emotion toward its own ends, it is only necessary to provide a target and then step back and let the anonymous mob do the work.

More positively, pseudonymity can be used to help people overcome the anger of those around them to learn from and contribute to communities that they couldn't openly join. Engineering statements from authority figures to make people take rather than relinquish responsibility can also lead to positive outcomes.

Anger is unusual among negative emotions. People induced to feel anger subsequently make more optimistic judgments and choices about themselves than do people induced to feel fear. The difference is that anger has a defined target and potential for resolution, whereas fear does not. A common persuasion technique involves inducing fear by scaring people, and then giving those people a target and a way to resolve the fear through anger. Again, by appealing to feelings rather than to thoughts, the persuader can bypass rational thought and directly target raw emotions. When people's emotions are stirred up, it takes only the suggestion of a possible solution for individuals to take it and run with it.

There's obviously a difference between blind rage, brooding sullenness, and the type of controlled anger that you can provide an outlet for. You must elicit the right level of anger, complete with an obvious target. Presenting a problem with an unknown cause creates fear, a problem with a more global cause that is not under the individual's control invokes sadness, and a problem for which the individual is responsible gives feelings of guilt or shame.

You must also show how individuals can influence the situation to remove the cause of their anger. Angry people are much more likely to want to change the situation than are people experiencing other negative emotions. Unlike other negative emotions, which tend to cause more introspection and insightful analysis, anger makes people fall back on their existing behavior patterns, tends to stereotype their perceptions of others, and focuses on superficial characteristics of individuals rather than the quality of their arguments. As a result, because they aren't processing deeply, angry people feel more certain about the choices they make.

Maybe the type of anger companies hope to induce shouldn't be classed as a sin. Its effects are closer to positive emotions than negative ones. Even though people look back on angry times as unpleasant and unrewarding, when they are in the throes of anger, they find it pleasant and rewarding, perhaps because they are anticipating revenge or Schadenfreude (the joy of seeing disliked others suffer).

Envy

Neither shalt thou desire thy neighbor's wife, neither shalt thou covet thy neighbor's house, his field, or his manservant, or his maidservant, his ox, or his ass, or any thing that is thy neighbor's.

DEUTERONOMY 5:21

ENVY IS SPECIFICALLY FORBIDDEN in the Ten Commandments of the Christian Bible. Still, as a race we humans seem to be almost hard-wired to react to other people's success with envy.

Sometimes envy can be benign. Seeing a famous musician playing in front of an admiring audience might be the inspiration that a child needs to practice her scales. However, as Mark Alicke and Ethan Zell point out in the book *Envy: Theory and Research*, "People who are more attractive, more popular, smarter, wealthier or more skilled cast other people's own qualities in a disadvantageous light. There is a fine line, therefore, between admiring people's superiors and basking in their accomplishments, and envying them and wishing them ill will."

And that's where envy gets nasty. Evolutionarily, to be seen as the most attractive mate, it's not sufficient to have a lot of something; you have to have more than others around you. That makes us *inequality averse* to use a term from economics. In other words, we hate feeling like we've lost out. That feeling of deprivation, inferiority, or shame is the basis of destructive envy.

With *destructive envy*, it's not just that we want the thing that someone else has; we also want that other person to not have it because their having it makes us feel inferior. In these situations, we make decisions based not just on benefit to ourselves, but also to make gains over others around us. So, even if we found ourselves in a situation in which we could gain more by cooperating with someone, destructive envy dictates that we'd often rather not work together than be in a position in which that other person benefitted more than we did.

Whether the root of someone's envy is benign or destructive, it's a powerful motivating force. That means it can be harnessed to make customers do things.

Manufacturing envy through desire and aspiration

To use envy as a motivating force, it has to first exist. The precursors of envy are aspiration and desire, and much of the publicity around products is designed to create those feelings.

> *Publicity persuades … by showing us people who have apparently been transformed and are, as a result, enviable. The state of being envied is what constitutes glamour. Publicity is always about the future buyer. It offers him an image of himself made glamorous by the product or opportunity it is trying to sell. The image then makes him envious of himself as he might be.*

> JOHN BERGER: WAYS OF SEEING

Aspiration leads to benign envy by creating a wish to emulate what we see. Desire can lead to benign or destructive envy by creating a wish to have what we see, and to even stop others from having it.

 Create desirability to produce envy

An object must be desirable for envy to work as a motivating force.

If nobody desires an object, that object is unlikely to create envy. Because envy is such a strong motivator, persuasion works by first creating desire and then leveraging that desire with envy. Some ways to create desire include:

» **Secrecy**: Being one of the few in the know about an item.

» **Scarcity**: Small numbers, low availability of the item.

» **Identity**: Identify the item with a desirable lifestyle, person, or activity.

» **Aesthetics**: The item is pleasing to look at, hold, and use.

» **Functionality**: The item solves a problem nobody else is solving.

Apple hits all these marks with its hardware. It is secretive leading up to a launch, which creates large quantities of speculation. People stand in line for days waiting to be the first to have the new product. The newly launched product then typically sells out fast, creating scarcity. Celebrities tweet about or are seen with the product, which is typically pleasing to look at and has a unique interaction design that solves problems in an elegant manner, especially if it provides functionality that solves a problem that people didn't previously know they had.

The aesthetics of Apple products work on a visceral level. People respond positively to attractive faces, symmetrical and rounded objects, and soothing colors and sounds. Even the front-facing camera mimics the beauty spot from another aesthetic icon.

The end result is large quantities of desire. That desire leads to envy, sometimes more than even Apple would have expected. In early 2012, criminals mugging people for their phones around Columbia University in Manhattan were not interested in Android devices, only iPhones. New York mayor Michael Bloomberg even blamed the rise in the city's annual crime index on the 3890 extra iPhones that were stolen in the city in 2012. The thefts may have something to do with iPhones having higher resale values, but then resale values are also driven by desirability.

How to create desirability

Use one or more of the five desire paths—secrecy, scarcity, identity, aesthetics, functionality—to make people want what you offer.

» **Secrecy:** Provide little information about the substance or timing of a product release. Let a small group of well-connected individuals know what's happening, and wait for them to leak small details. This works best if your business has already established other elements of desirability.

» **Scarcity:** Make a release exclusive (through price or quantity) or just hard to find. Have sufficient product waiting in the wings for when the panic buying starts.

» **Identity:** The staple of print advertising. You don't get a bikini-clad model free with every bottle of sunscreen you buy, but you'd expect this to be the case given the frequency of association in ads.

» **Aesthetics:** The design, feel, and usability of the product must resonate with your target audience. This is hard to fake—it takes real work to make an aesthetically pleasing product.

» **Functionality:** Identify and then solve a problem that nobody else has solved. Although not easy, this is extremely effective. Even solving small problems can have a big payoff.

 ## Create something aspirational

Give your users something to aspire to. Benign envy is a powerful motivator.

Lifestyle magazines aren't aimed at who they say they are: *Cosmo* is aimed at 17-year-olds; *Just 17* is aimed at 13-year-olds who aspire to be as grown up as 17-year-olds.

Although there is a big aspirational market for a magazine called *Better Homes and Gardens*, you wouldn't expect to find one called *Double Wide Weekly* or *Mobile Home Monthly* because mobile homes are often the first step on the property ladder. Actually though there is such a magazine: it's called *Upwardly Mobile Home Magazine, the magazine of mobile, manufactured, and modular home living*, and it's all about making mobile homes posher. In other words, it's still totally aspirational.

Aspiration—a form of benign envy—encourages people to emulate their idols and fuels ambition. Creating desirability through association with a famous person (desirability through identity) is the basis of celebrity endorsements and the reason why movie stars don't pay for the dresses they wear on the red carpet at the Oscars award ceremony.

Fashion from Paris catwalks and the red carpet at the Oscars makes its way into high street stores and big box retailers quickly because wearing something visibly similar to the haute couture clothes is aspirational.

Given that people will emulate their idols, there is obviously a place for idols to endorse products online in more creative ways than just appearing in advertisements. Leveraging aspiration online has even extended to Twitter. Now, companies can pay celebrities to tweet 140 characters about their brand or latest campaign. Sponsoredtweets.com has a sliding payment scale based on the popularity of the celebrity. Jamie Oliver (celebrity chef) costs $3,250 per tweet, Khloe Kardashian (reality TV star) is $9,100, and Bob Vila (house repair TV host) is a bargain at just $910. If you have to ask how much Paris Hilton costs, you can't afford her.

What happens when you approach envy from the other side? Susan Fiske, a professor of psychology at Princeton, argues that while we look up to the "haves" with envy, we look down on the "have nots" with scorn, especially around economic issues. Rich people are viewed as competent yet cold, poor people as incompetent yet warm. We are always comparing ourselves against others, and when we look down with scorn, we're saying "You aren't worthy of my attention."

Clever marketing embraces both aspiration and scorn. Ad campaigns showing someone giving his spouse a luxury car wrapped in a big red ribbon as a Christmas present speak volumes about the prestige associated with driving one of these vehicles. Viewers compare themselves to the couple in the advertisement. This reinforces the aspirational feelings that envious would-be buyers have about the brand. For those who can already afford the car, the message still resonates and creates scorn for those who can't.

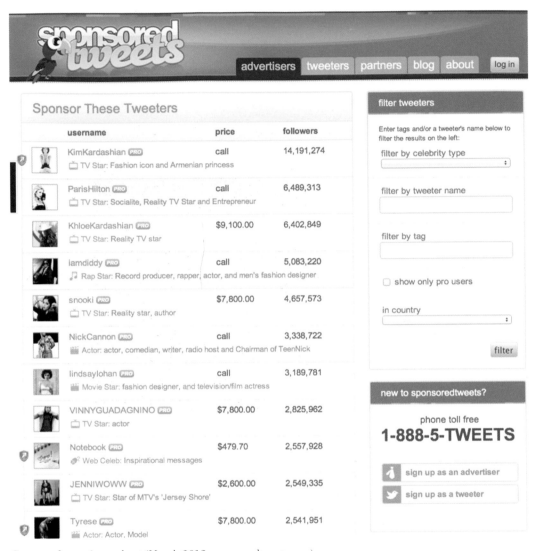

Sponsoredtweets' rate sheet (March 2012; sponsoredtweets.com)

The trick in providing a balance that allows both envy and scorn is that you mustn't be too out of range. Nokia's deluxe Vertu handsets have keys individually cut and ground from sapphire, gliding on ruby bearings similar to the internals of expensive watches. The cases are clad in 18-carat gold, alligator leather, and precious stones. The London Symphony Orchestra creates the phones' ringtones. This type of manufacturing obviously comes at a price. Handsets range from $3,500 up to $310,000 (yes, for a phone).

The musician Seal apparently uses a Constellation Quest phone. This model retails for $8,400. A USB data cable costs just $190. Is this aspirational, or so inaccessible to just be scornful? Either strategy can work as a marketing technique. (vertu.com)

Of course, wherever there is aspiration that is so obviously out of reach, there is the opportunity to make money from affordable fakes, which let people "live the dream" of the expensive brands without taking out a second mortgage. For less than one-tenth of the price of the real item, you can purchase a knockoff that carries the name, if not the quality, of the original and unachievable product.

The less virtuous Vertu is the knockoff available on this site. People who aspire to own a Vertu still pay more for this fake than they would for a full-function brand-name smartphone. (amatory.biz)

How to create something aspirational

» Show your product in settings that would be aspirational for your target audience. This may include showing it being used by aspirational individuals or to achieve end results that your audience aspires to.

» Provide a comparison point: What does your product provide "more" of for customers? Will users be richer, more popular, smarter, or all three?

» Be careful of leveraging scorn. Being envious gives people feelings of guilt, but being scornful often leads to dehumanizing of the scorned group, which can have dangerous repercussions.

» Consider as a secondary audience any group who is one or more notches lower on the scale (age, income, leisure time, and so on) than your current target audience. Develop a product offering for that group that helps them meet their aspirational goals. If you don't, someone else will.

Make people feel ownership before they've bought

They will value the item more, increasing their desire to purchase.

In his book *Emotional Design*, Don Norman states that we are much more emotionally attached to products for which we feel some involvement. This is true even before we own the product. Clever sites invite us in and make us feel like a member of the family before we even part with our cash.

BioLite is a revolutionary camping stove design that burns wood and other biomatter cleanly and efficiently through gasification. The idea is old (cars used similar gasification burners in post-war Germany where petrol was scarce), but the technology needed to create a small, portable, reliable stove was untested.

The company first promised an early 2010 release, which subsequently slipped to late 2011 and then Spring 2012. Its design finally came to market in May 2012.

What kept people interested enough during that time? The company could have worked in stealth mode. After all, there was always the potential for another company to "borrow" the idea and get to market sooner. Instead, it chose to keep its website updated at each stage of the journey. It showed video of early prototypes used in the woods, listed the design awards it was winning, and consistently tied the commercial camping stove product back in with its charitable work to develop low-carbon, high-efficiency cooking stoves for developing nations. It also updated the design by making the stove lighter and adding a USB port to recharge electronic devices using the excess energy generated by the clever heat-to-electricity generator that powers the stove's fan.

This constant communication, coupled with well-placed PR mentions in *Outdoor* magazine, *Wired* magazine, and on influential sites such as TechCrunch and Gizmodo meant that people who were interested in purchasing the camping stove could see regular updates. The charitable work acted as proof of concept, and the fact that sales of the camping stove would subsidize creation of the larger home stove for developing nations gave potential customers the feeling that they'd be supporting a worthwhile cause. The videos allowed people to see how the product could apply to them before it was available.

All-in-all, the company's site made potential customers feel like they were already part of the BioLite "family" even though there was no tangible product to purchase.

This story isn't unique. In the digital realm, three months prior to releasing the game *Spore* in September 2008, Electronic Arts made the *Spore Creature Creator* (a way to build characters for the game) available as a free download. The *Creature Creator* was a game in itself. After choosing a body, limbs, features, and decoration, users could make the monster that they had plugged together dance, sing, and react. This was one of the first times that players could easily build their own fully rendered game characters from the ground up. Experiencing the smooth animation of a custom-built monster fuelled desire among potential customers to see how the character they'd built would perform in the game world. This in turn drove sales of the game, which moved more than two million copies in the first three weeks and was a top-10 PC game through 2009. Will Wright, the creator of *Spore*, observed that it took *Spore* fans just 18 days to create the same number of species as exist on earth, which meant they were working at 38 percent of the efficiency of God.

The *Spore creature creator* gave users a feeling of "owning" the character they developed before the full game was available. (spore.com/trial)

Kickstarter's whole business model could be described as making people feel ownership before they've bought a product, or indeed before it's even been made. The idea is that you pledge money and become a backer of a proposed creative project. Obviously, if the project doesn't meet its funding goals you aren't billed. That means that if you want the product, it's in your interest to persuade as many other people as you can that they too should get involved.

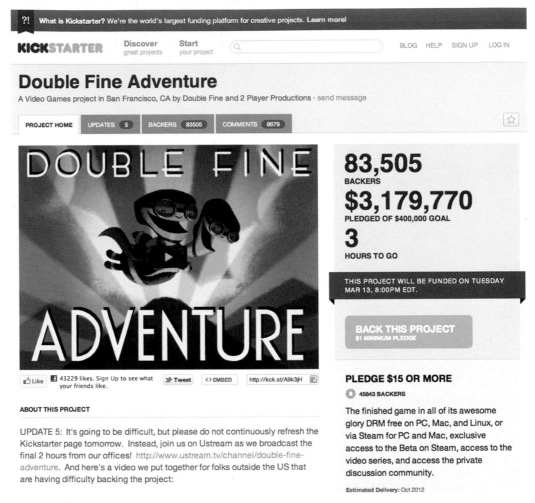

With three hours to go, Double Fine had already easily become the highest financed Kickstarter project in the site's history. The Double Fine project pushed all the right pre-ownership buttons. (kickstarter.com)

One example of a successful Kickstarter project is *Double Fine Adventure*, a point-and-click computer game. At the time of funding, backers knew only that Tim Schafer, the project's leader, had a history of producing engaging adventure games. No work had been done on a script, character development, or any other aspects of the game. Based on nothing more than reputation and a promise to include backers in regular updates as the game development process progressed, Tim met his funding goal of $400,000 in just eight hours. Even he was surprised when funding topped the one million dollar mark within twenty-four hours. By the time the Kickstarter project closed, he had 87,142 backers for a total donation of more than $3.3 million. That left him 834 percent funded, and therefore he could add more characters and better technical effects, and release on more platforms and in more languages than he had ever intended.

To increase the chances of success, most Kickstarter projects draw people in with escalating rewards for pledges at different levels of involvement. Double Fine Adventure promised a copy of the game to people pledging at the $15 level, with various stages including signed books and posters at $500 up to lunch and a tour of the offices at the $10,000 level. Variable pledge levels allow people to "buy in" to the project at different levels of support. Especially at the higher levels, the money that people give is almost definitely more than the value of the goods, yet for Double Fine Adventure all one hundred of the $1,000 level pledges and all four of the $10,000 level pledges sold.

How to make people feel pre-ownership

» Show people how your product can apply to their lives so that they get and remain excited about it through the prepurchase phase.

» For products that have yet to be released, provide frequent status updates, teases, and reveals (leaks). However, never over-promise.

» For physical products, provide a configurator that lets people play with product options and swap pieces in and out. This allows people to personalize the product, which can give them greater attachment to it. Make the configurator as visual as possible so that people can easily fall in love with their creations.

(continues)

(continued)

» Offer demonstration versions of your product so that people can give it a trial run. Although you might feel the urge to remove some functionality or create a time limit on the demo version's life, users must be able to create and share output from the demo to feel a desire to own the full product.

» Less sexy products can also create prepurchase desire. Testimonials, reviews, and white papers serve this purpose so long as they describe real use cases and quantifiable outcomes.

» Encourage potential customers to participate in a forum where they can get their questions answered by people who already use the product. When they feel like part of the community, they'll slip more easily into the purchase process.

» Create different levels of reward for different levels of engagement; the more people engage, the closer they get to being "family."

Status envy: demonstrating achievement and importance

In a totally egalitarian universe, envy couldn't exist. There need to be differences in status for envy to work. If you want to use (benign) envy to drive people to a certain goal, then you need to show them the difference between their current status and the status they can achieve if they reach the goal.

There are indications of status—and status differences—everywhere. Even in supposedly "classless" societies such as the USA, there exists a wide range of social strata, as brought to light by the Occupy movement, and plenty of opportunity for envy, as shown by talk of the "one percent."

Employing envy as a motivating factor therefore means highlighting the differences in status. You can do this effectively by showing successful users' achievements and importance in a public manner.

Create status differences to drive behavior

Without differentiation, there can be no envy.

Envy and scorn work because there are two groups: those that have and those that have not. Members of the group who do not have the thing are envious of the group who does have it, who in turn scorn those who do not.

One group who you wouldn't expect to see using status differences as a sales point is religious organizations. That however doesn't stop some people from offering services that play on status differentiation to a particularly religious group.

The site youvebeenleftbehind.com enables Christians who believe in a relatively imminent Rapture event (true believers are suddenly taken up to Heaven, everyone else remains behind in Tribulation) to make contact with those who are "left behind."

As status differentiators go, this is quite big. It's hard not to see this as a form of inverted envy, or scorn. Indeed, the site plays on this:

> *Imagine how taken aback [your friends and family] will be by the millions of missing Christians and devastation at the rapture. They will know it was true and that they have blown it. There will be a small window of time where they might be reached for the Kingdom of God. We have made it possible for you to send them a letter of love and a plea to receive Christ one last time.*

YOUVEBEENLEFTBEHIND.COM/WHY.HTML

So from this perspective, the Rapture is something exclusive. If you live by a certain set of rules, you get the special treatment and many others do not. The promise of special treatment might be a good enough reason for some people to choose to live by those rules in the first place, but last time I checked, piety is typically one of the rules and smugness is not. Especially not when it leads to presumptuous bumper stickers like "Warning: in case of Rapture this car will be unmanned."

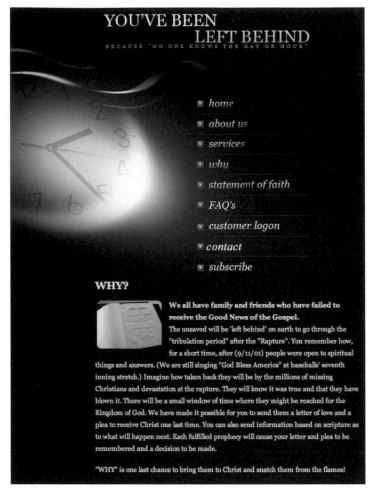

youvebeenleftbehind.com makes a clear distinction between the haves and the have-nots. It then exhorts the haves to "pity" the have-nots by sending a last invitation to join the club.

The security researcher Bruce Schneier pointed out an especially clever aspect of the youvebeenleftbehind.com business model. Although the site provides few clues about the owners' backgrounds, these owners suggest that their servers are an ideal place to store details on every aspect of your financial life. Indeed, until Schneier called it out, the site used to have a sales pitch directed clearly at this point:

In the encrypted portion of your account you can give them access to your banking, brokerage, hidden valuables, and powers of attorneys' (you won't be needing them anymore, and the gift will drive home the message of love). There won't be any bodies, so probate court will take 7 years to clear your assets to your next of Kin. 7 years of course is all the time that will be left. So, basically the Government of the AntiChrist gets your stuff, unless you make it available in another way.

YOUVEBEENLEFTBEHIND.COM
(THIS TEXT WAS REMOVED IN 2008, BUT THE SENTIMENT REMAINS.)

Given the highly trusting nature of the potential audience for this service, it's hard to know whether the service is an example of good gone wrong, or just plain evil.

In a nice counterpoint, a group of atheists has got in on the act as well. Eternal Earth-Bound Pets are "a group of dedicated animal lovers and atheists. Each Eternal Earth-Bound Pet representative is a confirmed atheist and as such will still be here on Earth after you've received your reward. Our network of animal activists are committed to step in when you step up to Jesus."

Bart Centre, who runs the service, doesn't mince his words: "I'm trying to figure out how to cash in on this hysteria to supplement my income." And at $135 per pet, he's likely to do quite well, given that he has nothing to lose: "If we thought the Rapture was really going to happen, obviously our rate structure would be much higher."

How to create status differences

» Show how your group is different—and better—than other groups.

» Create opportunities for users to pity or scorn the other groups.

» Offer a service that is exclusive to the group.

» Bonus points for creating a differentiation in which people pay to pour scorn on you (for instance atheists offering a service to believers).

Emphasize achievement as a form of status

Give users more status when they achieve certain (company-serving) goals. This trains them to keep coming back for more.

You wouldn't pay $20 at the departure gate to board an airplane earlier, but you might choose to fly with an airline that gives you that privilege as part of a mileage rewards plan, even if the ticket ends up costing you $20 more. Why? Because you too can be "Elite" and get that extra five inches of legroom if you just slug it out in cattle class for another fifteen trips.

The airline is counting on the envy that all the other passengers feel as they watch the early boarders fill up the overhead bins, and as they traipse past the frequent fliers who got first class upgrades on the way to their seats at the back of the plane.

By encouraging the desired behavior in passengers time after time, passengers start to develop habits around that company. After a while, the habit becomes sufficiently ingrained, and the impending reward becomes sufficiently achievable, that passengers stop comparing prices so diligently and just go with the familiar airline.

The strength of this perceived reward is all in how you show it, though. The member-only perks must be seen as sufficiently valuable. For something like grocery store reward cards, the differential pricing is sufficient reward, even if it works more as a punishment for nonmembers than an incentive for members. The lure of airline rewards is that by being loyal to the airline rather than using price-check sites like Kayak or Orbitz, you can gain more creature comforts and even free flights in the future.

Loyalty programs need to seem enticing right from the beginning, so it's important to "prime" an account. Joseph Nunes and Xavier Dreze ran experiments that determined that car wash loyalty cards were more likely to be redeemed if they were given to customers with 10 purchases required of which two were already clipped than if they were just a straight 8 purchases required.

Mileage plans and awards-based credit cards work the same way by giving a signing bonus, for instance by adding a large number of awards upon opening a credit card account. Bagchi and Li found that it's also better to give people large numbers of points, even if the goal is equally distant. Offering 10 points per dollar, with 1,000 points needed, works better than offering 1 point per dollar, with 100 points needed because as they get closer, people see a bigger progression toward their goal.

The reward doesn't have to be financial. Xbox achievement points, while not a draw for all gamers, might make a game more appealing to purchase and play for obsessive achievement unlockers. PlayStation3 has a similar achievement-based system using trophies. Even Visual Studio—a software development platform for writing code—now has achievements built in.

Achievements make it apparent what skills somebody possesses. By unlocking certain achievements within a game, that individual obviously managed to master a particular set of moves or demonstrate a specific level of skill. Now, rather than just being "good" at a game, it's possible for players to quantify exactly how good and at what specific things. Although this probably doesn't mean that programmers are going to start writing their Visual Studio achievement scores on their resumes, it does give others who care about such things a measure of the status of an individual.

Achievement unlocked. © *Derek Lieu, Kick in the Head Jan. 18, 2011.* (kickinthehead.org)

Achievements also benefit the game companies in several ways. First, the obsessives will buy each new game based on the number of achievement points it allows them to collect. Because points accrue per game, the more games you play, the more achievement points you can collect. Playing more games means buying more games.

But even regular gamers will unlock some achievements as they play. Information on which achievements get unlocked frequently and which are avoided helps the game developers to create future titles that fit better with gamers' expectations. Often achievements will also have funny names based on in-jokes, so they provide entertainment value as well as collection value.

How to emphasize achievement

» Focus users' attention on how many points they've gained, not how many they need for a reward.

» Help people on the way to achieving by priming their account to start with.

» Ensure that people can relate to the longer-term end goal they get with the awards system. Remind them constantly of the benefits that accrue with awards.

» Set and control the exchange rate so that people find it sufficiently valuable to stay with the program despite cheaper alternatives.

» If you offer several different types of achievement, tracking the popular achievements may give you an indication of which types of status are important to your audience, allowing you to make future offerings more attractive.

Encourage payment as an alternative to achievement

Show impatient people a shortcut to improved status via their wallets.

Part of the fun of playing *World of Warcraft* (*WOW*) is the social aspect of being online with ten million of your closest friends. The part that turns it into a game is the achievement and status that comes with successful quests.

However, it takes time and patience to reach a high enough level to make the game really fun. Luckily it's easy enough to bypass the boring achievement part if you want instant status. You just have to pay someone else to do the hard work for you. The World Bank says that gold farming (the act of sitting in front of a computer performing repetitive tasks to "earn" in-game rewards) and power leveling (playing with the intent of gaining enough character status to then sell the character) was a $3B market in 2009, with a surprising proportion of that money actually going to the developing countries where the clicking takes place.

Characters.net is just one of many sites selling prebuilt characters to players who have more money than time.

Now obviously the gold is valuable because the game developers made it take many hours of "grinding" to create goods that can be exchanged for gold. Characters are valuable only because of the time and experience it takes to nurture them through to sufficiently high status levels. When enough people start offering these third-party gaming services (the 2011 World Bank report suggests that 100,000 people may have been earning their primary income this way in 2009), the game companies must ensure that players don't get disheartened by seeing their competition buying their way to success.

The official line from companies such as Blizzard, the makers of WOW, is that the virtual economy is wrong, that much of the gold on offer is stolen from compromised player accounts, and that people who buy rather than achieving are cheating. Blizzard specifically chose to build the game as a subscription rather than freemium (free to play, buy the extras you need) platform, and it suggests that players want to see it kept that way.

Unfortunately, new players have a harder time "leveling up" than experienced higher-level players who already have powerful magical tools, weapons, and armor at their disposal, and who can complete more complex quests that provide higher rewards. As Cory Doctorow (who researched gold farming for his novel *For the Win*) says "so long as [Massively Multiplayer Online games] look the way they do now, where there's that leveling path, and so long as the ways MMOs incentive players to go on playing after a long time is by creating lots of new levels they can ascend to, and so long as ascending to new levels gives you exponentially more access to power, wealth and sorts of enjoyment than you would have had otherwise, then that market will exist."

Other games such as *Farmville* use a freemium approach, but the items you can buy in-game are typically tools to help you succeed or vanity items such as gifts, rather than the capacity to instantly level up. This type of purchasing is likely to continue and even increase after players reach higher levels in the game, whereas the need for out-of-game purchases of gold and status will diminish as the player's in-game character becomes more powerful.

Encouraging payment rather than achievement also works for real-world tasks. GymPact (also mentioned in the chapter on Pride) "lets you set the financial stakes of not getting to the gym, plus earn cash rewards and real prizes for fulfilling your Pact." The company is basically betting on laziness, despite encouraging people to work out. Dan Ariely, in his book *Predictably Irrational*, shows how providing the offer of payment (even in the sense of a fine) counterintuitively legitimizes an otherwise punishable activity, allowing people to feel OK about doing it because they paid for it. Ariely's example is parents who were happy to pay a late fee for leaving their kids in daycare too long. It would be interesting to see whether GymPact has users who behave the same way, seeing payment as an alternative to achievement or even as a way of justifying not achieving.

How to encourage payment instead of achievement

» If your game or product revolves around escalating levels of achievement, it's likely that people with more money than time will want to pay for a shortcut. Try to find a way to enable this out-of-game purchasing without alienating players who have more time than money.

» Own the exchange: Make sure that if people can pay to achieve status, they are paying you (or at least performing the transaction via your systems) rather than somebody else. This also allows you to set the exchange rate to maintain the value of status. Achievers should never feel disheartened, and payers shouldn't stop paying.

» Ensure that there is a sufficient flow of items within the game/product to satisfy demand without oversaturating the market. That may mean creating a steady flow of new items over time.

» Try to minimize the guilt that people feel about paying instead of achieving. For instance, by donating a certain percentage of payments to a charitable cause, or by giving them the opportunity to "buy back" their payment with later achievements on a credit-like system. (It's doubtful they ever will.)

» Allow payments as an excuse for not achieving.

Let users advertise their status

Encourage users to build and advertise their status within a community.

In the real world, people advertise their status by the clothes they wear, the cars they drive, and even the places they choose to congregate. Online, many of those cues aren't available, so they are replaced instead with other (potentially more democratic) measures of status such as reputation.

Reputation can be summarized in different ways depending upon the online context. For instance, in online games it might be the level and experience points that a character possesses. In social media circles it might be the number of "likes," recommendations, mentions, back links, badges, or followers. In forums, it might be the number of posts or thanks received.

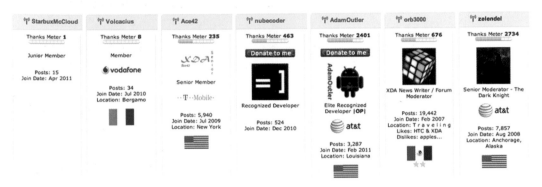

The xda-developers.com forum has different status levels. Posters start off as junior members and progress to senior members. Developers have special status levels (they are the reason the forum exists), and moderators are chosen from within the community based on participation. Thanks, posts, join date, and the ability to add a signature and image are all additional indicators of status.

Online communities require participation to be useful, fun places to hang out. With increased participation comes an increased requirement to police what is being discussed. Although people employed by the community provider to prevent abuse must undertake some of this policing, other community members often want to step in to an informal overseer role. It makes sense to encourage this as much as possible. It appears that most of the time status is a sufficient reward for these individuals. In other words, they are doing a job that would normally require payment just for the opportunity to have the title of "moderator."

Other people see these higher levels of status and want to attain them because of the perceived benefits, so differentiating and displaying status levels creates an aspirational goal.

Awarding status is also a major retention opportunity because the status was hard-won and is difficult to transfer elsewhere. People are typically loss averse, so they will continue using a system rather than "losing" the status they have accumulated, even if there is no physical value attached to that status.

How to design for status advertisement

» People care about their status and the status of others in the environment. Make sure it's easy for them to show and see the status of people they interact with.

» If you want to migrate to a new forum system, or entice forum moderators from a different platform, make sure that you give them an equal or better status in the new system.

» Try to make the status worthwhile achieving. For instance, in forums, status can also come with access to more tools such as the ability to ban users and promote, edit, or move postings.

» Higher status levels should require an element of work to achieve. The highest levels should be relatively exclusive to make them more desirable.

Let people feel important

Giving people a little bit of recognition makes them love you more, and do more for you.

What do Dale Carnegie, author of *How to Win Friends and Influence People* and Mary Kay Ash, founder of Mary Kay Cosmetics, have in common? Other than both starting their careers as door-to-door salespeople, both also realized the potential of making customers feel special.

Mary Kay Ash said, "Pretend that every single person you meet has a sign around his or her neck that says 'Make Me Feel Important.' Not only will you succeed in sales, you will succeed in life." This advice helped create a 1.8 million-person strong worldwide multilevel sales force.

People who you make feel important will do more for you because they see you as someone who affirms their importance. Yes, that is a circular statement. It's also a powerful yet insidious way to get what you want.

Dale Carnegie mentions letting people feel important in several of his key points. In his book he suggests that you should call people by their name, acknowledge them, show appreciation, be encouraging, and "give them a fine reputation to live up to." In other words, if you compliment people on possessing a positive trait, you can then later ask them to apply that trait (generosity, for instance) in your direction.

The large opportunity for social interaction online today can easily give people the illusion of being important. Andy Warhol's 1968 comment that "in the future, everyone will be world-famous for 15 minutes" has more potential to be true today, as everyone pastes their fifteen megabytes of (potential) fame online. Perhaps more realistic is Nick Currie's 1991 statement that "in the future, everyone will be famous for fifteen people."

Zappos is a master of making customers feel important. Surprising people with complimentary shipping upgrades, good customer service including live agents, and fast no-hassle returns are wonderful features, but they are just well-crafted implementations of traditional e-commerce principles. Where Zappos truly excels at making customers feel important is through embracing social interaction. The Fan of the Week feature on its Facebook site allows visitors to vote for the image that will be displayed on the Facebook page that week, chosen from people who post pictures of themselves with a Zappos box to their Facebook wall. Customers submit photos that serve Zappos' advertising needs at least as much as they serve the individuals' desire to feel important. Zappos also solicits images of pets or babies for their site—with one condition: The animal or child must be sitting in a Zappos-branded box.

Threadless.com is a site that sells T-shirts. However, it's the process of finding T-shirt designs to sell that sets them apart from other online stores. Anyone can upload a design, and then Threadless members rate those design submissions. On a weekly basis, the Threadless team chooses from the highest-rated designs to determine the few that will get made into T-shirts.

Why would a shoe company have a place on their site to show baby and pet photos? Because pets and children are two of the most important things to people, so by displaying them online it makes their customers feel important. Note that the images all contain free advertising for the brand. (zappos.com)

Creators of the chosen designs get a $2,000 cash prize plus $500 in store credit, but judging from comments posted on the site and elsewhere, its true value to contributors appears to be in the recognition, not the cash. The whole process from submission, through voting, to production of the chosen designs focuses on a sense of community, making customers feel important, central to the process, and powerful too. What better incentive could these customers have to purchase a T-shirt than having personally shepherded it through from design to finished product?

Submit an idea for a chance at fame, friends & TWENTY-FIVE HUNDRED DOLLARS!*

Design

1. Get your idea ready to submit

Take some time to come up with the best original idea you can think of. We're not talking your fraternity's logo or a photo of your new puppy. We're talking an idea so amazing that your eyeballs may explode if you stare too long!

Template Files

- T-shirt Kit (11.8MB zip)
- Hoodies (4.2MB zip)
- Tanks (2.6MB zip)
- Messenger Bags (1MB zip)
- Totes (10.4MB zip)
- Wall Patterns (1.4MB zip)
- Girly Styles (10.5MB zip)
- Crew Sweatshirt (2.8MB zip)
- Scarves (2.2MB zip)
- Laptop Cases (2MB zip)
- Wallets (2MB zip)
- Kids Styles (2.8MB zip)
- Polos (2.7MB zip)
- Backpacks (2.2MB zip)
- Pencil Cases (1.9MB zip)
- Notebooks (3.3MB zip)

2. Submit your idea

Use the templates provided to prepare your design presentation files. Click the "Submit a design" button below, follow the instructions and fill out the form to submit your design for presentation to the Threadless community.

3. The community scores and comments on your idea

Over a period of 7 days, the Threadless community will score and comment on your design. These scores and comments will help us decide which designs should become the next Threadless product!

4. If your idea is selected as a Threadless t-shirt*, you'll receive

- $2,000 in cash
- $500 Threadless Gift Certificate (can be redeemed for $200 cash)
- $500 in cash each time your design is reprinted
- Alumni Club membership including a Medal of Honor and other goodies
* payments vary for other product lines

Critique

Not sure if your design is ready? Why don'tcha submit it for a critique!? You can get community feedback on your ideas to help you finalize your design before submitting it for scoring!

Submit a critique

Submit a slogan!
If we print it, you get
$500

Did you know that every TypeTee began as a slogan submission? Think you got one?

Click here to submit!

Threadless.com's community gives T-shirt designers direct feedback on how likely it is that people would pay for their work. This helps the designers improve, but it also gives the company very strong indicators of which images to turn into products to sell online.

The community involvement doesn't stop there. Much of Threadless' advertising happens by word-of-mouth (although obviously every T-shirt is a walking billboard), and Threadless members' feedback gets turned into product features in a visible way through the founder's blog. Jake Nickell, the co-founder of Threadless, put it this way: "We are so much driven by our community that we don't really make the decisions. We look at what the community wants and react to it, but we don't make plans five years in advance. This company will grow to where customers want to take it."

One of their popular artists, Brent Schoepf says, "I hope that the trend continues where anybody can make art and put it in the world for people to see and explore."

The site has seen more than 200,000 submissions, which have been voted on more than 100 million times by their more than one and a half million registered users. They sell more than 10,000 T-shirts per month at prices ranging from $15 to $17. There's obviously profit in making your users feel important.

How to make people feel important

» Give something away free to customers "because you are so important to us." This could be a month's free membership, free shipping, or any number of other low-cost (to you) items that still serve as a pleasant surprise to customers.

» Have an exclusive thing that only certain individuals get. Each "certain individual" need not know how many other "certain individuals" there are. It can be something mutually beneficial like an early-warning e-mail list that is open only to repeat customers, letting them know about deals before they are generally announced.

» Harness the power of your customers—so long as they feel like their opinions are respected, they will do free work for you, such as choosing the best items from a selection or policing your forums.

» Make it clear that your customers are important by giving them a place on your site. It could be something as simple as the capacity to comment on blog postings, but why not get more creative and choose "featured customers" or ask for customer submissions?

Manufacturing and maintaining envy in your products

I hope that the person who created the default "Sent from my iPhone" e-mail signature text for iOS devices got well rewarded for their work. It is the perfect embodiment of effortlessly viral aspirational content. Taken at face value it is little more than an advertisement for a product—something that benefits the company more than the customer. Yet users seem strangely reluctant to change it. This inertia stems at least in part from what that small phrase says about them as an individual. Even more than half a decade after the device's release the phrase is still prevalent at the bottom of people's e-mails, and it can't just be because none of them can find out where to change the setting. It remains there because it's boastful in a socially acceptable way.

Full-on destructive envy is the desire to have more than those around you. While that could lead to some pretty antisocial behavior, we've seen that its milder form—aspiration—can actually be quite a powerful motivational and persuasive factor.

We've covered ways to create desire for a product and to ensure that the product is one that people aspire to own by showing it in aspirational settings or being used by aspirational individuals so that people can visualize what it might give them "more" of. It's possible to get people bought in before they've made the purchase by inviting them to be part of the family even in small ways like receiving news updates, playing with configuration options, or using demo versions.

Staying in benign envy is probably more useful than moving to destructive envy. A little bit of inequality aversion probably won't hurt too much, but when people start making decisions based on limiting others' gains, the community aspect of your product will suffer. A product that rewards individuals for helping others attain their aspirations helps keep envy under control, like the multiple levels of sales people in the Mary Kay hierarchy, where people higher in the chain are reliant on the success of those beneath them. Interestingly Mary Kay shares a feature with the online game World of Warcraft here, because both are smart enough to provide several interim levels of attainment to aspire to. There's always a viable goal, and once it's reached there's another one just ahead to work towards. In both cases that means everyone who participates can have realistic and achievable aspirations.

Having achievable aspirations doesn't mean completely leveling out the playing field. You can maintain benign envy by making differences in status and achievement apparent. Help customers advertise their status so they feel important. This advertising can occur simply by their overt use of your product ("Sent from my iPhone") or by encouraging them to share their experiences using the product in the form of reviews or something more obtuse like Zappos' dog photo gallery. This gives you free publicity and good review content. To moderate the amount of envy that is generated and to keep it aspirational, be sure to show how other people can achieve that goal themselves either through working for it (with constant reminders of their progress) or by paying to gain the status.

It's very hard to make people desire and aspire to use products that are aesthetic duds, undifferentiated, or just plain broken. However, if you have a pleasing product that solves an interesting problem there are plenty of ways to build a buzz that creates a level of benign envy that will drive sales and adoption.

Lust

Lust and greed are more gullible than innocence.

Mason Cooley

WE MIGHT OFTEN THINK of lust as sexual, but it actually describes an intense desire for any item. When we lust after something we stop thinking rationally. We look only for additional reasons to have it, not for reasons to abstain. So, when people have that craving, it doesn't take much of a nudge to turn desire into action by convincing them to fulfill those lustful feelings.

Lust is a strong emotion. Tapping into that emotion gives control over many elements of a person's life. Without lust, it's unlikely we'd feel the irrational need to possess things that others have or keep more stuff than we actually need. Lust is the starting point; envy and greed are the results.

To harness lust, companies must first get people to like them so that they are inclined to do what the company wants. Then the company can create feelings of obligation in its customers using reciprocation; giving customers a small gift to get a larger commitment from them in the future. The gift doesn't need to be anything tangible, so long as it fuels lust and thus breaks down the barriers of rational thought.

Creating lust: Using emotion to shape behavior

You'd think that when discussing lust, the many online dating sites would be a good source of examples. Unfortunately, the "science" behind the sites isn't necessarily scientific. To start with, nobody actually knows what constitutes a good match. Individuals with different tastes and attributes can and do have wonderful relationships. Secondly, over-analyzing compatibility leads people to hold unachievably high expectations of potential partners. Meeting anybody after spending too long vetting them beforehand is likely to lead to disappointment.

What does work is being likeable. Making an effort to be likeable before some-one has created high expectations is even more likely to work. This isn't dating advice; it's persuasion advice.

Liking, or in its stronger form, lust, can be manipulated much like other feel-ings. Flattery does work, even if we think we're immune to it. It's also possible to insert ideas into people's minds that lead them to liking or disliking an individual or idea. We favor people that we see as similar to us, so it's incredibly easy to cre-ate a self-reinforcing group based on even the most flimsy of criteria. Of course, it's possible for people to be so perfect that we end up disliking them because they are a threat to our self-esteem, so there are some steps that companies take to be seen as good enough rather than too good.

Say "I love you"

Flattery makes people more responsive to persuasion.

Everyone wants to be loved. On May 4, 2000, people all over the world started receiving an e-mail purporting to be from one of their friends telling them that yes, the friend did love them. That prompted enough people to open the e-mail attach-ment that 10 percent of all computers attached to the Internet were infected with the virus lurking in the message, causing an estimated $5.5 billion of damage.

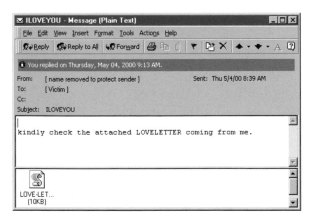

A love letter? For me? From a friend? Of course I'll open it!

Social engineering techniques for getting people to open infected e-mail attachments or click links have become progressively more sophisticated since this early attempt, but many still resort to the same basic method, namely flattery.

Flattery, which is actually just an insincere form of praise, makes recipients feel good, even if the flattery isn't particularly accurate and even when recipients know the motive for praising them was insincere. It also leads to recipients liking the flatterer more than they did before.

When recipients of the flattery see the person delivering it in a more positive light, they are then more open to persuasion from that individual. Although people might say they discount the type of false flattery they see in marketing literature, it still affects them. Elaine Chan and Jaideep Sengupta found that consumers are still influenced subconsciously by flattery even when they consciously try and correct for the influence. That's because they do still get warm, fuzzy feelings from the esteem-boosting compliment, and they have a subconscious positive response toward the marketer, even while stating that the compliment had no effect. Interestingly, the pleasant, unconscious response lasts longer than the conscious memory that the flattery was just a marketing ploy, making it more likely that the consumer will make a purchase in the future.

You might expect that messages delivered via a computer system would have less capacity to flatter, but B.J. Fogg and Clifford Nass found that even when they told study participants that the computer was giving them praise regardless of their actual performance, those participants still liked the flattering computer better than control participants, found the session more enjoyable, were more willing to continue working with the computer, and rated themselves as performing better than the control group. Actually, flattery worked as well as sincere praise that was demonstrably linked to participants' actions.

It seems we're so desperate for praise that we don't filter it in the same way that we do with criticism. Even if we're aware that the praise is synthetic, we still accept it on a subconscious level.

Welcome to the Nest Community.

Matt Rogers

Matt Rogers is Nest's founder and VP of Engineering.

We like you. We think you're smart, funny and, frankly, have excellent taste in thermostats. But we'd like to get to know you better, so today we're unveiling the Nest Community.

The Nest Community is a forum where you can talk to us and, more importantly, talk to each other. We hope you'll make this community your own, whether you're sharing installation stories, cool photos of Nest in your home, your energy bills, product ideas, what you've named your Nest, or even things completely unrelated to Nest. The sky's the limit.

For those of you who've become obsessed (in a good way!) with Energy History, the Energy Report and other Nest data, we've created an Energy board where you can find and share rebates for your Nest, post tips for how to save more energy, tell us how you've optimized your schedule or your solar panels, or share your thoughts on smart meters.

We've also created a Product Suggestions section for suggesting and voting on new features for your Nest thermostat. It's already filling up with great ideas.

Related articles

● Company
January 14, 2013

Tom vonReichbauer & Shige Honjo join exec team.

● Company
December 11, 2012

Nest Gift Guide 2012.

Labeling its audience enables Nest.com to flatter in a noncommittal way. Note that the labels (smart, funny, and have excellent taste) are all relatively safe because they are generic and easy for almost anyone to identify with.

Of course, some people are prepared to go beyond just clicking to see who loves them and will actually pay to see who has viewed their profile or read their messages. Tagged.com, "The social network for meeting new people," has VIP accounts that give additional benefits over regular accounts, such as seeing who is viewing your profile, for $20 per month. On the other end of the personal/professional spectrum, LinkedIn charges you for the same privilege. They have premium accounts that enable you to see who has checked out your profile, and guarantee that your messages to people go through, again for $20 per month.

Although they are at opposite ends of the social network spectrum, LinkedIn and Tagged both use the same technique: For just $20/month you can find out who loves you. (linkedin.com, tagged.com)

How to use flattery

» Flatter people and they will see you more favorably (and thus be more likely to purchase from you), even if they are conscious that the flattery is insincere or undeserved.

» Make sure the flattery you provide is the first piece of esteem building that takes place. Chan and Sengupta found that if consumers' self-esteem were raised before the flattery occurred, then the conscious recognition that this was insincere flattery outweighed and overruled the subconscious longer-term positive effect.

» Label people and then make a request of that label. For instance, tell people they are obviously discerning, environmentally conscious, and likeably geeky. Then, ask them to buy your green gadgets. The labels can be relatively generic, based on the typical positive characteristics of site visitors.

» Monetize anxiety and insecurity by allowing people to pay you to see more details about their relationship with other site members.

Be the second best

Game theory and self-esteem dictate that in a competitive space, you'll avoid the top of the pack.

In the early 1960s, the car rental company Avis ran an ad campaign claiming, "We're number 2, We Try Harder."

Doyle, Dane, and Bernbach, the same agency that created the VW ads mentioned in "Show the problems" in the chapter on Gluttony, managed the campaign. The agency focused each advert on frank and truthful statements about Avis' business philosophy. This was a shockingly refreshing approach for the time, and it did wonders for the brand. One year into the campaign, the company showed its first ever profit. Four years in, market share grew from 11 percent to 35 percent. The tag line "We try harder" was used for 50 years until being replaced in 2012. These days it seems Avis just isn't seen as a scrappy underdog any more.

Avis is only No.2 in rent a cars. So why go with us?

We try damned hard.

(When you're not the biggest, you have to.)

We just can't afford dirty ash-trays. Or half-empty gas tanks. Or worn wipers. Or unwashed cars. Or low tires. Or anything less than seat-adjusters that adjust. Heaters that heat. Defrost-ers that defrost.

Obviously, the thing we try hardest for is just to be nice. To start you out right with a new car, like a lively, super-torque Ford, and a pleasant smile. To know, say, where you get a good pastrami sandwich in Duluth.

Why?

Because we can't afford to take you for granted.

Go with us next time.

The line at our counter is shorter.

An example print advert from Avis' "We're number 2" campaign (Doyle, Dane, and Bernbach for Avis)

There might be another reason that Avis was successful in its number two position, and it centers on how we make comparisons to others.

In 1966, Elliot Aronson ran an experiment to study the relative likeability of people. His participants were told they would be listening to audio recordings of people who were auditioning for a college quiz show. Participants heard recordings of either a nearly perfect person (honor student and member of the track team who got 92 percent of the quiz questions right) or a mediocre person (answered 30 percent of the quiz questions correctly, nothing distinguishing about his academic career). Half of the participants in each condition also heard what appeared to be the auditioning student accidentally spilling coffee over himself at the end of the interview.

This blunder made a difference. Of the four experimental conditions (near perfect, near perfect with blunder, mediocre, and mediocre with blunder), the superior person was rated most attractive *when the person blundered,* followed by the nonblundering superior person, the nonblundering mediocre person, and finally the blundering mediocre person. So it wasn't the coffee spilling itself that caused the attractiveness rating to rise. The spill actually caused the mediocre person to be rated less attractive. Instead, Aronson proposed that although high levels of competence make us attractive, if we also appear slightly fallible we are seen as more attractive still. The blunder humanizes the superior person and makes him more approachable, less likely to hurt our self-esteem, and therefore more likeable.

The *pratfall effect* as it has become known affects men more than women. The effect is also stronger when the observer feels at least some level of social comparison with the blunderer. When the individual being rated is completely out of the observer's league, observers prefer the nonblundering superior person.

More recent research suggests that we are attracted most to people who emulate the person we want to be, rather than who we truly are. But, how we *rate* people and who we actually *date* are two separate things. Analysis shows that we date people who match our level of physical attractiveness.

In other words we lust for someone or something that meets our vision of our ideal selves, but we end up settling for something closer to our actual selves.

This effect plays out online. Although we don't normally get insight into the workings of dating sites, Christian Rudder, co-founder of the online dating site OKCupid.com published blog entries where he mined the company's database to discover interesting behavioral quirks.

Members of the site rate each other's attractiveness on a 5-point scale. One thing Christian found is that for a given average attractiveness rating, some women were receiving a lot more messages (a measure of "liking") than others.

It turns out that a woman with more polarized scores (more "1" and "5" ratings) receives a greater number of messages from men than a woman with an identical average rating, but whose average results from ratings all clustered around a single score, even a high one, such as a 4. As Christian says, "When some men think you're ugly, other men are more likely to message you. And when some men think you're cute, other men become less interested."

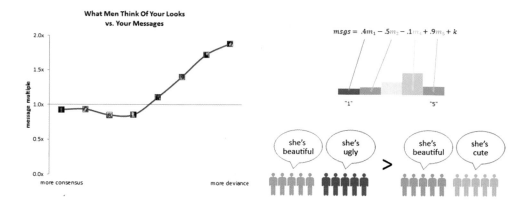

The more consensus there is about a woman's looks, the less messages she receives. When men can't agree on her appeal, she gets more messages overall. A multiple regression analysis shows that getting rated a 1 ("not my type") or a 5 ("definitely my type") by men voting on her looks both contribute positively to the overall number of messages a woman receives. (Graphics from OKCupid.com)

Christian explains this using game theory. If a man on the dating site suspects that other men are less likely to be interested in a woman, as evidenced by a certain number of "1" or "2" ratings, he interprets it as less competition. Conversely, if that man sees a woman with a preponderance of "4" ratings, he gets the impression that lots of other guys are likely to be competing for her attention.

So Christian's advice is to take whatever you think some guys won't like and play it up. "We now have mathematical evidence that minimizing your 'flaws' is the opposite of what you should do. If you're a little chubby, play it up. If you have a big nose, play it up. If you have a weird snaggletooth, play it up: Statistically, the guys who don't like it can only help you, and the ones who do like it will be all the more excited."

It turns out that both game theory and models of self-esteem indicate that regardless of our idealized desires, we will end up choosing the most likeable rather than the objectively best person.

How to benefit from being second best

» If you must convince a predominantly male audience who may see you as too perfect, doing something that comparatively improves their self-esteem (the pratfall effect) can increase their attraction to you.

» If your product is likely to incite polarizing opinions, let people whine. The things that some people hate will be the things that other people love.

» Show people how choosing your option requires less competition than choosing the number 1 option; for instance less waiting in line, shorter delivery times, lower cost, but just as much satisfaction.

Frame your message as a question

"Have you considered why so many people are switching to our brand from the competition?"

In the United States, polling companies have an exemption from the do-not-call register. In other words, even if you've explicitly stated that you don't want random callers bothering you, polling companies can do so.

At some point a devious political campaign manager realized that telephone surveys are a way of communicating directly with the voting population, despite that population's individual wishes. The campaign didn't have to actually do anything with the results of a poll. All that was important was to insert its message into the body of the questions. And because the questions often covered theoretical events, the inserted message could contain completely unsubstantiated rumors without fear of reprisal.

These surveys are called *push polls* because of their habit of pushing respondents toward a viewpoint. Some may just be attempting to bring an issue to voters' attention: "Please rank the following three candidates on their support for [the issue]." Others are more sinister, using the questioning to commit character assassination.

Here are some questions taken from a push poll conducted in Texas just before Dan Morales, the Attorney General, was up for re-election in 1996. Morales was launching a $4 billion lawsuit against tobacco companies to reclaim Medicaid costs spent on smoking-related illnesses.

As you know, elected officials are held to high standards in public life. Here are some reasons people are giving to vote against Dan Morales for Attorney General. Please tell me if each statement makes you much more likely to vote against Dan Morales, somewhat more likely to vote against Dan Morales, or if it makes no difference at all?

Morales supports affirmative action.

Morales supports gun control.

Morales' political campaign purchased two tickets to a fundraiser for Louis Farrakhan's Nation of Islam organization.

Juvenile crime has increased by one-third in Texas since Morales became Attorney General.

Conservative political groups rate Morales as a liberal Democrat.

As Attorney General, Morales has made consumer issues a higher priority than fighting violent crime.

Morales has said that young gang members don't need harsh treatment and prison, but that they need nicer recreational facilities, drug counseling, and summer jobs.

Victims' Rights activists say Morales sold out crime victims when he settled a prisoner's lawsuit without even taking the case to court.

Now that you've had a chance learn more about Dan Morales' record, do you think Dan Morales has performed his job as Attorney General well enough to deserve reelection, or do you think it's time to give a new person a chance to do a better job?

Another group of respondents were asked to rate questions that addressed Morales' relationship with donors and claimed that the tobacco suit would benefit only a few wealthy personal injury lawyers.

Interestingly this survey, while acting as a push poll, also produced statistics that demonstrated the effects of awareness-raising (even if the awareness being raised was of questionable truthiness). Before being "asked" about Morales' attitudes toward various events, 42 percent of the 800 respondents said that he deserved re-election. Twenty-seven percent said a new person should do the job, and 30 percent said they didn't know. Immediately after the list of reasons not to re-elect Morales was read to respondents, those figures changed to 21 percent in favor of re-electing him, 58 percent in favor of dropping him, and 20 percent still on the fence. In other words the leading questions had "pushed" both those in favor of Morales and those who hadn't expressed an opinion toward not re-electing him.

The survey was conducted by Public Opinion Strategies, a market research company whose site explains, "Here's who we are not: a passive participant that simply produces numbers. … About half of our research is conducted in the realm of public affairs. … The other half of our work continues to be dedicated to winning elections." This survey appears to have been dedicated to winning the election for anyone but Morales.

The survey was commissioned by lobbyists representing the tobacco industry. They delivered the results to Morales directly, ostensibly to show how public opinion was against the lawsuit but with an additional not-so-subtle warning of their demonstrated ability to manipulate voter perception of the issue and of the man himself. There's nothing quite like the threat of losing an election to make a politician drop an issue, but Morales went ahead anyway and won a $17 billion settlement for Texas.

That should be the happy end to a scary story, but unfortunately the survey's insinuations were marginally prescient. There is an irony to the push poll questions on "enriching wealthy personal injury lawyers" as Morales was later convicted of falsifying documents to funnel $260 million of the state's tobacco settlement money to another lawyer, Marc Murr, and spent several years in prison.

Push polling works because it raises awareness of issues that people may not have previously considered, regardless of whether the issues are real or fake. It subtly slips emotions into something that people expect to be rational. It creates cognitive dissonance, which people will seek to remove either by ignoring what they hear or by changing their perspective. This misinformation works its way deep into people's minds and blends with their actual memories of events in the same way that asking suggestive questions of eyewitnesses can change their memory of the event.

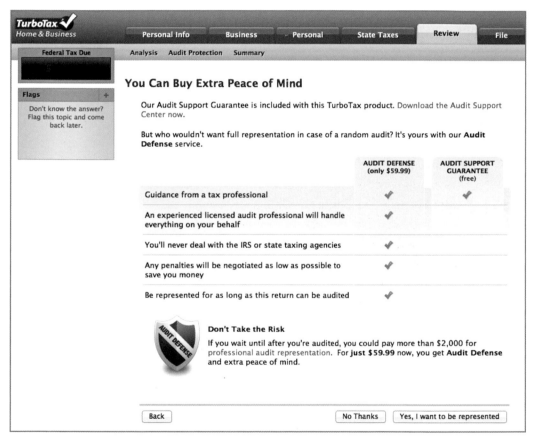

Who wouldn't want audit protection? The true message in TurboTax is, "You'd be crazy not to" but by framing it as a question, it forces users to think about and agree with the proposition. (Intuit's TurboTax)

How to use push polling

» Lead with a question that puts doubt about your competitors into customers' minds. *Have you considered why more people are switching to our brand from the competition?*

» Provide a reason to buy your product as part of the push question. *Could it be because [insert fear mongering trait we can resolve]?*

» The question doesn't have to be based in fact. *What would you do if you learned your current antivirus product wasn't fully protecting you? Try our antivirus, anti-malware, and antispyware all-in-one for full protection.* It's enough to raise the question, regardless of the actual abilities of the questioned product.

» If possible, avoid naming competitors directly. Just disparaging the competition isn't useful, makes you look petty, and gives them an extra brand impression.

Create an in-group

Show customers that they belong to your preferred group, and they will take on and defend its traits.

If you follow sports of any description, you'll be familiar with the great feelings you experience when "your" team wins. Why is this the case? You weren't out there competing. You didn't train for months beforehand. You may not even have been in the same city as the sporting event. Actually, you were probably sitting at home in front of the TV with a beer in one hand and the remote control in the other.

The truth is that you get feelings of self-esteem by associating with the successful team. You like basking in the reflected glory. The team's success contributes to your sense of identity. If you are at the game, you feel great comradeship with the other fans supporting your team, and you feel the pain of a foul and the joy of a win almost as much as the players themselves. Watching with other supporters, you feel disinhibited. You call the referee names you'd never normally use when he makes a bad call. You taunt the opposition.

But you are fickle. Robert Cialdini found that university students were three times more likely to wear T-shirts showing support of the school football team on the day after they won a game than they were on the day after the team lost a game. After the team does something that fails to boost self-esteem, you will try and find an external reason for the loss, or talk trash about the opposition as a way to retain that self-esteem. You also start to disassociate yourself from the team at that point; for instance, you might say "the team" lost whereas you would have said "we" won.

What has happened? You have joined an *in-group* (your team and other supporters) and at the same time created an *out-group* (the opposing team and their supporters) to focus your negative feelings on.

It doesn't take much to create an in-group/out-group distinction. In some of the early social psychological research in this area, Henri Tajfel and his colleagues assigned participants to one of two groups by flipping a coin, but told the participants that the assignment was based on the results of a preference test (for instance their preference for a certain style of art). Subsequently, even though they never interacted with other members of the group they'd been placed in or of the other group, participants favored other members of their own group when asked to allocate money between members of the two groups. Actually, they would even take a lower level of reward for their group if that meant they could maximize the difference in the reward between their group and the out-group.

This *in-group bias*, the tendency for people to give preferential treatment to others they perceive to be members of their own groups, also leads to generalization and stereotyping of out-group members. ("They all behave like that.")

Decisions that people make as part of their in-group tend to be more extreme than those of the individuals that make up the group, and group members' beliefs can also shift to correspond with the in-group's norms. Coupled with the disinhibition of being part of the group, this can lead to people taking on and defending views that they may not otherwise have held.

The Seattle Seahawks foster in-group feelings from their fans by officially recognizing them as "The 12th Man" (on a team of 11 players). Reading the in-group community forum pages at seahawks.net shows plenty of the disinhibition and adoption of the group's views that often goes along with feelings of in-group membership. In return, by feeling like they are part of the team, fans are more likely to embrace the behaviors of the team, including dressing like them (with items conveniently available from the team's store), and engaging in Seattle's notorious high crowd noise levels to confuse and intimidate the opposing team.

The Seattle Seahawks' "12th Man" designation for fans shows how much they embrace supporters as part of the in-group. Note the prominent link to the store, where people can show their in-group affiliation by purchasing jerseys and other Seahawk logo items. (seahawks.com)

How to use in-group bias

» Provide a clear differentiating factor between in-group and out-group members. This distinction is the most important step in creating and maintaining an in-group.

» Clearly identify the out-group because that's what provides the focus for the in-group to cooperate and self-identify. Increase the in-group/out-group contrast by exaggerating the perceived difference between the groups' characteristics.

» Make it easy for individuals to identify with your group's philosophies. They will then see your group in a more positive light and be biased against those who are defined as being in an out-group.

» Attribute positive behaviors to in-group members and negative behaviors to out-group members. Then, emphasize the positive behaviors that lead to your desired behavior in the in-group.

» It helps if the in-group can see themselves as the winners rather than being the underdog, and as the heroes rather than the villains. Emphasize the thing that makes them positive, even if it's just a different wording of the same trait ("loyalty to our family" versus "nepotism") or two sides of the same coin ("We treat our members well" versus "they are hostile toward outsiders.")

Controlling lust: Using desire to get a commitment

Because it has its roots in desire, lust has a tendency to bypass rational behavior. That is useful for companies that want to turn desire into action without the filters that logic and an even disposition provide.

The nudge from desire to action can be achieved by relying on social norms or by breaking market norms. The social norm of reciprocity, where giving a gift makes people indebted to the giver, works at a level below rational thought. Making something "free" goes so far against market norms that people stop making rational comparisons because they see nothing but benefits to an offer that has no cost to them.

Companies can also appeal to the emotional desires that people have and sell them the intangible value. Between two ostensibly identical services, the one that best demonstrates its intangible value will be seen as more desirable.

Alternatively, companies can turn things on their head and use good old cognitive dissonance to get people to favor them by making a request of their customers that they later use as proof that the customer must actually like them.

Give something to get something

People will feel obliged to reciprocate.

The chapter on Gluttony discussed how foot-in-the-door and door-in-the-face techniques work at least in part through reciprocity. Foot-in-the-door creates cognitive dissonance in the customer at the thought of refusing to do a larger favor after first doing a smaller one. In door-in-the-face the customer makes a reciprocal concession to the smaller second request after denying the large first request.

In each case, the customer feels obliged to reciprocate. Actually, reciprocation is a social norm. We also tend to like people who help us, and dislike those who ask for help but don't return it. There is an implicit obligation to repay someone who does us a favor, whether we asked for the favor or not.

In 1971 Dennis Regan ran an experiment where participants were paired with an accomplice of the experimenter ostensibly to undertake a study of aesthetic enjoyment but actually to better understand reciprocity. It's worthwhile describing the procedure in some detail because it led to several interesting findings.

Before the study started, the participant had either overheard the accomplice be nice or be nasty on the phone. This was done to manipulate whether the participant subsequently liked the accomplice. Both "participants" (the true participant and the accomplice) were then paid for their participation in advance. This ensured that the participant had money available for the subsequent true experiment.

After the first round of critiquing paintings for the dummy aesthetic enjoyment study, the accomplice asked to leave the room briefly, and he and the experimenter left the participant alone. When they returned, one of three events took place. Either the accomplice brought with him two soft drinks and gave one to the participant (a favor), the experimenter brought two soft drinks and gave one to each of the "participants" (an irrelevant favor) or no drinks were handed out.

After the next round of the dummy study, the experimenter again left the room. At this time, the accomplice asked the participant to buy some raffle tickets for a relatively worthy cause, "Any would help; the more the better." When the experimenter reappeared he asked each "participant" to fill in a quick questionnaire, explaining it was to check whether their mood state might affect their ratings of the paintings. Parts of the questionnaire asked for ratings of the other participant, including likeability, generosity, and politeness.

At this point the true experiment was over. Participants were debriefed and given back any money they'd spent on the raffle tickets. The amount they spent was used as a measure of how much they would reciprocate for the accomplice's earlier gift of the drink. In 1971, the drink would have cost 10 cents and each raffle ticket was priced at 25 cents. The participants were paid $1.75 for their time. So even purchasing one ticket meant that participants were giving back more than they had received from the accomplice.

What did the results show?

>> Doing a favor did increase reciprocation. More tickets were purchased when the confederate had brought the drink.

>> There was no real difference between the experimenter bringing a drink and the no-drink condition. That means the effect was due to reciprocation rather than just being happier or less thirsty.

>> Participants bought more raffle tickets if they said they liked the confederate than if they didn't, *unless* the confederate had given them the drink. Then, it didn't matter whether they liked him; they still bought more tickets.

>> Buying just one ticket would have repaid the favor. However, receiving the favor doubled the amount of times that participants bought more than one ticket (from 25 to 58 percent).

>> Accomplices that did the favor were liked more, regardless of participants' initial experiences overhearing a nice or nasty phone call. This manipulation of liking didn't have a significant effect on reciprocation.

To drive that home, let's say it again. It doesn't matter whether you like the person who did you a favor, you still feel obliged to reciprocate and often to do so above the level of the initial favor. You will also like the person more because they did the favor for you, regardless of how "nice" they were to start with.

Subsequent studies have backed up these findings multiple times. Reciprocity isn't gratitude. There may be gratitude in the reciprocal act, but there doesn't have to be. Indeed, tit-for-tat fights are an example of negative reciprocity. What seems to happen is that recipients feel obligation until they reciprocate. The obligation is so strong that the giver can even make requests based on having given, rather than waiting for the recipient to act.

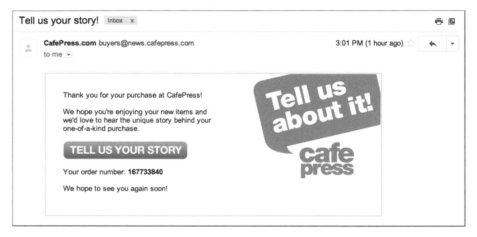

In this e-mail, Café Press "reminds" me they just did me a favor ("We hope you're enjoying your new items") and asks for a reciprocal favor ("write us a testimonial"). Wait; wasn't it me doing Café Press a favor by making a purchase on its site? Apparently not. (e-mail from cafepress.com)

Reciprocity is powerful. If you can be perceived to have given someone something, even something as inconsequential as a free whitepaper or report; then people will feel more obliged to give you something back. In other words, it makes sense to put the request for visitors' e-mail addresses *after* you've given them the free item, not before it.

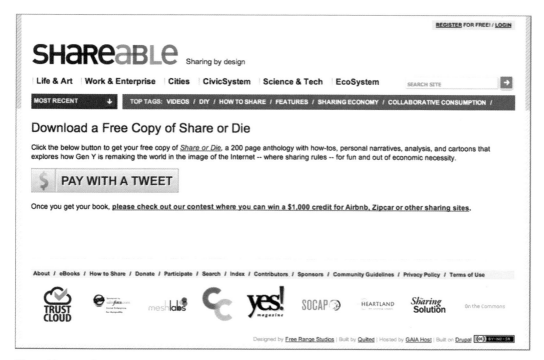

Shareable.net asks you to give it some free marketing in the form of a tweet as the reciprocal action of downloading a report. This is true reciprocity in contrast to the usual bribery approach of "Give us your details; then we'll give you the report."

How to use reciprocity

» Give the gift first, and only then ask for something in return. Typically sites make people register before they can have the "free" report, but this is counter to the principles of reciprocity.

» The reciprocal favor is often proportional to the perceived value of what you give, so it's useful to place a value on the item you're giving them ("Normally $150, but you can download it free today") so that they feel comparatively generous in return.

(continues)

(continued)

» If time elapses between your gift and your requested response, recipients will have reduced the value of that gift in their mind. Remind them of the value and prompt them to think about one or two of the benefits that your gift gave them before you ask for the reciprocal favor.

» Reciprocity doesn't have to be symmetrical. In other words, the favor can also be paid forwards. For that reason, if you say you have donated to a charity on a customer's behalf, the customer will feel the same reciprocal pull.

 ## Make something free

Make something free, and rationality disappears. You can recoup the money elsewhere.

Amazon.com first started offering year-round free shipping on purchases of $99 or more in 2002. By the end of that year, it had reduced the trigger point to $49. In 2003, it reduced it again to $25. At this time, the company stopped running print and TV ads, and put the money it would have spent on advertising into free shipping instead because it saw better returns from the goodwill of free shipping than it did from a 16-month study into the benefits of TV advertising.

Over the course of 2 years, free shipping had moved from being a limited time promotional offer to becoming Amazon.com's primary differentiator. As the company said in a recent SEC filing, "While costs associated with Amazon Prime memberships and other shipping offers are not included in marketing expense, we view these offers as effective worldwide marketing tools, and intend to continue offering them indefinitely."

Now, approximately 40 percent of e-commerce transactions have free shipping. To differentiate further, some companies such as Nordstrom and Zappos also offer free return shipping. Free shipping is obviously a strong persuasive force.

Offering free shipping also makes business sense. During Third Quarter 2010 the average order value for transactions involving free shipping was 41 percent higher than transactions without free shipping. Higher volume can quickly make up for lower margins.

It also makes psychological sense, as people respond differently to "free" than they do to simple price reductions.

As Dan Ariely points out in his book *Predictably Irrational*, the move from cheap to free appears much bigger than the move from expensive to cheap, so making something about the transaction free (shipping in the previous example) removes any remnants of rational thought from the shopper's mind. It seems that people do not simply subtract costs from benefits. Instead, they see free products as having more benefits.

Ariely explains that when buying things, consumers compare the upside and the downside. When something is free, the downside disappears. You can't lose anything from making that choice, even if you ultimately end up with something that is less suitable for your needs.

There are different variations on the "free" theme:

» Free as an incentive to buy, or to spend more (such as free shipping, free gifts, and two-for-one deals)

» Free with the cost moved elsewhere (free shipping with an annual subscription)

» Free with the cost disguised (free use of a service in return for use of your data)

Let's explore each of these approaches in turn. The first approach involves enticing customers with an offer of something extra if they buy a product.

Free shipping and free gifts are different from the "Give something to get something" pattern previously described. In that pattern, companies rely on the social norms of reciprocity. Here, however, we're discussing market norms.

Giving gifts normally works within the realms of social norms. If someone gives me a birthday present, I can't reciprocate at their birthday party by giving them an envelope containing the exact cash value of the gift she gave me. To do so would be to move outside the social norms and into an area where we can put direct value on each transaction, namely the world of market norms.

But because in this pattern the gift was used as an incentive rather than to create reciprocity, companies can make it clear exactly what the value of the "free" gift is.

Companies can afford to promote this type of offer by charging enough for the base product to cover the expense of the "free" accessories being offered. Any accessory, additional product, warranty, or service that costs less than the margin on the base product is in effect not truly free but just an alternate form of discount. Because of the irrational response that customers have to the word "free" however, they may well perceive an additional product or service as a better deal than a straight percentage price reduction.

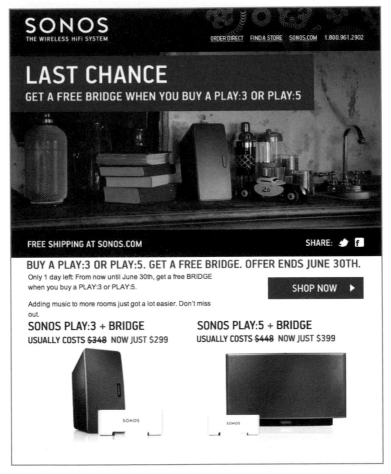

Sonos offers a small component for free at certain times of the year to persuade you to buy a more expensive item. The company could just have said "12 percent off" but using the word "Free" is much more attractive. (e-mail from sonos.com)

The second approach to offering something free is to move the cost elsewhere. Amazon.com's Prime service offers free 2-day shipping for $79/year. So it's actually not free at all. In direct terms serious shoppers may well save money by subscribing to this service, but that discounts the value that Amazon.com accrues from the additional purchases those individuals make as a result of the "free" shipping. The siren call of "free" probably also encourages many people to sign up for the service despite not actually accruing $80 of shipping costs in a year.

The third approach is to disguise the cost by making interaction with the service free, in return for viewing targeted advertisements. Many products that give you access to their service free of charge and without apparently asking for anything in return are using this approach to "free."

As a user, if you aren't paying to access the service, you're most likely the product, not the customer. The implicit contract with companies such as Facebook, Instagram, Twitter, and the like is that users provide their eyeballs and behavioral data in return for use of the system. In turn, the companies sell that information to advertisers, who are their true customers.

Social media services hype the ability to share information with your friends, but their true goal is to get you to unintentionally share with people who aren't your friends; the marketers who want to profile you for targeted ads. Users typically see sufficient value from using the service to go along with this, at least until the advertisements become too intrusive.

This approach to "free" works best when the true nature of the deal remains implicit rather than becoming explicit. Instagram, the photo sharing app owned by Facebook, tried changing its Terms of Service in a way that commentators suggested would allow it to sell users' photographs to advertisers. The big problem was that the wording of the change exposed the until-then implicit nature of users' contracts with the company.

Even though Instagram denied that it was ever its intention to sell users' photos, many users reacted in the only manner available to them, by deleting their accounts. Instagram quickly reversed the controversial areas in the Terms of Service; although, the updated version used many more vague weasel words that made it much harder to understand its true intentions. Apparently it's OK to monetize users so long as you obfuscate the ways in which you do it sufficiently well to keep the methods implicit rather than explicit.

Social commentary on users' lack of awareness of their status with social media services. "Instagram" ©
Randall Munroe, xkcd. (xkcd.com/1150)

How to use "free"

» Free has a magnetic attraction. Offer free shipping but only on orders above
a certain amount so that shoppers add more to their cart. The free shipping doesn't even have to be of the same quality as the paid-for shipping,
so you can still show differentiation, which gives you the chance to upsell
(for instance from free economy shipping to 2-day or overnight shipping).

» Ensure that "free" items you give have an obvious value. Gifts must have value
to be seen as an incentive.

» Instead of discounting the cost of your product or service, add an accessory
or additional service for "free." The additional emotional response of "free"
creates more value than a straight discount.

» Use the lure of a free service to attract a secondary audience who provide
the incentive for your primary audience to use your product. For instance,
Facebook's secondary audience is its user base, which provides eyeballs for
its primary audience's ad impressions.

Sell the intangible value

Reality is costly to change, perception less so.

The NeuesMuseum in Berlin displays a late Bronze age (1000—800 BCE) golden hat that probably originated in Swabia or Switzerland. I'm sure that the *Goldhut* is insured for far more than its weight in gold. One of only four such items ever found, the hat contains symbols that allow calculation of lunar and solar events (such as solstices) and its method of manufacture tells us much about the culture that made it. The emotional implications of these intangible factors make it priceless.

The 75cm (30-inch) tall Goldhut (Gold hat), in the Neues Museum, Berlin, has an intangible value beyond that of the material it's constructed from.

In the same museum are excavated hoards of precious metals that were at some point in the past buried by their owners for safekeeping. The chunks of metal in those piles are sometimes called *hacksilver* because they have been chopped from larger items such as plates, icons, or even maybe gold hats. To marauders sharing spoils or traders accepting payment, those chunks of metal probably had no emotional value, only a tangible value. They were worth whatever they could be exchanged for.

Why the history lesson? Because it demonstrates that sometimes items have only a tangible value relating to their utility, and sometimes items have much higher intangible value. Despite the fact that it may once have been jewelry or ornamental tableware, hacksilver's utility was that it could be traded for other goods. In comparison, the gold hat had little utility as headgear but probably a high emotional value in religious ceremonies. The intangible value isn't inherent in the materials used, or necessarily in the time and care taken to create the object. Instead the intangible value is assigned by our perceptions of and relationship with the object. It's the emotional aspect of this intangible part of the value equation that generates lust.

Rory Sutherland, the executive creative director at Oglivy & Mather UK, suggests that most value-related problems are problems of perception rather than function, and so it's often much more productive to tinker with perceptions rather than reality.

Disney theme parks, for instance, just don't have sufficient space on their rides to seat every visitor at the same time. Rather than trying to resolve that problem, which would be prohibitively expensive, they have made the act of traveling between rides and waiting in line for a ride into an intangibly valuable experience. Rather than being a chore, it's actually fun to walk between rides, taking in the sights as you go. Costumed characters keep people entertained, the path of the ride waiting line gives visitors glimpses of what they are about to experience; sometimes booths along the way provide information or let them play mini-games, and mileposts give them regular progress updates.

Making lemonade from wait-time lemons actually added to the intangible value of spending a day at a Disney theme park. Instead of just going for the rides, people go for the emotional ambience of the entire park. Disney cleverly found a way to make people value the thing that could have been its downfall.

The same is true in the online world. Instead of just going for the service, a site with high levels of intangible value will have an ambience that encourages you to stick around. One example is Angie's List, an online review site that charges $40+ per year for membership in a space that sees competition from several free services such as Yelp, Kudzu, and Ratemycontractor.com.

Angie's List managed to create sufficient intangible value compared to these other sites by focusing on the quality and impartiality of the content the site provides. Each member is named, so there is no opportunity for inflammatory or fake anonymous reviews. Companies who have been reviewed get a chance to respond to reports so that review readers can hear both sides of the story, and the site also offers a complaint resolution service that acts as a guarantee in the event that a rated contractor doesn't perform as expected.

While ostensibly offering the same basic service as other review sites, Angie's List manages to create the perception that it is more professional, less open to bias, and generally a trustworthier source for reviews. By highlighting the intangibles in a way that hits the right emotional tone, it has created a perception of value that allows it to charge for a service that others offer for free.

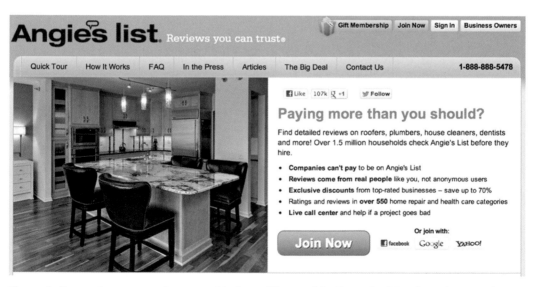

The angieslist.com homepage makes some of its intangibles tangible. By emphasizing these elements of its service, it creates an environment that people favor over other review sites. Note also the use of a push poll question ("Paying more than you should?") to frame its main message.

How to sell the intangible value

» Don't change what you do, change how you position it. You can create differentiation from your competitors by focusing on the intangible, emotional element of your product or service.

» List the features that differentiate you from competitors in a way that appeals to people's emotions as well as to their rational thought processes. Emotional responses, although intangible, can be powerful.

» Focus on the relationship that people have with your brand rather than the direct functionality of your products. For instance, Angie's List's tagline is "reviews you can trust®." Lots of sites offer reviews, but only Angie's List owns *trusted* reviews.

» Find ways to turn negatives into positives. Wait time is an opportunity for brand messaging or entertainment; subscription fees imply higher quality content.

Make a request in order to be seen more favorably

The Ben Franklin effect shows that people who have done us a favor see us in a better light.

In his autobiography, Benjamin Franklin describes how he turned around the feelings of someone who had spoken up against him in the Pennsylvania State legislature.

Having heard that he had in his library a certain very scarce and curious book I wrote a note to him, expressing my desire of perusing that book, and requesting he would do me the favour of lending it to me for a few days. He sent it immediately and I return'd it in about a week with another note, expressing strongly my sense of the favour. When we next met in the House he spoke to me (which he had never done before), and with great civility; and he ever after manifested a readiness to serve me on all occasions, so that we became great friends and our friendship continued to his death.

By asking a favor of the previously combative legislator, he made that person resolve the cognitive dissonance of lending a book to an enemy by thinking "I must not have hated him too much because I lent him that book. And he obviously shares some of my interests, so he can't be too terrible a person."

It's a nice story, but can people without Ben Franklin's charisma replicate it? Apparently so. Jon Jecker and David Landy asked students to participate in an experimental task, for which they were paid. However, as they left, the experimenter approached one-third of the participants and explained that his funds for paying them were coming from his own pocket, and that he was running low. He asked, "As a special favor to me, would you mind returning the money you won?" Another third of the participants were given the same request, but by a different member of the department's staff. The remaining participants were not asked to return their reward. All the participants subsequently filled out a questionnaire that included ratings of the experimenter. The participants who had been asked to do a favor and return the money rated the experimenter as more attractive.

This is different from the foot-in-the-door and door-in-the-face effects described in the chapter on Gluttony. When asking for a small favor and then a larger favor, or vice versa, guilt can play a role. The aim here is to ask only for a single favor, thank the favor-giver (removing any possibility for guilt), and then leave the favor-giver hanging in a state of cognitive dissonance. The favor-giver didn't think they liked the individual, but they still performed the favor. Something must change in the favor-giver's minds to resolve the dissonance this pair of thoughts causes. The most appropriate way for individuals to justify their actions to themselves in this situation is to decide that they like the person for whom they performed the favor. Of course, this happens on a subconscious level.

A lovely online example of the Ben Franklin effect at work is in reporting bugs. Take for example Blogger, the blog publishing tool owned by Google. It has a simple "Send feedback" flash in the bottom-right corner of each blog administration page. Clicking this flash opens a dialog box on the page, which has now become a highlightable image. Users can quickly show which area they are concerned about without knowing its technical name and can easily remove personal information by blanking it out. After typing a short problem description and reviewing the information that will be sent, users can submit the bug. Google then thanks the users for their input.

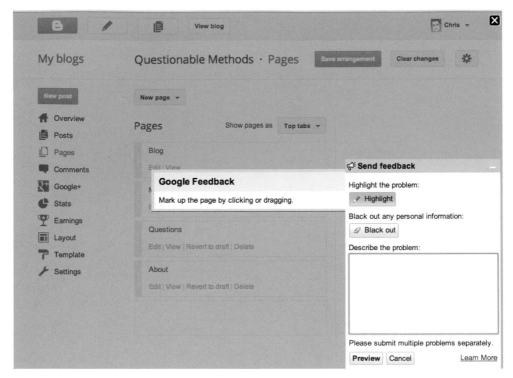

Reporting bugs on Blogger is interactive and relatively pain free. The Ben Franklin effect suggests that after successfully reporting the bug and being thanked, customers will like the company more. (blogger.com)

At this point, users who have submitted feedback will realize they have done Google a favor. It is likely that they will rationalize this dissonance and justify their continued use of the product that they just complained about by liking it more. There is a sweet irony in the fact that when done correctly the act of reporting a bug—something that has just caused problems—has the potential to make customers like a company more than they did before.

How to use the Ben Franklin effect

» Ask customers to do a small favor for you. Thank them for it after they are done, but don't return the favor immediately. Now, having done an unreciprocated favor for you, they must justify it to themselves by believing that they truly like you.

» Be sure that the favor is successfully completed. Without that, there will be no increase in liking. That suggests you should make the favor easy to perform.

Lustful behavior

Mae West was right when she said that flattery will get you everywhere. This chapter has shown that if you are smart, but not *too* smart, you're in a good position to be liked because you are subconsciously raising the self-esteem of your audience. Creating an in-group of "believers" and giving them a reason to believe will subsequently create defenders of your awesomeness.

Of course, this doesn't just happen for free. You have to give to get, and sometimes as Ben Franklin demonstrated in extreme cases you might even have to get to get.

Luckily there are people out there to help you with the giving of flattery. Flatterme.ca will do it for a small fee. For just $5 in North America, or $10 for international destinations, they will telephone an individual and give them a flattering message on your behalf.

You may be scoffing at this point, thinking that although others may fall for these cheap persuasive tricks, you never would. You are wrong. The *third-person effect* shows that we tend to over-predict the influence that these techniques have on others, but feel that the technique will have less effect on us. However, in reality the flattery does affect us, as we've seen in both Elaine Chan's and B.J. Fogg's research, and as demonstrated in the psychological literature on the *sleeper effect*, where impact of the flattering message lives on long after we've forgotten that we shouldn't be swayed by it.

Yes, you can buy flattery. (flatterme.ca)

Lust reveals itself through anticipation. Materialistic customers experience this anticipation so strongly that they might get more pleasure from the desire for a new product than they do after purchasing it. They experience strong positive emotions when they think about the transformation that future purchases will bring about in their lives, enhancing their self-esteem. Because of their materialist mentality, they think about the purchases a lot, so they get frequent mood boosts.

This anticipation of the intangible value of items is, in some respects, the ultimate embodiment of commercial lust. Luxury brands work hard to create lust and direct it toward purchase of their items. Just owning the item is marketed as sufficient to improve our standing in the world and thus our self-esteem.

Greed

The point is, you can't be too greedy.

DONALD TRUMP

GREED IS THE DESIRE to get or keep more stuff than you need, either accumulating money or possessions ("whoever has the most toys wins") or just to feel better than someone else does.

Because greed prevents other people from having access to a thing that they could use more than the greedy individual could, it's seen as selfish or spiteful. The reason it's seen as one of the seven deadly sins is that greedy people obviously distrust that God will provide all they need.

All talk of sin aside, there does seem to be a correlation between having more than one needs and being selfish. When talking about haves and have-nots, there are four possible behaviors: selfishness, altruism, spite, and cooperation.

Greed happens when people pursue their own agenda at the expense of others, leading to selfish or spiteful behavior. Paul Piff, a social psychologist at UC Berkeley, found that people who "had more" (those in higher social classes) were less ethical, and more likely to lie, cheat, or steal. Interestingly, it wasn't that more greedy people made it to a higher social class, but that getting to a higher social class reinforced those behaviors, making people more likely to be greedy. As Piff puts it, "Upper-class individuals' unethical tendencies are accounted for, in part, by their more favorable attitudes toward greed."

The reverse is also true. In another set of studies, Piff found that people in lower social classes are more generous, charitable, trusting, and helpful even at cost to themselves. This helpful have-not behavior is classic altruism. Others in Piff's team ran a study that found lower-class individuals were more compassionate and less selfish.

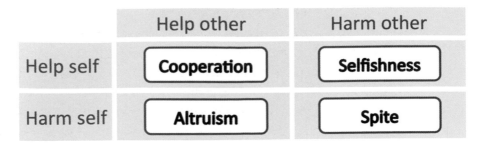

	Help other	Harm other
Help self	**Cooperation**	**Selfishness**
Harm self	**Altruism**	**Spite**

The four possible behaviors between two people who want access to the same resources

It seems that the more you have, the less you need to rely on others. The less you need to rely on others, the less you care about them. The more you have, the more likely it is that you are surrounded by others who also have more, and so the less likely it is that you will need help. Greed therefore feeds upon itself, helping people to justify their increasingly selfish and spiteful behaviors.

So how does greed happen? How does it get reinforced? What triggers cause people to be greedy, and how do companies benefit from this behavior?

Learning from casinos: Luck, probability, and partial reinforcement schedules

Imagine that you are a game show contestant about to make a play for the grand prize. You are shown three doors. The host tells you that a new car waits behind one door, and the other two doors hide goats. The host asks you to choose a door. After you choose it, the host opens one of the two doors that you didn't choose, revealing a goat. Now, to add an element of excitement, the host gives you the option to switch your choice to the other unopened door. Assuming you're more interested in winning a car than a goat, what do you do?

After the game show host opens the door, most people expect that there's a 50-50 chance that they have already chosen the correct door. Because they have already made their choice, they are attached to their current door (the *endowment effect*) and so they stick with it.

However, the correct answer is to always switch because there is actually a two-in-three probability that the car is behind the other door.

Think of it this way: Before you made a choice, there was an equal one-in-three probability that the car was behind any door. That means there was always a two-in-three probability that the car was behind one of the two doors that you didn't choose. That fact doesn't change after you make your choice, and it doesn't even change when the host opens one of the doors you didn't choose. Even though you now know which door is not hiding the car, the other unchosen door retains its two-in-three probability because you could still theoretically choose the door that has already been opened.

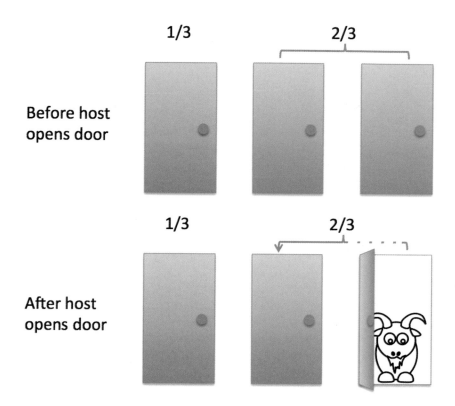

Say you first choose the left door. The probability of the car being behind one of the other doors is 2/3. It stays at 2/3 even after the host opens the right door. By switching, you keep the 2/3 probability with the added benefit of having one of the options eliminated.

If that explanation made your brain hurt, welcome to the world that most people inhabit. The previous example is called the *Monty Hall problem* after the host who popularized it on the *Let's Make a Deal* game show, and yes, they really did use goats. It is a great demonstration of the difference between mathematical probability and common sense. And yet strangely, despite the confusion that most people feel when dealing with questions of probability, they feel qualified to play the odds every time they enter a casino or buy a lottery ticket.

In North America, lotteries created $66 billion in sales, resulting in a $20 billion profit in 2010. Forty-three states, DC, and Puerto Rico run lotteries, as does every Canadian province. Sixty percent of adults in states with lotteries report playing at least once per year.

Between them, casinos and lotteries account for 72 percent of all gambling in the United States. Americans spend more than $1 billion/day on slot machines in the 38 states where they're legal.

On one level the people walking in to the casino to play the machines must know that their odds are low and that the house always wins. On another level, however, they are willing participants in the systematic removal of their money because they cling to a vague hope that they might just "win big." Lotteries have the worst odds of all forms of gambling, but also the highest potential payout proportionate to investment. As the Kentucky state lottery slogan points out, "Somebody's gotta win, might as well be you."

The casinos' and lottery providers' job is just to reinforce this belief. How do they do this? As just pointed out, a large part of the problem is the players' inability to properly measure risk.

We aren't good at understanding randomness either. Consider the outcry when on July 11th 2007, the five numbers picked for North Carolina's Cash-5 lottery were identical to the numbers picked on July 9th. There were cries of tampering and calls for investigations. The state lottery director even had to be dragged out to explain that different machines and different balls had been used on the two occasions, so it was impossible that tampering had caused the repeat. The thing is, although it looks strange, there's no reason for the numbers not to repeat. That's the nature of randomness. The same numbers are just as likely to come up again as are different ones. The probability of it happening in any given 3-day period is only 1 in 191,919.

And it has happened at least a couple of times subsequently. In September 2009, a Bulgarian lottery drew the same six numbers two times in the same week.

In 2010, the Israel National Lottery produced the same numbers, pulled out in the exact reverse order, just seven draws apart.

Because it is hard to measure risk, and because we like to think we see patterns where there is only randomness, we're susceptible to the *gambler's fallacy*. That is, we believe that a win becomes more likely after a series of losses. And despite the cognitive dissonance you'd think it causes, we also believe that there is a "winning streak" effect, where after we've won once, we're more likely to continue winning.

And that's where the casinos draw us in. It's okay to lose most of the time, just so long as we win occasionally, or at least are surrounded by people who appear to be winning.

The appearance of winning—or nearly winning—is what makes casinos so appealing to many. (mandalaybay.com, excalibur.com, bellagio.com, luxor.com)

This occasional winning in among multiple losses is called a *partial reinforcement schedule*. To understand reinforcement schedules we should begin with Ivan Pavlov and his dogs. Pavlov was collecting dogs' saliva to study their gastric function. He noticed that his dogs would start drooling more when they heard the sounds associated with food preparation. He experimented further, pairing the concept of food with the sound of a bell. When he subsequently rang the bell, the dogs would drool even though no food was present.

This was a *continuous reinforcement schedule*—every stimulus was associated with a reward. The dogs would stop responding (drooling) quickly if no food appeared after the bell was rung.

Later, B. F. Skinner was performing learning experiments with rats and pigeons when he found that sometimes withholding the reward for a correct behavior led to the animals continuing to exhibit the behavior for longer.

This became known as a partial reinforcement schedule. Unlike Pavlov's dogs, who quickly stopped responding to the bell if no food was given to them, Skinner's rats and pigeons would continue at the task for much longer if they were only rewarded (reinforced) occasionally rather than every time. For this reason, a partial reinforcement schedule is much harder to break than a continuous reinforcement schedule.

And what type of schedule do the casinos and lottery providers use? A partial reinforcement schedule. Humans respond in similar ways to rats and pigeons when given an occasional reward for repetitive behavior.

Casinos are a visual indication of the ways that companies can benefit from greed through creating aspirational, conditioned behavior and emphasizing the "luck" of winning. This section talks about several of the other ways that this is exploited.

Use a partial reinforcement schedule

You'll keep people playing longer.

The principles used when training animals are not that different to those used when designing successful computer games. During an initial learning period, there must be a sufficient reward for the participant (animal or player) to continue exhibiting the correct behavior. Over time though, the rewards can be given further apart or only for certain combinations of behaviors.

When the rewards are backed off, they can either be given once every certain number of times the behavior is shown (a *fixed ratio* schedule), or on average once within a certain number of times the behavior is shown (a *variable ratio* schedule). Rewarding in a specific timeframe, again either *fixed interval* or *variable interval*, can do the same; although, this does not provide such a strong reinforcement.

In dog training, you start by rewarding everything that looks like the behavior you want with a treat. Subsequently, you reward only the exact behavior you want. When the behavior is set, you can move to a partial reinforcement schedule where the dog is only given a treat occasionally. The dog will continue to perform the exact behavior even though it is not rewarded every time.

Computer games are designed to keep us playing. Reinforcement might come in the form of points, leveling up, or getting better equipment or in-game skills. As John Hopson puts it in an article for *Gamasutra*, that reinforcement isn't random. It happens in response to actions the player performs. Early in the game, it might happen frequently to reward players for mastering a certain type of move or just to keep them interested as they learn the game mechanics. Later in the game, the frequency of reward may drop off. The more invested the player, the less reinforcement they need. Actually, sometimes just reaching the next piece of the puzzle after struggling through a particular stage can be a sufficient reward. What has happened is that the motivation to continue has moved from being *extrinsic*, based on the rewards being given by the game, to being *intrinsic*, based on the personal challenges of mastering the game.

A fixed ratio or fixed interval schedule leads to times when the reward seems a long way off—such as just after leveling up, when it takes a lot more points before the next opportunity. To keep people playing during this time, it makes sense to use a variable ratio schedule for some other activity in the game, such as killing enemies, so that they feel there's always a chance of being rewarded for some minor goal they're working toward rather than being disheartened by the far-off major goal.

Another approach for game designers is to produce events that are negatively reinforcing. In other words, players work to prevent them from happening. An example might be going too long without logging in to *Farmville*, only to find spoiled crops and rampant animals. To prevent this, players must remember to tend to their farms frequently. Negative reinforcement rewards people by *taking away* a bad outcome. You reinforce the behavior by associating it with bad things *not* happening. This is very different from punishment, where you try and stop a behavior by associating it with bad things happening.

And as it is in games, so it is on the Internet. Facebook users checking to see how many Likes they received for a post and Twitter users counting followers are working on a variable ratio partial reinforcement schedule. People hunting for bargains in Amazon.com's Gold Box are working on a fixed interval partial reinforcement schedule.

That leads to a simple way to break online habits. Often it's enough just to visualize ourselves as a pigeon in a box, pecking in response to the rewards being fed to us by the online sites, for us to realize that we're being rewarded for actions that potentially benefit the site more than they benefit us.

How to design for a partial reinforcement schedule

» Keep people engaged by creating multiple goals that can be worked on simultaneously.

> » Some should be longer-term *fixed interval/ratio* events, which happen after a certain time has elapsed or a number of items have been collected.

> » Others should be shorter-term *variable interval/ratio* events, which happen within a certain time range or after a number of enemies have been killed, but with an element of uncertainty built in, so it's not always clear exactly when the reward will be given.

» Prevent people from ignoring you by using negative reinforcement. Design the interaction so that bad things happen if the user doesn't visit regularly. Using a variable interval before the bad things occur will mean they don't know exactly when to return, increasing anxiety and the likelihood of checking in.

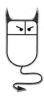

Make it into a game

Turn onerous tasks into a game by providing (minimal) rewards for participation.

How do you convince people to take the stairs rather than an escalator? Or recycle bottles? Or obey the speed limit? In 2009, Volkswagen ran a competition to find the best ideas for changing people's behavior for the better. One entry showed how installing touch-sensitive strips arranged like piano keys on the staircase exit from a train station in Odenplan, Stockholm led 66 percent more people to choose the stairs than the escalator, simply so they could "play" the piano as they walked. Adding a choose-the-right-hole game to a bottle recycling container (and displaying a high score) led to 100 versus 2 uses in one evening. The winning entry was a speed camera lottery that redistributes fines levied for disobeying the speed limit to the people who actually obeyed it. The pilot implementation resulted in a 22 percent reduction in speed from an average of 32km/h to 25km/h.

So it appears that when given the right reasons or rewards, people can be persuaded to perform real-world tasks they otherwise wouldn't.

Considering how easy it is to capture, count, and reward behaviors electronically, it should come as no surprise that there are similar games in the online space.

Some are actual games, such as *Fold.it* and *DigitalKoot*. *Fold.it* uses a game-like reward system to help show that humans can be more effective than computers at folding proteins into correct structures. The protein folding work is important for discoveries in many fields including combatting AIDS and cancers, and the *Fold.it* team hopes that any advances in folding strategies that the players create can be fed back into computer algorithms, making those algorithms better at doing their job.

DigitalKoot was an effort run by the National Library of Finland to correct words that had been poorly digitized when the National Library moved its newspaper archive online. Players typed in words as they were presented onscreen by in-game mole characters, thus allowing the moles to build a bridge and cross the water. The game-like elements (tasks and scores) led to some individuals volunteering more than 100 hours of their time, with the top-ranked player completing almost 350,000 tasks over 395 hours. That's the equivalent of 10 full-time work weeks spent identifying blurry Finnish words. All told, the game's participants fixed more than 8 million words in under 2 years.

Other online game-like applications use *crowdsourcing* to complete trivial tasks. Google until recently ran the *Image Labeler* application, which pitted two players against each other producing descriptive words for a picture. If both chose the same word, they would be awarded points based on the specificity of the word, and thus its suitability as an image label. This obviously helped Google provide more appropriate images in its image search results, but the game approach, with a set time to complete the task, a variable score based on answer quality, and a high score table, made it fun for users, too.

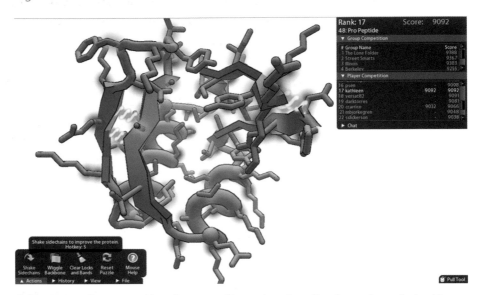

Fold.it is an online game with real purpose. Players have been listed as authors of scientific papers for their contributions to preventing or treating diseases, despite having no formal scientific training (image courtesy of the fold.it site).

Waze is a GPS navigation app for mobile devices that integrates a social element into the route finding process. Users of the app ("Wazers") can see each other on the map interface. Any user can report traffic jams, speed traps, and other slowdowns and can update map information such as points of interest, addresses, and road changes. Reporting changes gives Wazers points, which unlock different avatars and denote status in the *Waze* community. Just the act of running the application while driving provides real-time speed information to the *Waze* servers, which is then used to help other users choose the best route.

All these elements are designed in a way that makes them appear game-like, but *Waze*'s real innovation was in getting users to help create the base maps for the service. When the company starts in a new location, it relies on open source or commercial map information that might be out of date or inaccurate. After a *Waze* user has driven a route, *Waze* can be more confident that the roads are actually where the map said they were, so the company has found an interesting way to incent people to take a route they maybe wouldn't have normally used. Roads that *Waze* needs more information about display with dots overlaid on them, much like the original *Pac-Man* game. To incent people to take those routes, items such as cupcakes appear in tempting locations. Driving the route "eats" the dots and cupcakes in real time and simultaneously increases the Wazer's score. As a result the Wazer is happy because they get more points, and *Waze* is happy because it has more accurate map and route information.

None of the rewards mentioned in this section have any monetary value. Instead they have societal value—at least within the community of fellow game-players. That societal value is enough to keep people coming back and participating, earning points in exchange for their time and effort.

How to turn it into a game

» Find a way to let two individuals compare their abilities at the task you want them to complete. After you have the comparison point, turn it into a scoring mechanism, and keep track of individuals' scores. The very fact that there is a high-score table will encourage competition.

» Publicly broadcast the top scores so that players can claim bragging rights.

» Make the underlying reason for performing the task clear, especially if it is for a charitable cause or for the greater good. That gives people more reason to participate.

» Add an element of fun to the task process. For instance, *DigitalKoot* chose to use moles holding up placards with the scanned words on them. That created much more whimsy than merely showing the word on the screen. *Waze* has drivers chasing dots onscreen like a version of *Pac-Man*, with occasional cupcakes as a special reward.

Customers should "win" rather than "finish" or "buy"

Tap into the fear of losing out by describing events as competitions rather than as lotteries.

What's the difference between a lottery and an auction? When you look at the fMRI images of people winning either a lottery or an auction, the same reward centers light up. But, when people *don't* win, things look quite different. The brain activity in these reward centers decreases much more when losing an auction than losing a lottery. Actually, the more the activity decreases, the higher the likelihood that someone will bid more for the auction item than it is actually worth.

Because of the comparable brain activity when participants won their auctions and lotteries and the differences in activity when they lost, the researchers put the overbidding behavior down to fear of losing rather than joy of winning.

In other words, when the activity has an element of skill or competition (auctions), people feel more of a sense of loss than if it were purely luck-based (lotteries and sweepstakes).

JCPenney (a U.S. department store) experimented with removing the word "sale" from its vocabulary and instead emphasized "month-long value." Their reasoning was that consumers couldn't be expected to keep track of the 590 unique annual sales events. Instead it grouped discounts into three categories: *everyday low prices* reduced the artificially high mark-up from some items; *month long deals* dropped prices on select items for a longer period of time; and *best price* was the new name for clearance sales.

The result of this strategy was that revenue dropped 20 percent at the same time that it was rising at rival Macy's stores in the same malls. Apparently people like their sales. Why? Maybe because sales reward bargain hunters—the people who go specifically out of their way to find cheaper items rather than just stumbling upon them by chance. They like to feel they've won and that there was an element of skill, rather than feeling like they were lucky.

Paco Underhill, who researches consumer behavior in stores, suggests, "Sales are just like heroin." Stores' strategy of moving to every-day low prices when they used to offer specific sales events takes some of the fun away.

That might explain the success of eBay's 2008 "Don't just shop, win!" ad campaign and of sites such as Groupon, an online coupon site whose tag line is "Find great deals on fun things to do."

Groupon has built its whole business around sharing deals with its subscribers. Every day, Groupon sends out an e-mail with local deals. Its offers are only available for a certain time period, and Groupon requires a certain number of participants to sign up to unlock the discount. In other words, if in-store sales are like heroin, Groupon is a bargain hunter's crack cocaine.

Part of the draw of Groupon is discovering new deals, and to reach the requisite number of individuals to "unlock" the discount, it behooves bargain hunters to tell all their friends about the offers as well, doing Groupon's advertising. All the elements of fear of losing are present. Limited time, exclusive offers, limited access to certain merchants, a minimum participation requirement, sometimes a quantity limit, and upfront payment to secure the discount. Although it doesn't take much skill, there's still a feeling of "winning" the deal.

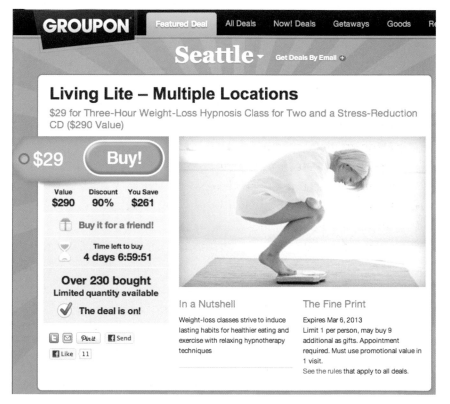

Groupon relies on the thrill of the bargain hunt. Customers are highly motivated to tell their friends about offers because that helps ensure that the minimum number of people sign up to "unlock" the deal. Of course, Groupon makes sharing easy by integrating with Facebook and other social media platforms. (groupon.com)

Groupon benefits on the seller side as well. Merchants typically offer a 50 percent price reduction on Groupons and then split the remaining revenue 50/50 with Groupon, in exchange for Groupon's promotion and handling of payments. This means that merchants are offering services for one-quarter or less of the regular price. That might not seem like a great deal to merchants, but because Groupon only offers a limited number of deals per day in each market, and because there are enough merchants desperate to get involved, Groupon can play the exclusivity card and define the terms.

As Rocky Agrawal at TechCrunch points out, what Groupon offers to merchants is cash now in return for deeply discounted goods later. The most successful businesses might not need the cash infusion and wouldn't choose to play on Groupon's terms. The ones who are struggling and need some quick cash will be much more willing customers. That doesn't actually bode too well for consumers.

Some merchants have been so swamped with bargain hunters (now known as the Groupon effect) that they have been unable to properly service the deals, and their overall customer service has suffered as a result. And the marketing benefits might not always be there. Fast Company reports survey results that show more than one-half of past deal-participating businesses don't plan on doing another offer in the next 6 months.

It seems that people are only in it for the deals. Because they are motivated more by the thrill of the hunt and the fear of losing out than by the actual products they're getting at a discount, deal seekers are unlikely to become long-term customers. So they'll continue to visit Groupon for new deals but not form a sustainable relationship with Groupon's merchant partners.

How to design for winning

» Play upon the fear of losing out. Make people aware that their skill or perseverance determines their success.

» Introduce a (manageable) challenge that must be completed to obtain the "prize."

» Even for plentiful items, make people "qualify" to purchase them.

» Manipulate availability variables such as time, quantity, or escalating cost to trigger fear of losing out.

Further inflate people's (already overconfident) feelings of skill and mastery

Ease unskilled individuals into a task with some quick wins. Enhancing their feelings of "illusive superiority" will make them more likely to continue when the stakes are higher.

As Bertrand Russell said, "One of the painful things about our time is that those who feel certainty are stupid, and those with any imagination and understanding are filled with doubt and indecision."

In 1999, David Dunning and Justin Kruger backed up Russell's assertion with some seminal research in this field (which, incidentally, won them an Ig Nobel prize in Psychology), showing that indeed those individuals who performed worst on a series of skill tests thought they had performed much better than they actually had. Test participants who had performed well had a tendency to believe they had performed comparatively poorly. Even after showing test participants their own results, whereas the individuals who had scored well could correctly estimate their own ranking, those who scored in the 12th percentile (that's quite bad) still placed themselves above average.

It was only after the low-performing participants were given some training in their lacking skills that they could better estimate their actual rank. Their estimating skills improved regardless of whether the training they received actually improved their performance. In other words, it was only when they became aware of what they didn't know that those people could correctly identify themselves as poor performers.

So the poor performers needed to be given an understanding of what it took to have real skill before they could make a good estimate of their own skill level. The higher performers similarly didn't understand that they really do have higher skill levels than other people—they believed that others were better than they actually were.

This behavior—unskilled individuals suffering from *illusive superiority*, whereas skilled individuals suffer from *illusive inferiority*—is now known as the Dunning-Kruger effect.

Dunning and Kruger's studies used tests of logical reasoning, grammar, and humor, but the same effect holds across other domains, at least for a Western audience.

There are several online activities that are open to anyone to participate in, but which require some serious skills to actually succeed at. One of the most obvious areas is online financial trading. Although it's probably true that you could observe the Dunning-Kruger effect in action with simple stock trading sites, the most fun occurs on sites that broker trades in the derivatives market: options and futures.

Options and futures are two financial instruments that—on a basic level—enable speculators to place bets based on their expectations of how a commodity will perform in the future. In other words, they are showing their expectation of how the *derivative* of the commodity will perform. Of course, the term "bet" is not used because that would suggest that participating in this market is akin to gambling. Institutional players prefer the terms "hedging" and "speculating."

And now it gets interesting. Along with trading in derivatives of regular commodities (precious metals, wheat, pork bellies, and such), you can also trade in things such as future housing prices, gasoline prices, or even in nontangibles such as weather derivatives to hedge against bad ticket sales if an open-air concert takes place on a rainy day.

Although the primary reason for trading in derivatives used to be to hedge other investments (the rainy day example for instance, or airlines hedging on future fuel prices), the high potential returns of 60 percent or more also encourage speculative trading in futures in their own right.

Just to warn you; if you're thinking at this point that you'd like to participate in this type of market, unless you have degree-level understanding of advanced financial instruments, you're probably in Dunning and Kruger's "illusive superiority" group. But as a member of that group you won't believe that you're a member of that group, and plenty of websites exist to indulge your desires.

Many of these sites, such as TradeRush.com and 24option.com are housed in countries outside the direct regulatory control of the United States, but the North American Derivatives Exchange (nadex.com) is Chicago-based and has Commodity Future Trading Commission oversight. These aren't fly-by-night concerns. Remember however that the site's legitimacy doesn't ensure your success as an investor.

24option's site offers several reassurances that trading derivatives is easy. It offers tutorials, a sandboxed practice area, and low-cost trades. It's easy to see how newcomers could get a sense of illusive superiority. (24option.com)

Most of these sites include a sandboxed practice area and tutorials that describe a simple set of rules for success. The tutorial rules tend to emphasize what happens when your option expires "in the money" but not what happens if it doesn't.

For instance, on its overview page, 24option.com describes a three-step process:

1) Among 24option's assets, you choose to invest $500 in Google.

2) You are NOT buying Google stock, you just need to decide if the Google's price will rise or fall.

3) You click Buy. If you are right, you've just made $445!

However they conveniently left out the most important part of step 3: "…and, if you're wrong, you just lost $500!" They also failed to mention that, either way, 24option will be making money through their commission.

The setup of the site, instructional material, and trading interface is such that novice traders are likely to feel overconfident. Because options trading can occur in short time frames (puts and calls can be for time periods as short as 1 minute), people can lose money quickly.

Even with indicators that things aren't going as well as they should, people might be tempted to stick with the program because often the training information suggests that it takes time to develop a winning strategy. Dunning and Kruger caution that "poor performers do not learn from feedback suggesting a need to improve"—just the sort of people who'll plow money into a financial vehicle they stand little chance of understanding.

Derivatives trading without serious experience and industry knowledge is likely to lead to an illusion of control. Even with that experience you can still seriously lose your way. Just ask Nick Leeson, who single-handedly brought Barings Bank to bankruptcy in 1995 by losing $1.2 billion through trading equity derivatives.

You can get some quick wins, and the low minimum investment makes it easy to gloss over early losses. The interfaces used by the web-based exchanges make the experience feel much like a game of chance with some added pseudo-skill built in. There are pretty graphs and glossy buttons with an invitation to enter a call if the derivative looks like it's going up, or a put if it's going down. Unfortunately, if it were that simple, there would be no spread and therefore no money to be made.

Warren Buffet calls derivatives "financial weapons of mass destruction." After the large part that derivatives played in the global financial melt-down of 2008, who do you prefer to believe: the people who get rich from you playing the options game or the man who remains rich from not playing it?

How to increase feelings of mastery

» Give people a set of relatively simple-looking rules to follow and a sand-boxed area to practice in. This way, they'll soon feel like they understand the principles of the task they are performing and feel qualified to play with the "big boys."

» Provide social proof that it's possible to win by encouraging customers to boast about their successes on a message board or other special area of the site.

» Keep ignorant people ignorant. In other words, don't make people aware of what they don't know. That way they will continue to overestimate their competence.

» Reward people early with "quick wins" so that they feel they're getting the hang of the task.

» Make it possible to play with small levels of investment so that initial losses don't feel too discouraging.

» Convince people that it may take time before they truly feel like they understand the process, but that they are doing great anyway.

 ## Make rewards seem due to skill, not luck

Requiring action to get a reward increases the perceived value of the reward.

Let's go back to Pavlov's dogs and Skinner's pigeons. There was a difference in how Pavlov and Skinner introduced new behaviors in their animals, and that difference is important because it has implications for how long the behaviors last.

Pavlov made use of a built-in reflexive behavior (drooling) to form an association with a preceding condition (a bell ringing). In contrast, Skinner was performing *operant conditioning*. If the bird did the right thing, it received a reward as a consequence.

What does that mean for us? Well, Skinner's conditioning was active, whereas Pavlov's was passive. The dog wasn't in control of its behavior in the same way as the pigeon was. The dog didn't have to do anything conscious to get the reward, whereas the pigeon did. Making the animal take an explicit action produced a stronger, longer lasting effect.

Skinner also showed that making rewards happen on a purely random "luck"-based schedule leads to weird, superstitious behaviors. He found that if he rewarded pigeons on a random schedule, regardless of what they were doing at the time, it would condition them to start performing some seemingly strange actions. For instance, one pigeon would perform a dance, whereas another might bow or turn its neck in a certain direction. This happened because the pigeon would try repeating whatever action it was performing when it received the reward. Thus it was more likely it would be doing this same thing when the next reward arrived, and so on, until the random behavior had become superstitiously associated with the reward.

This may seem at odds with the appeal of gambling. After all, gambling is addictive at least in part because of its randomness. However, what makes gambling enjoyable is the addition of a gaming element to make people think they are offsetting the randomness.

In other words, giving people pseudo-control in where they place their chips, or how they play their cards gives them a level of perceived mastery over the randomness. At its most basic, this is the difference between pushing a button to see if you've won and choosing the correct one of *two* buttons to win. Giving people choices, and making them take an action, gives them pseudo-control.

There is also a higher perceived value in getting rewarded for something you did, over something that happened to you. The emotional component of investing time or skill to obtain the coupon makes it appear more valuable. You feel like you "deserve" your reward. As a result, people are more likely to value a coupon or discount when claiming that discount requires some skill-based activity than if they had just been given something that anyone could receive.

Some of the simplest online examples of this are giving discounts to people who have signed up to receive e-mail newsletters, or to frequent purchasers via reward point programs. These individuals took an action, and now they are being rewarded for it. Others who didn't take that action are missing out. Of course, it doesn't hurt that the actions people undertake to get the reward also help the retailer.

Some companies have built skill-based rewards in to their core functionality. Groupon is a coupon based discount site, but the skill element manifests through being on the site at the right time and with sufficient other people to trigger the discount. Foursquare users must attend a location to check in, and frequent attendance is rewarded with both in-app status (badges and mayorship) and real-world perks such as discounts.

Some companies have built their entire business around skill-based rewards. SCVNGR.com gets participants to do challenges at places to unlock rewards. The challenges mainly revolve around broadcasting something positive about the location on social media, or about performing actions that make it more likely that players will return in the future. Each action also gives a certain number of rewards, which can then be redeemed for discounts or free items at the participating locations.

Shopkick.com encourages shoppers to browse online and then earn points when they subsequently buy the items they browsed in a physical store. Shoppers earn a combination of location-based points (walk-in "kicks"), plus purchase-based points and rewards on linked credit cards. By getting participants to state a goal upfront, Shopkick encourages future actions by showing progress toward their wanted reward.

In all these examples there is a level of customer involvement—either action or risk—that gives the appearance of skill. The result is that recipients of the reward value it more than they otherwise would.

Obviously, the more value the user perceives in the reward above and beyond its face value, the more value there is to the business. A hard-won $1 discount may be worth disproportionately more in terms of loyalty than handing out $5 vouchers to everyone who enters the store.

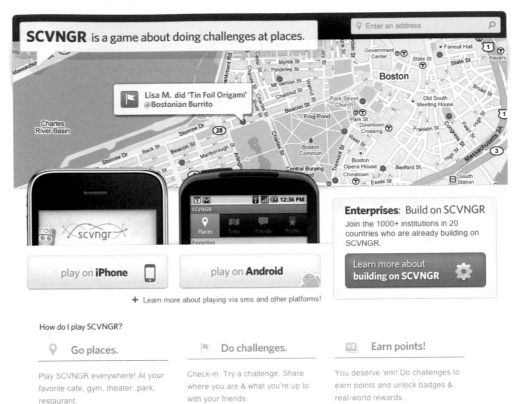

SCVNGR uses a location-aware app to tell players what challenges are available in the vicinity. Performing challenges earns rewards in the form of coupons or free products. Having performed a task makes the reward seem more worthwhile. (scvngr.com)

The best perceived value thus occurs when the barrier to winning requires just less than the amount of effort or risk that would make a customer decide not to act (play the game). Interestingly, it's also likely to be the most ardent (hopefully, this equates to most valuable too) customers who are prepared to jump through the most hoops.

How to design for skill, not luck

» Make customers perceive that they have worked for their discount, but keep the effort at a suitably low level that it doesn't become a barrier.

» The "work" that customers do could involve a game of skill or a simple challenge such as being present at a certain time or displaying a specific item.

» Challenges and games should be biased to reward your target group. For instance, frequent customers should be challenged to take a picture of a past purchase whereas new members should be challenged to visit at least two store locations in a week.

» It's okay to include a random element in the reward, but the randomness should appear to be controllable (that is, everyone wins, but the size of the reward is random within a set of parameters).

» Make it clear that the reward is only available to people who have completed the action, maintaining its exclusivity.

» Rewards need not be large—no more than the discount that a good customer might get anyway.

Create a walled garden

If you own the infrastructure, ensure that people have little reason to leave, and that they return frequently.

Back in the days of dial-up internet access, America Online (AOL) was synonymous with "The Internet" for many people. Subscribers found themselves within the walled garden of AOL's content. Ostensibly the idea of these walls was to keep non-subscribers out, but actually the true value was in keeping subscribers in. That way they could be shown more of AOL's advertisements rather than viewing content (and advertisements) on other sites.

It wasn't just AOL doing this. Individual sites would have interstitial pages asking users whether they were sure they wanted to leave the site. Landing pages would have HTTP redirects so that if a user hit the browser's back button, they'd be popped straight back into the site again.

Some sites still use these redirect tricks but users have grown less tolerant of them. Now, sites have realized the same thing as the TV companies. You need to have just enough content to keep users engaged so they'll put up with the adverts you throw at them. For TV, that amounts to about 42 minutes of programming in every hour, the remaining 18 minutes being advertisements. Prime spots can have even more minutes of advertising, as can exclusive broadcasts.

In the future, we won't need ad breaks because the advertisements will be there all the time, walling in our content [*Idiocracy* (2006), 20th Century Fox, directed by Mike Judge].

So is there still space for walled gardens online? Apparently so. Facebook has done this well and continues to offer users even more reasons to perform most of their actions within the confines of Facebook's properties. Twitter does something similar. YouTube has become synonymous with video, but since 2008 it has also been the second most used search engine in the USA, second only to its parent Google.

The same thing can be true anywhere where people need to use the provided infrastructure rather than an open alternative – either because that's where all their friends are, because that's where all the tools are, or because that's where they are guided when they start on their journey (like the original dial-up AOL).

There is however a difference between walled gardens and paywalls. Subscription sites such as the New York Times or Wall Street Journal have erected a wall to keep undesirable people *out*. That is very different from a wall designed to keep desirable people *in*.

Just ensure that the garden walls are elastic rather than rigid; clever companies let people out, but make it clear there's more fun stuff waiting for them back in the garden. Facebook, Twitter, and Google achieve this by extending their presence outside their own walls, with "Like," "+1," and "Tweet" buttons on other sites, and with the option to use Facebook, Google or Twitter credentials to log in to other sites. Providing these features as a convenience to users also allows each company to track individuals as they venture beyond its walls, and then target behavioral ads based on their actions once they return to the walled garden.

How to design a walled garden:

» Own the infrastructure. AOL used to own the dial-up infrastructure for getting online, so users were directed to their content. Facebook owns the software infrastructure for posts, likes and walls in locations where everyone's friends hang out, so users are tied to their environment.

» Carefully test your users' advertising tolerance. The purpose of the walled garden is to maximize ad revenue (you own all the ad locations inside the garden), but if advertising is too intrusive users will leave.

» Let people leave the garden, but provide features that let you track them while they are out so that you can give them more targeted advertisements when they return.

» Constantly test your garden for completeness, and, when it fails to cater to your user's wants and needs, grow it to once again so that users see no need to leave. (For instance, Facebook's acquisition of Instagram to add photo-editing features.)

Anchoring and arbitrary coherence

The gas tank needle is on empty, but we drive right past a couple of gas stations simply because their prices are more expensive than what we paid the last time we filled up. It's only when the car is running on fumes that we realize maybe we will have to fork over more cash than we want to.

What has happened? We formed an opinion on the price of gasoline (an *anchor*) when we last filled up. Now we compare the new prices that we see against this anchor. We are looking for coherence between the new price and the last price we paid. With a product that varies in price over time and over location, it's hardly surprising to see price hikes but still we rely on our internal anchor until the evidence of several gas stations tells us that it's time to perform a reset.

How much you last paid for gas creates an anchor for how much you expect to pay next time.

Still, when we perform this reset we don't have a "gold standard" of gas prices that we are calibrating against. It's unlikely that we even refer to government statistics describing current national average prices. The new anchor price that we create is instead somewhat arbitrary—it's based just on our recent experiences. Thus, when we next need to fill up the car with gas, we'll be applying our new arbitrary anchor because we seek *arbitrary coherence*, as behavioral economist Dan Ariely puts it.

To illustrate just how arbitrary this coherence-seeking can be, consider the prices of gasoline in the United States in recent history. In February 1999, the average cost of a gallon of regular unleaded gasoline was 91 cents. If at this time you saw a gas station selling even premium unleaded for $3/gallon, you'd just laugh, shake your head and drive on by. However, by July 2008, gas was at $4.11, a record 20-year high. If you saw a station selling it for $3/gallon, you'd join the line that wound around the block.

Now say that during this time you took a trip to England. You'd see prices of more than $6.75 per United States gallon. Setting this new anchor point means that when you returned home after your holiday, filling up would suddenly appear to be a bargain.

So our seemingly rational coherent view is anchored in both time and space. There's little that we can do about it without finding a friendly Time Lord with a spare TARDIS, but then we wouldn't need the gasoline anyway. It shows that the view we form on what is cheap and what is expensive is somewhat arbitrary.

How do designers of software and websites use this anchoring and arbitrary coherence seeking? An understanding of anchoring enables us to more easily reset people's expectations, and by studying coherence we can find ways to either increase or decrease the set of items that people seek to compare.

Resetting people's expectations can make them greedier. This is basically what happened to the people in Paul Piff's studies mentioned at the beginning of this chapter. As they became richer and surrounded by other richer people, they changed their expectations of what behaviors were acceptable. Changing the set of items that people compare has a similar effect. By excluding items that provide a more considered baseline, companies can encourage consumers to justify their greedy impulses.

Own the anchor

Create the anchor point that describes the value of your offering so that you control the terms.

Say you're looking to buy a new toaster. You haven't started your research yet, but you have a vague idea of the price range you would expect to pay. Imagine that in the store, the first thing the sales assistant does is gets you to write down the last two digits of your Social Security number, and then asks whether you'd be willing to pay that price for the toaster. Next, regardless of your answer, the sales assistant asks what is the maximum price you'd be prepared to pay.

Now, the last two digits of a Social Security number (SSN) range from 00 to 99 and might as well be randomly distributed. What possible effect could this number have on toaster purchases? Interestingly, when used this way as an anchor number, the answer is "quite a bit."

Itamar Simonson and Aimee Drolet at Stanford University found that even an anchor point as arbitrary as an SSN can influence how much people are subsequently prepared to pay for an item. Study participants whose last two SSN digits were in the 00–49 range subsequently proposed lower maximum purchase prices than participants whose last two SSN digits were in the 50–99 range. It seems that this totally unrelated number, when put in the correct context, was enough to create an anchor point even if the person with high SSN digits said they wouldn't pay that price for the item.

Considering how easy it is to use even arbitrary numbers as an anchoring point, it should come as no surprise that companies use more realistic anchors as a regular sales technique.

Anchoring in a retail environment normally works by displaying a range of products, each with a similar aura of quality, but with progressively more features and progressively higher prices. The cheapest item now becomes the anchor point. It is this one that is advertised in sales fliers. The most expensive item becomes the high-end anchor point against which all others are compared. It is relatively simple for sales staff to move a customer up through the range of items by showing the comparative benefits of each subsequently higher priced option, all of which still seem cheap in comparison to the high-end anchor point.

An alternative approach is to set a fancifully overpriced high-end anchor so that all other prices seem reasonable in comparison. Restaurant menus do this, showing the expensive cuts of steak and seafood dishes at the top of the menu, and cheaper pasta dishes further down. Even if the pasta is expensive, it'll seem cheap in comparison to the steak.

In a retail environment, this is nowhere more apparent than with high-end audio equipment, where spending $500 per speaker seems positively reasonable in comparison to the $25,000 alternatives on offer.

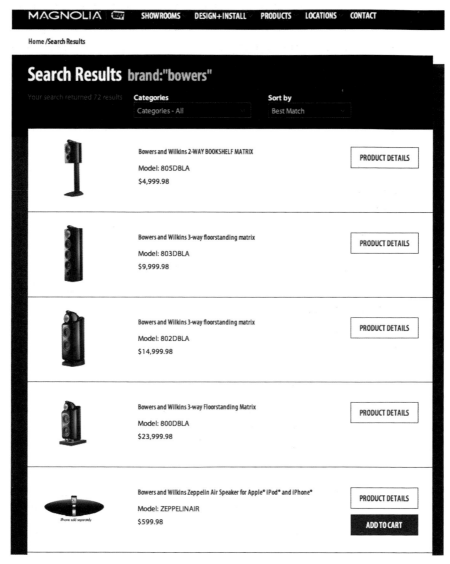

Bowers and Wilkins products at Magnolia HiFi. Seeing the Zeppelin iPod dock in comparison to the high-end speakers makes it seem cheap. What's not clear here is that it's still ten times more expensive than other available iPod docks. (magnoliaav.com)

A more common situation is purchasing accessories to go with a new product. Stores often offer a discount on accessories bought in the same transaction as the product, and for good reason. The product provides the anchor point, so any accessory looks cheap in comparison. Coming back the next day to purchase accessories, we'd be comparing them against each other rather than against the price of the original product.

You can even reset an anchor point on multiple occasions if you are selling something that people don't buy frequently, or don't research as much as they should. In 2010, Best Buy started raising the price of one computer every week, and then advertised that computer in their paper flyers with the price highlighted. They never used the word "Sale," just the term "New Price." Thus, they managed to set a new anchor point for many customers that was actually higher than the previous product price.

How to own the anchor

» For a high-end anchor:

  » Show a range of comparable products, with the most expensive setting a high-end anchor price sufficiently large to make the rest of your products look cheap by comparison.

  » Make frequent comparison to the high-end anchor when describing other products' prices.

» For a low-end anchor:

  » Show a range of comparable products, with the cheapest setting the lowest price that you are comfortable with.

  » Ensure that the low-end anchor price does not deviate substantially from customers' expectations, or that comparison with other vendors is difficult.

  » Start from the anchor point and then work customers upward toward more expensive products in the range.

Move from money to tokens

Tokens can have an arbitrary value. People respond to price points (99 cents rather than $1), so if you move them to a token-based currency, you can charge 99 tokens even if that equates to $1.50.

Capcom made the news in late 2011 after a child racked up $1,400 in in-application purchases of the Smurfs iPad game. The 8 year old, Madison Kay, had purchased Smurfberries and other items in the game, which were then charged to her mother's (the iPad owner's) iTunes account.

As a result of this and other similar news items, Arkansas Senator Mark Pryor wrote to the FTC saying "children, in particular, appear to be confused by in-app purchases, leaving parents with an unexpected bill for virtual smurfberries, snow-flakes, or other products. In the end, it would appear that these app companies may be the ones having all the fun and games at our children's expense."

The FTC has so far investigated the app descriptions on the Apple and Google app stores and concluded that the stores "must do more to ensure that parents have access to clear, concise, and timely information about the apps they down-load for their children" but has not yet evaluated what protections should be put in place to prevent unauthorized in-app purchases. In March 2013, Apple pro-posed a class-action settlement that allows parents who did not authorize their children's in-app purchases to claim refunds.

The way that the in-app purchases break coherence is by exchanging dollars for tokens. Individual games might use Smurfberries or snowflakes as their cur-rency, but each of the major games companies also uses a token-based economy rather than stating costs in dollars. Partly this system enables children and others without credit cards to make online purchases when somebody with a credit card has populated the account with points, but it also has other benefits, mostly for the token issuers.

Using points allows companies like Nintendo to manage their online digital assets for the Wii and DSi gaming systems more easily because all prices are quoted in points, not local currency. It's probably a good thing that points cards are not redeemable outside their country of purchase because otherwise with the current spread, Nintendo Points would be trading on foreign exchanges worldwide. Nintendo Points officially cost $1 per 100. However, in the UK the same 100 points cost £0.70, which is about $1.20 at the time of writing. In Europe, 100 points cost €1 ($1.30). Now Nintendo isn't responsible for global currency fluctuations, but sometimes it appears to pay to be an American rather than a European gamer.

By converting currency to points, the real-world coherence is removed. The Smurf game is free to download from the iTunes store, but if you want to progress you'll need lots of Smurfberries, which are conveniently available for in-game purchase. Players trading in Smurfberries are probably not considering the dollar equivalent of their purchases.

Microsoft Points mix things up a bit more—using these points to buy songs on the Zune music player (yes kids, it's a bit like an iPod only not so hip) costs 79 Microsoft Points. That sounds cheaper than Apple's 99 cents per song until you realize that a Microsoft Point costs more than 1 cent—you get 80 points to the (US) dollar. Microsoft also sells cards with different numbers of points in different countries. This way, the card can still hit a "magic" price point such as 19.99 or 39.99 when it is sold in each local currency.

So the link between dollars and points is quickly cut. This makes the cost of items within the company's infrastructure much more arbitrary than it would have been if direct dollar comparison was possible.

In addition, with all these systems, consumers must prepay for content. To purchase a single song or game, they must first buy a points card with several thousand points (1,600 or 4,000 for Microsoft, 1,000, 2,000, or 5,000 for Nintendo). That leaves the points issuing company holding on to a large portion of the users' cash until such time as they choose to redeem the points (if ever—see the "Encourage breakage" pattern).

How to design for a token economy

» Decouple the token value from a specific dollar value. When prices are listed in token currency, people will forget that the magic 99-token price point actually cost them $1.20.

» Sell tokens in large blocks, corresponding to price points that consumers see as valuable (19.99, 39.99).

» Keep the process of replenishing tokens separate from the process of spending them so that people are less likely to consider the real price of tokens.

  » This also allows separate people in a household to be responsible for replenishment than are responsible for spending, further removing any concept of the dollar value of tokens.

» Ensure that tokens can be used only within the jurisdiction where they are purchased to prevent speculative trading.

» Use tokens as rewards within the system. Offer a certain limited number of tokens when users achieve specific goals.

  » Potentially only allow redemption of these earned tokens after customers have also purchased tokens outright.

Encourage breakage

If unredeemed tokens have a value in your jurisdiction, profit by requiring purchase of more tokens than are necessary for immediate redemption, but not sufficient to purchase more items.

Gift cards are a win-win proposition for retailers. Customers tend to either never redeem gift cards they have been given, redeem only part of the card, or spend an additional 15–40 percent in the process of redeeming the card.

Gift cards are popular presents, but redeeming them is fraught with difficulties that end up leaving the issuing companies as the winners. Amazon.com counters this fear by clearly stating that their cards have no fees and never expire.

The industry term for the dollar value of unredeemed prepaid items is *breakage*. Breakage is big business for retailers who offer gift cards. In 2011, the electronics retailer BestBuy reported $53 million in income on the value of unredeemed gift cards. Estimates suggest that anywhere from 10 percent to 19 percent of card balances go unredeemed, for a total of approximately $41 billion dollars in the period from 2005 to 2011.

The currency doesn't have to be dollars for this tactic to work. Any prepaid gift card, such as Microsoft Points or Facebook Credits, can suffer from breakage.

It's also a common technique in other industries, such as cell phone service providers who "bundle" prepaid services that consumers don't actually want or use, or who require prepayment for highly variable items such as data usage. In these circumstances the breakage is either the number of text messages or voice minutes that expire every month because you didn't use them, or the megabytes of data that you didn't consume. Yet if in one month you use more than your allowance, the penalties for "overages" can be extreme.

To maximize breakage, unscrupulous companies make it hard to redeem the full value of the prepaid item without either leaving money behind or contributing more money to complete the purchase. This can be done by coordinating gift card denominations to always be slightly less or slightly more than the cost of in-store items. For instance, a coffee chain may sell gift cards in increments of $5, knowing that the average drink purchase is $3. This either leaves $2 on the card, or requires the customer to spend an additional $1 (20 percent) to clear the card's value.

Procrastinating about spending a gift card can also be a bad idea. Forcing an expiration date on cards to increase breakage was so lucrative for a time that in 2009 the U.S. Federal Government stepped in and pinned expiration dates at 5 years to prevent companies from "reclaiming" unused gift card value before that time had elapsed. That didn't stop Amway from putting a "redeem before" date on their gift cards, claiming it wasn't an expiration date, just a suggestion. Luckily for consumers, the courts disagreed with Amway's interpretation. However, companies can still charge fees after a gift card has been inactive for more than 1 year. Those fees can, over time, completely remove the value of the card.

How to design for breakage

» Ensure the smallest denomination of points card is at least 10–15 times the cost of the cheapest available item.

» Make sure that points cards and refills are offered in denominations that leave remainders. For instance, if individual items cost 79 points, then a 1,000 point card will leave 52 points—insufficient to purchase a thirteenth item, thus requiring purchase of a new card or forfeiture of the remaining points.

» Make points expire after a set period, or start charging administration fees.

Make it expensive

Increasing cost can increase people's appreciation of a product.

People typically buy more expensive products because they expect them to have higher quality and be more enjoyable than cheaper alternatives. For instance, when buying tools and other hardware products, the advice is often to buy the item that is one price point up from the tool that would actually get the job done. The implication is that the higher price point item will be nicer to use and of a higher quality, so it will provide a better long-term experience than the merely utilitarian option.

When it comes to wine, however, the American Association of Wine Economists found that in blind tastings, regular consumers on average showed a slight preference for cheaper wines over more expensive ones. Expert tasters in the same blind tests did tend to enjoy expensive wines slightly more, but for the average customer, the findings from this study suggest that price and expert recommendations aren't the best predictors of enjoyment.

What's interesting is that even after you read about this finding you aren't likely to change your alcohol purchasing behavior. That's because part of the pleasure we get from drinking wine comes from external attributes such as its price and how it is presented. My wife, for instance, admits to buying wine at least partly on the strength of how pretty the label looks. When price is introduced as a variable, people tend to rate the more expensive wine as more pleasant, and it's not just their subjective self-reports that bear this out. fMRI scans of the brain show more "pleasantness" response to the wine with the higher price tag, even when both glasses were actually poured from the same bottle.

Why is this? Scarcity boosts appeal, and maybe either people associate higher price with greater scarcity, or because they can afford to buy fewer bottles, the wine will actually be scarce for them, so they will savor it more.

It may also be that we like to indulge—splurge on something "because we can"—or to show off by purchasing something that not everyone can afford. And there is a subtle twist. It seems that consuming indulgent food reduces the pain of paying for it. People consume more indulgent foods when they are more aware of what they are paying, for instance when they pay using cash (an instant transaction) than they do when the cost is hidden, such as the delayed transaction of a credit card.

Perhaps the most expensive production bicycle available, the Specialized McLaren Venge exists to increase your appreciation of the brand, even if you can't afford the bike. (venge.specialized.com)

Whatever the reason, cost is firmly linked in people's minds with quality. Charging more for an item sets in motion a psychological flow that in turn leads us to appreciate the item more.

Specialized created a bike so expensive that it gets its own marketing site. The bike is shown next to a Formula 1 racecar and the McLaren supercar. It looks more like a stealth fighter plane than a bike. The S-Works McLaren Venge costs $18,000. That's for a bicycle, not a motorbike. It is sufficiently exclusive that outside the professionals racing it in the Tour de France, only 60 were destined for sale in the United States in 2012. The site contains many details about the quality of the components and the research that went into making the frame lighter and stiffer than any previous Specialized bike.

What's interesting is that like the findings about wine appreciation, the average cyclist would probably actually be happier and more comfortable on a lower-end bike that was more forgiving in the corners and more compliant in its frame. So why does Specialized produce this model? The company has several reasons.

First, there are people out there who'll buy the bike just for its exclusivity. Second, there is a technological trickle-down effect that sees all the manufacturer's other bikes benefitting from the research done on this one. Third is the psychological trickle-down effect on the bike-buying public's perception of other models from the same company. Advertising the superbike brings brand awareness and knowledge that similar engineering is used to build the other bikes in the line, including the ones that cost only $1,800. This psychological trickle-down is known as the *halo effect*.

Is it worth it for Specialized? Well, the company managed to sell all its available superbikes despite that price tag, and if nothing else it makes the other bikes in their line-up seem like comparative bargains.

How to benefit from expensiveness

» Just raising the price of a product may be sufficient, but it helps if it also looks the part: Use packaging and associated imagery that implies the item is more scarce or valuable.

» Use cost as a product differentiator; make it apparent that you charge more for your item because you think it has higher quality.

» If your product is a luxury good that people would find indulgent, make customers aware of the cost rather than hiding it. Consumers often believe that indulging can compensate for the pain of payment.

» Leverage the halo effect. Other cheaper products in your line-up will receive a psychological benefit from association with the expensive product.

 ## Show your second-best option first

Create a frame of reference and contrast for the best option.

A quick side-question for you: How long do you think the dashed lines are in the middle of the road? Most people say they're approximately 2 feet long. They are actually between 10 and 15 feet long in the United States. The thing is, you don't actually have good reference values for this figure. You normally see the lines only in the distance when you're moving fast in a car. You never see three people lying head-to-toe alongside the line so that you can get a feel of its comparative length.

And that's the problem. Humans aren't good at judging absolutes. They're better at judging comparative values. This *perceptual contrast* can play tricks on you. If you put one hand in a bowl of cold water and the other in a bowl of warm water, and then move both to a bowl of room temperature water, the cold water hand will feel hot and the hot water hand will feel cold.

Perceptual contrast is all about tricking the brain into perceiving a bigger difference than actually exists by making comparisons between less and more desirable options that tend to inflate the characteristics of the more desirable option.

The central square is the same shade of gray in each box. It appears lighter in the middle and right boxes due to perceptual contrast. It appears even lighter in the middle than in the right box because contrast between the foreground and background shades is higher. Simply by changing the level of contrast (background shade) our brains perceive the central square to be different.

Salespeople take advantage of this trick. Robert Cialdini describes how during his field research into sales techniques he observed real estate agents showing buyers a dilapidated and overpriced house before showing them the property they actually wanted to sell. The contrast between the state of the two houses made the second one more desirable than it otherwise might have been. The agent had placed his clients' hands in cold water before moving them to room temperature water, and so their hands felt hot.

This works best when the second-best option is shown first, and in minimal but sufficient detail. This second-best option should be "good enough"—sufficiently similar to allow comparison—but the second option should be sufficiently better for contrast.

It's also useful to discuss the preferred option in more detail than the less-preferred option. Giving more information is associated with feeling more knowledgeable, which in turn leads to better feelings about that product.

The Wall Street Journal uses perceptual contrast to encourage subscribers to pick the bundled option. Choosing just print or just online delivery seems crazy when you can get both for just $10 more. The artificial pricing of the individual options allows the bundled subscription to appear comparatively more enticing. (wsj.com)

How to create a frame of reference in your design

» Always have a secondary object that is sufficiently similar to your primary object to be considered a good comparison, but sufficiently less desirable to create perceptual contrast.

» Introduce the secondary object before the primary object. Even if they appear on the same page, make the secondary object appear first or to the left of the primary object.

» Share information about your secondary object, but not as much information or in as much detail as you subsequently share about your primary object.

» Artificially inflate the cost of your secondary object or reduce its feature set/desirability to make the primary object appear as a comparatively good value for money, even though it is more expensive.

 ## Break coherence to justify prices

Make the new option appear sufficiently different that it can't be compared to other options.

If you want to charge higher prices for an item, it helps if you can break its ties with other similar options. That way, people are less inclined to comparison shop and are more likely to set a new anchor point for your product.

As part of the national move to metric weights and measures, the UK finally changed over to selling all groceries in metric weights in January 2000. Many consumers complained at the time that this move appeared to have been accompanied by a corresponding hike in prices, or rather a shrinking of product packaging. For instance, when moving milk cartons from pints to liters, the price stayed the same, but the carton size changed from 4 UK pints to 2 liters, equivalent to 3½ UK pints.

The metrication process managed to break coherence and the anchor point at the same time. By completely redefining the measurement scale, consumers had little opportunity to compare pre- and post-change value.

You can also break coherence by introducing a new product line and claiming that it doesn't fit the traditional mold. Adjustment to change is accelerated by introduction of a new type of product or a new category that can be used to justify the increased price. That's exactly what happened when 100 percent biodiesel (B100) first became widely commercially available.

Biodiesel appeals to people who want to be slightly more environmentally conscious without actually giving up their internal combustion engines. Although prices have stabilized in recent years, especially with the introduction of federal tax incentives, biodiesel initially cost approximately 50 cents more per gallon than regular diesel.

Now, biofuel may well cost more to produce because it doesn't have the economies of scale or distribution. It also may not hurt to pay so much for fuel if you think that you're doing something laudable for the environment. But it's not the actual cost that is at issue here. Instead, it's the ability to charge more for the product because it's sufficiently different from other available products.

The key differentiator that allowed the price increase to exist was that the new product, *bio*diesel, was sufficiently different from regular old *diesel*diesel. Putting the product in its own separate category meant that coherence was broken and the price hike was less painful. Could this be one reason why the mainstream brands have moved to 5 percent biodiesel (B5) so that they can market their fuel in the same category and re-introduce coherence even if their product is only marginally green?

Gap, Inc. has five different brands. Along with Gap stores, it also owns Banana Republic, Old Navy, Piperlime, and Athleta. Athleta is its premium sporty brand, and it sells yoga pants for $80. Old Navy could never get away with charging this much for a pair of yoga pants. Instead, it charges $20 and lets the Gap brand split the difference with a $55 pair. Piperlime and Banana Republic customers just don't do yoga (or don't want to *look* like they do yoga), apparently.

Women's Boot-Cut Yoga Pants
~~$19.50~~
$18.00

GapFit gDance contrast waist pants
$54.95

Fusion Pant
$79.00

Gap, Inc. breaks coherence by creating different brands to sell similar style clothes at different prices. (left to right: oldnavy.com, gap.com, athleta.com)

This is important primarily because it allows them to remove coherence between their brands' products. At the mall you'd have to walk between stores to compare similar items. Online, you have to pull up two browser windows to show similar products side by side. Coherence is also broken by the implicit style of each site, summed up on Gap, Inc.'s corporate site as "Fun fashion and value" (Old Navy), "Iconic retail" (Gap), and "Ultimate performance apparel" (Athleta). This allows Gap to bill its Athleta yoga pants as "high performance," whereas its Old Navy ones are "sassy" and "fashion-forward."

Undoubtedly there are differences in materials, cut, and quality between the variously priced items, but by segregating them into their own sites, Gap, Inc. can also reset comparison points. For instance, the Fusion yoga pants on the Athleta site are the *cheap* option—Revelation yoga pants cost an extra $20. However, that extra $20 is only a 25 percent price increase rather than the 100 percent increase it would be on the Old Navy site. By breaking coherence, Gap, Inc. can reset customers' price expectations.

How to break coherence

» Change the name or appearance of your product to separate it from other options that could be seen as similar.

 » Use more up-market names. For instance, "gourmet chocolate confections" rather than "candy" or "imported artisanal cheese" rather than "Velveeta."

 » Make both the shape and color of the product's packaging distinct. Use more luxurious or exclusive colors (typically purple or black) and packaging with curves or more angles (facets).

» Place the product in a different category or area of your site. Physically separate it from other products that could be considered similar.

 » Create separate sites—either microsites or entire brands—to ensure differentiation.

» Use different metrics as comparison points. For instance, green credentials, plant oil source, and clean-burning capabilities for biodiesel versus sulphur content and gel point for regular diesel.

 » Bonus points if the comparison points for your higher-end product are more luxury-related than for your lower-end products (for instance, fabric choice versus free shipping).

Feeling greedy?

In the introduction to this chapter we mentioned the four possible behaviors between haves and have-nots. Altruism and cooperation happen when individuals are made aware of the needs of others in their community. Selfishness and spite happen when people are surrounded by others who also don't need help, leading to the assumption that nobody else in the community needs assistance.

Companies can use this same effect of separating people from reality to develop systems that amplify greed. It's possible to change the anchor points of what people consider to be "normal," and to change the comparison items that they use when making decisions, by either creating or removing coherence with other items.

Normally we rely on comparisons to keep greed in check: comparison with what we have now, with what our neighbors have, or with what we can afford given our budget. By warping or removing our capacity to use these reference points of what's rationally correct, companies can set new anchor points for us that make us think it's OK to do things we'd otherwise consider spiteful or selfish.

Another way that people are separated from reality is in terms of the level of mastery they feel. Counterintuitively, as the Dunning-Kruger effect demonstrates, it takes at least a degree of skill to know that you aren't very skillful. Without understanding their true level of skill, people can easily get drawn in to working with systems they do not truly understand. It's easy for companies to convince us that we can win by downplaying luck and emphasizing the skill and mastery we already think we have, even when we don't.

Most individuals don't understand the basis of chance and probability. They tend to think luck and skill equate, so they easily get caught up in games of chance. Even small terminology changes (like *winning* rather than *finishing*) really appeal to individuals' competitive nature, so it's easy to reinforce this type of behavior and set the greed machine in motion. Our competitive nature takes over and then all bets are off (or actually, on).

Once people are on the path to greed they seldom stray. There are techniques to keep them pointed in the right direction by giving them encouragement (reinforcement) and by removing distractions, such as indications of how much they are spending, through a move to using tokens instead of currency.

Operant conditioning relies on *extrinsic* motivation. Skinner's pigeons pecked because that led to a food pellet appearing, not because it was inherently enjoyable (an *intrinsic* motivation). Many of the "gamification" rewards in the online space rely on this extrinsic motivation principle. By making the reward extrinsic rather than intrinsic, we come to expect something in return for our actions so we're less likely to do things altruistically, again reinforcing greed.

Moving us to a different value structure through the use of tokens rather than money means we're reliant on cues in the company's built environment for cost comparisons rather than our real-world knowledge. Just like people who become greedier when they are surrounded by other greedy people, companies can encourage us to spend more just by changing the currency to one without suitable reference points. Just how many Smurfberries is a mushroom house really worth, anyway? Everyone else has mushroom houses, so why shouldn't I?

Greed happens when we lose sight of reality to the degree that we forget charity. It's reinforced by companies changing our comparison points from ones that benefit the community at large to ones that benefit us as individuals, and which in the process might just happen to benefit the company as well.

Evil by Design

THE ADJECTIVE "MACHIAVELLIAN" IS used to describe someone who aims to deceive and manipulate others for personal advantage. However Niccolò Machiavelli just used his observations of contemporary and historical affairs to suggest the courses of action that were most likely to help 16th-century states-men ("princes," or more accurately "merchant princes") succeed. As such, he was a data-driven commentator. Some of the courses of action he recommends are less virtuous, but the more virtuous princes, as he mentions, did not often succeed. He was interested in setting down the facts and leaving the actions and moral judgments to someone else.

This book gathers observations from contemporary and historical computer applications and websites to suggest the courses of design action that are most likely to help modern-day entrepreneurs (the merchant princes of Silicon Valley) succeed.

The principles laid out in each of the seven deadly sin chapters can be applied either for good or for evil. How far you take it is up to you. There is a continuum from persuasion to deception. That continuum takes in everything from being totally open, through being economical with (or neglecting to mention) certain truths, through bent truths and white lies, to all-out deception. I would not go so far as to advocate lies—if nothing else because lies are difficult to recover from if you are found out. However, this book wouldn't sell half so well if it were called *Slightly Naughty by Design*.

In addition, you can use this information to recognize and avoid being person-ally persuaded by these principles when they appear on sites you use.

Should you feel bad about deception?

My grandfather was a grocer. He owned a store in a small village. This was in the days when you would enter a store with your shopping list, and the grocer would fetch all the items for you off the shelves, rather than making you walk around and collect them yourself. Among the many products he sold, my grandfather was renowned for his Cheddar cheese. Certain customers liked their cheese mild, whereas others liked it strong. My grandfather knew their preferences and, like all good salesmen, he would talk up how good the cheese was. "Ah, Mrs. Jones, we have some lovely creamy mild Cheddar this week—in fact I've got some set aside for you," or "Mr. Smith, how about some more of that sharp Cheddar? It's good stuff, isn't it?"

My grandfather would disappear into the back of the store and reappear with a hunk of cheese wrapped in greaseproof paper to be weighed on his balance scales. What the customers didn't know was that sometimes the farmer who supplied the Cheddar would run low, meaning that there was only one round of cheese available in the cold room. In those instances both the strong and the mild cheese were cut from the same block. Undoubtedly, Mrs. Jones still enjoyed her mild Cheddar just as much as Mr. Smith enjoyed his sharp Cheddar.

Was my grandfather, a decorated veteran, being deceitful? Maybe. Was there more benefit to him than to his customers? In some respects yes—no lengthy explanations were required, and he still made the sale. Were his customers hurt by his actions? Quite the contrary. They probably savored their cheese even more, knowing that it had been chosen especially for them by their favorite grocer. Much of the effectiveness of the transaction was tied up in the *suggestion* of the cheese—what it represented—rather than the actual article itself.

On the outside, a typical quiet village grocer's store. On the inside, a den of deception.

Deception helps this cute kid sleep well at night

Young children often worry about monsters under the bed or in the closet. Pixar even created a successful movie franchise around this idea. Rather than resorting to rational reassurance ("there's no such thing as monsters"), researchers Liat Sayfan and Kristin Hansen Lagattuta at the Center for Mind and Brain at the University of California, Davis, suggest that especially for younger children it is more useful to resolve the issue by staying within their imaginary world. Giving the child a way to be powerful against the monsters, or to see the monsters as less scary, helps much more than dismissing the idea of monsters.

This, of course, is deception. It appears from their research that the kids are willing participants in the deception. Even the 4-year-olds in the study knew that monsters weren't real, but they coped better when resolution was framed in terms of the imaginary world.

And that willing complicity in the deception leads to product opportunities. "Monster Go Away!" spray is a dilute mix of lavender oil in water, packaged specifically with monster banishing in mind.

A shot from the monstergoaway.com site in 2009. The site is no longer active, but the product is still sold.

Deception helps the elderly and infirm stay safe

Many Alzheimer's patients living in care get distressed when their long-term memories conflict with their current situation. As dementia sets in, they are less able to remember current events and get concerned that they should be returning to the house or companions of their past. Richard Neureither, the director of the Benrath Senior Center in Dusseldorf, suggests that rather than fight this "People with dementia live in their own world. They are not open to rational arguments. One must meet them in their own version of reality."

Fake bus stop outside the Sana care facility for Alzheimer's sufferers (Dusseldorf, Germany). *Photo © Associated Press.*

The answer, pioneered by Franz-Josef Goebel, chairman of the Dusseldorf Old Lions Benefit Society, was to create a fake bus stop outside the care facility. Because the residents are free people, they cannot be locked up or restrained with drugs. Some can also get violent when told they can't leave. By walking the residents to the bus stop—a symbol that many associate with returning to their home—staff can give the residents a sense of accomplishment. Because their short-term memory is not sharp, the residents soon forget why they were waiting for the bus. "We invite them in for a coffee and after five minutes they forget they even intended to leave."

The idea, first implemented at two locations in 2008, was sufficiently successful to be repeated at care homes in Munich, Remscheid, Wuppertal, Herten, Dortmund, and Hamburg.

These three examples, the cheese, the monster spray, and the bus stop, all come from the physical world. However companies practice benign deception in the digital realm as well. As part of their "Real Beauty" online awareness raising campaign, the skincare company Dove created a Photoshop action (a downloadable feature that automates a normally time-consuming photo editing activity) that claimed to add "glow" to models' skin. They distributed it on several online

Photoshop forums. They were however being deceptive. The action was really designed to revert all changes to the image it was applied to, and to display the message "Don't manipulate our perceptions of real beauty" on-screen. The action could subsequently be undone, so that photo retouchers' work wouldn't be lost. In reality it's unlikely that professional photo retouchers would be downloading free Photoshop actions. It's more likely that Dove's ad agency Oglivy spotted an opportunity for a feel-good story. However, the advert is deceptive on either level.

It's fair to say that most of the design patterns in this book don't need to be deceptive in order to be persuasive. In the introduction I said that the truly great evil designs are ones where people will enter willingly into the deal even when the terms are exposed to them. However, many of the patterns become easier to implement when they are disguised or when they use misdirection.

Should you feel bad about using the principles in this book?

In 1999, Daniel Berdichevsky and Erik Neuenschwander, both at Stanford's Captology lab, proposed eight Principles of Persuasive Technology Design. These principles have subsequently become a mainstay in the realm of persuasive design. Their eighth and "Golden" Rule of Persuasion is that "The creators of a persuasive technology should never seek to persuade a person or persons of something they themselves would not consent to be persuaded to do."

This may not always be the case. Is it okay for a smoker to make an iPhone app to help others quit smoking? How about for an atheist to build a website for a church that seeks to recruit new members? Persuasion can be used to good or to bad effect. In both cases, the creator would not consent to be persuaded by the message yet many would see their actions as laudable.

Berdichevsky and Neuenschwander go on to state that deception and coercion are unethical. However, as we've already seen there are times when they can be very practically applied towards positive ends. Any parent will tell you about the numerous white lies they tell and the bargains they forge with their young children just to get through the day without resorting to infanticide. Humor often works by being deceptive. A joke is funny because the situation resolves in a different way than we anticipated. Warning people of this fact before telling them the joke would not be particularly effective.

Often the given test of whether a practice is deceptive or not is whether the individual would have consented to it if full information had been available. The implication is that individuals would not consent to deceit. But how does that help us when we encounter situations in which deception could be seen as both positive and necessary? The children in Sayfan and Lagattuta's monster studies responded better when they stayed in the world of monsters in order to address their fears, all the while knowing that the monster world was make-believe. The families of the Alzheimer's patients consented to use of the bus stop as a distress-reducing tool and most likely, if it had been explained to them before their condition became too advanced, so would the patients themselves. The alternatives—restraint or drugs—seem less ethically acceptable than the deceptive bus stop sign. In these scenarios, the individuals were fully complicit in their own deception.

So perhaps persuasive techniques that use deception or appeal to subconscious motivations can have positive or even ethical outcomes. The Golden Rule should probably be seen more as a Golden Guideline.

It's okay to make money

Capitalist enterprise suggests that it's okay to profit from business because it keeps you productive and it keeps you innovating. Economic theory suggests that it's in the capitalist's best interest to provide a satisfactory level of service to customers. There is not an implicit tension between these two goals. What you must decide is how far to push the benefit in your direction rather than in your users'.

Somewhere there is a boundary that distinguishes good business practice from evil design. There is a line to draw. Crossing that line puts you in the realm of con artists and criminals. However, the line is wavy. It moves based on public sentiment, political will, judicial powers, and personal moral imperatives.

It's easier to make money from happy customers

If you're doing things right, your users still value the service you provide because it is about more than just money. There's a large element of intangible benefit as well.

There are many kinds of intangible benefits. There is real value to users in providing hedonic satisfaction or the feeling of having worked hard to achieve something. If you provide users with a tangible product as well, then good for you.

Ultimately, you're making people happy. People part with their money for many other things in life that make them happy (and many that do not). In fact, the happier you make them, the more of their money they will offer you. Doing something that makes people unhappy is not a good business strategy.

Awareness is half the battle

Don Norman, in his book *Emotional Design*, states that we've always used *affordances* (how an item invites people to use it) and *intents* (what people want to achieve) to control user behavior. Often though, we've done so without knowing how or why the designs we created worked the way they did. This book lists the patterns that make the affordances and intents explicit. Now you know why you're doing what you're doing. You can be purposeful in your designs.

The introduction said evil design creates purposefully designed interfaces that make users emotionally involved in doing something that benefits the designer more than them.

Now perhaps some readers of this book care about more than just turning a quick profit and slinking off into the night. Maybe you want to create a sustainable business, or have even loftier goals such as getting people to lead healthier lifestyles or contribute to a charitable cause. You can extend the definition of evil design to accommodate these situations.

>> *Commercial design* creates purposefully designed interfaces that make users emotionally involved in doing something that provides an equitable benefit to the designer and the user.

>> *Motivational design* creates purposefully designed interfaces that make users emotionally involved in doing something that benefits them even though they would not chose to do it unaided.

» *Charitable design* creates purposefully designed interfaces that make users emotionally involved in doing something that benefits society more than either themselves or the designer.

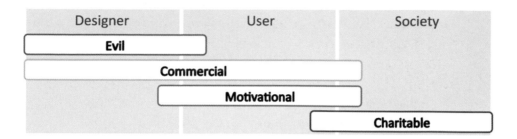

Who benefits? Your aims determine your approach. Are you just in it for the cash, do you want to create happy customers, do you want to motivate users to improve themselves, or do you want them to give to others?

How to use these persuasive design patterns in your work

» **Be purposeful:** Approach each area of your product or service with persuasion in mind. Actively consider which patterns might be beneficial in that area.

» **Appeal to emotions:** Remember that benefits don't have to be tangible in order to be appreciated.

» **Keep the benefit apparent:** Evolve the interface to maximize your desired outcome without removing the perceived benefits to your users.

» **Design for satisfaction:** Satisfied customers will be more likely to return. Charitable, motivational or commercial designs will be more likely to satisfy customers in the longer term than will evil designs.

» **Beware groupthink:** Discuss your plans with several not-like-minded individuals before implementation in order to check your ethical and business assumptions.

(continues)

(continued)

» **Measure success:** Test an early prototype with potential users to gauge reactions and tailor the interface. After release, capture feedback and metrics from real customers at every opportunity. It may take several iterations to fully achieve your desired effect.

Be purposefully persuasive

The patterns in this book are written so that you can take advantage of them for any of these different end goals: evil, commercial, motivational, or charitable persuasion. Some of the examples shown in this book might make you wince. Others might make you laugh. Still more of them might be sufficiently inspirational that you integrate them into your business practices.

Whether you intend to create evil, commercial, motivational, or charitable designs, make sure you do so purposefully rather than accidentally. Engaging users on an emotional rather than rational level is the key to persuading them to become involved.

The Persuasive Patterns Game

THE 57 PATTERNS DESCRIBED in this book are strong mechanisms for persuasion. They can be used in digital and physical products to increase customer loyalty or to attract new customers.

To foster creativity with the patterns, set aside an hour to play the following game with teammates, friends, or even on your own:

1. Think of a product (your own or a well-known brand).

2. Flip a coin. Heads is "good"; tails is "evil."

3. Choose one of the patterns at random.

4. Read the details about the pattern from this book, and make sure you understand the examples.

5. Individually write down as many [good or evil] future scenarios as you can that use this pattern for your chosen product.

6. Share your ideas with the group.

7. Work in pairs to turn your favorite ideas from the group into one new scenario.

8. Share your new scenario with the group.

9. Vote for the scenario that is most likely to influence customer behavior.

10. Repeat with a new coin toss and random pattern choice.

If your task is to create a "good" persuasive scenario, don't concern yourself with the potential cost/benefit ratio or practicality of implementing the persuasive technique. Go all out for creating a positive change.

For an "evil" scenario, the trick is to throw off the constraints of what you'd normally consider to be morally or ethically acceptable. Take the concept as far as you can. Embrace your inner archvillain.

When you have voted for the most influential scenario, discuss whether this scenario fits within your own boundaries for what is "good" or "evil" in the context of your product and your relationship with your customers. Are there gray areas? Do some people have very different interpretations? What does this say about your customer experience?

Even if you consider the resulting persuasion strategy to be too evil to implement or too costly for the possible returns, the act of working through the implications will most likely give you some insights into how you could make small changes that would nevertheless improve the product's persuasiveness. Those small improvements are sometimes all it takes to differentiate a product in customers' minds or to create a beneficial behavior change.

Following is a list of all the patterns.

Pride

Provide reasons for people to use. If you expect that users will be conflicted about the product or service you offer, provide them with many reasons they can use to resolve cognitive dissonance and keep their pride intact.

Dispel doubt by repeating positive messages. Hearing the same positive message several times from different trusted sources can provide the social proof that helps users form a decision.

Personal messages hit home. Messages aimed directly at the user grab attention. Messages that come from friends and trusted others have even more effect.

Gain public commitment to a decision. Make a user's decision public and they will feel more inclined to carry through with the action and defend the decision.

Change opinions by emphasizing general similarities. People don't like to change opinions and will ignore counterfactual information. Instead, show them how similar your desired position is to their current opinion.

Use images of certification and endorsement. Membership of third-party certification schemes is cheap in comparison to the conversions it can produce. Or just create your own certification, promise, or guarantee.

Help people complete a set. The compulsion to collect, to be complete, drives people to action. Give people some initial items "free," then set them to work completing the set.

Pander to people's desire for order. Capitalize on people's compulsion to be tidy. Make them "tidy up" by giving you the information you want or completing the tasks you require.

Sloth

Path of least resistance. Ensure that your desired end result is on the easiest path through the process. Hide disclaimers in locations away from this path.

Provide fewer options. The more items, the more likelihood of procrastination.

Pre-pick your preferred option. Prime people so that they are open to accepting the choice you highlight.

Make options hard to find or understand. Place opt-outs out of the way and obfuscate.

Negative options: Don't not sign up! Sign people up by default and make it harder for them to unsign than to continue down your preferred path. Use desire lines to hide the sign-up in plain sight.

Gluttony

Make customers work for a reward. People put more value on a reward that is not available to everyone.

Consider a small reward rather than a big one. Users will be forced to create justifications, which increase the perceived value of the reward.

Hide the math. People don't like doing sums, and so if you show them answers rather than the workings, they'll be inclined to believe you—even if the answers are only partial.

Show the problems. Mention weaknesses before customers find out. They'll trust you more.

Foot-in-the-door. Gain commitment to a small thing to convince about a big thing.

Door-in-the-face. Ask for a big thing, expecting to be turned down. Then ask for a small thing immediately afterward. Guilt at turning you down makes people more likely to agree to the small thing.

Present hard decisions only after investment. Ensure that users are hooked before you ask them to give you "valuable" information or perform hard tasks. Better to give something away free than lose the future value.

The Tom Sawyer effect. Scarcity breeds desire: "In order to make a man or a boy covet a thing, it is only necessary to make the thing difficult to attain."

Instill doubt to prevent cancellations. If customers want to cancel, instill doubt by tapping into loss aversion.

Impatience leads to compliance. Put a time constraint on a task and then offer to help users through it.

Anger

Use humor to deflect anger. If you mess up in a small way, convey your apology with humor to defuse the situation. However, for bigger issues or if you anticipate an angry response, use a calming and respectful tone instead.

Avoid overt anger with a slippery slope. Start small, and avoid a backlash by making several small sequential changes rather than one large one. If individual changes are sufficiently inoffensive, people won't become irate enough to revolt.

Use metaphysical arguments to beat opponents. When appeals to rational thought fail, side-step logic and use metaphysical constructs in your arguments. Claim to have something that science can't explain.

Use anonymity to encourage repressed behaviors. People will do more when they're anonymous than when they're identifiable.

Give people permission. If an authority figure tells people to do something, it removes individual responsibility.

Scare people (if you have the solution). Make people afraid, and then show them how to remove that fear using your product.

Envy

Create desirability to produce envy. An object must be desirable for envy to work as a motivating force.

Create something aspirational. Give your customers something to aspire to. Benign envy is a powerful motivator.

Make people feel ownership before they've bought. They will value the item more, increasing their desire to purchase.

Create status differences to drive behavior. Without differentiation, there can be no envy.

Emphasize achievement as a form of status. Give users more status when they achieve certain (company-serving) goals. This trains them to keep coming back for more.

Encourage payment as an alternative to achievement. Show impatient people a shortcut to improved status via their wallets.

Let users advertise their status. Encourage users to build and advertise their status within a community.

Let people feel important. Giving people a little bit of recognition makes them love you more—and do more for you.

Lust

Say "I love you." Flattery makes people more responsive to persuasion.

Be the second best. Game theory and self-esteem dictate that in a competitive space, you'll avoid the top of the pack.

Frame your message as a question. "Have you considered why so many people are switching to our brand from the competition?"

Create an in-group. Show customers that they belong to your preferred group, and they will take on and defend its traits.

Give something to get something. People will feel obliged to reciprocate.

Make something free. Make something free, and rationality disappears. You can recoup the money elsewhere.

Sell the intangible value. Reality is costly to change, perception less so.

Make a request in order to be seen more favorably. The Ben Franklin effect shows that people who have done us a favor see us in a better light.

Greed

Use a partial reinforcement schedule. You'll keep people playing longer.

Make it into a game. Turn onerous tasks into a game by providing (minimal) rewards for participation.

Customers should "win" rather than "finish" or "buy." Tap into the fear of losing out by describing events as competitions rather than as lotteries.

Further inflate people's (already overconfident) feelings of skill and mastery. Ease unskilled individuals into a task with some quick wins. Enhancing their feelings of "illusive superiority" will make them more likely to continue when the stakes are higher.

Make rewards seem due to skill, not luck. Requiring action to get a reward increases the perceived value of the reward.

Create a walled garden. If you own the infrastructure, ensure that people have little reason to leave, and that they return frequently.

Own the anchor. Create the anchor point that describes the value of your offering so that you control the terms.

Move from money to tokens. Tokens can have an arbitrary value. People respond to price points (99 cents rather than $1), so if you move them to a token-based currency, you can charge 99 tokens even if that equates to $1.50.

Encourage breakage. If unredeemed tokens have a value in your jurisdiction, profit by requiring purchase of more tokens than are necessary for immediate redemption, but not sufficient to purchase more items.

Make it expensive. Increasing cost can increase people's appreciation of a product.

Show your second-best option first. Create a frame of reference and contrast for the best option.

Break coherence to justify prices. Make the new option appear sufficiently different that it can't be compared to other options.

References

FOLLOWING ARE REFERENCES FOR the information provided in each chapter. Some articles are direct references to articles by authors whose work is called out within the text. Others provide material to reinforce statements made without direct attribution in an attempt to keep the content flowing.

You can find a hyperlinked version of this reference section online at `evilbydesign.info/references`.

About the Technical Editor

Dan Lockton's Design With Intent Toolkit: `requisitevariety.co.uk/ design-with-intent-toolkit/`.

Introduction

Tom Sawyer quote: Mark Twain (Samuel Clemens). *The Adventures of Tom Sawyer*. The American Publishing Company, 1884.

Pride

Saint Augustine quote: "*Humilitas homines sanctis angelis similes facit, et superbia ex angelis demones facit.*" as quoted in *Manipulus Florum* (c. 1306), edited by Thomas Hibernicus.

Cognitive dissonance

Leon Festinger proposed the theory of cognitive dissonance after he studied the aftermath of Dorothy Martin's December 21, 1954, end of the world prediction. Yes, these predictions seem to happen with alarming frequency: Leon Festinger. *A Theory of Cognitive Dissonance*. Illinois: Row, Peterson, 1957.

Harold Camping quote: `familyradio.com`. Retrieved January 2012.

Ig Nobel prize winners, by year: "Winners of the Ig Nobel Prize." *Improbable Research* (`improb.com`). Retrieved November 2012.

Social proof

Apple Store photo credit: Chris Nodder.

Repeat positive messages

Milgram's sky experiment (group size): Stanley Milgram, Leonard Bickman, and Lawrence Berkowitz. "Note on the drawing power of crowds of different size." *Journal of Personality and Social Psychology* 13.2 (1969): 79–82.

Testimonials suggestions come from my unpublished research into trust conducted at Microsoft Corp.

13 percent purchased without using Internet, number of bad reviews to deter shoppers: "When was the last time you made a purchase without researching online first?" *Lightspeed Research* (`lightspeedresearch.com`). April 11, 2011. Retrieved December 2012.

FTC guidelines: FEDERAL TRADE COMMISSION 16 CFR Part 255 *Guides Concerning the Use of Endorsements and Testimonials in Advertising*. Oct 2009.

Personal messages hit home

Hanakapiai Beach sign photos credit: Chris Nodder.

Jimmy Wales, Wikipedia appeal stats: "Fundraising 2011." *Wikimedia meta-wiki* (`meta.wikimedia.org`). Retrieved November 2012.

Facebook Sponsored Stories graphic: "Sponsored Stories in Marketplace" (PDF). *Facebook for Business site* (`facebook.com/business`). Retrieved November 2012.

Gain public commitment to a decision

Failing resolutions: John C. Norcross and Dominic J. Vangarelli. "The resolution solution: Longitudinal examination of New Year's change attempts." *Journal of Substance Abuse* 1.2 (1989): 127–134.

Change opinions by emphasizing similarities

Colbert seen as serious by Republicans: Heather L. LaMarre, Kristen D. Landreville, and Michael A. Beam. "The Irony of Satire: Political Ideology and the Motivation to See What You Want to See in The Colbert Report." *The International Journal of Press/Politics* 14.2 (2009): 212–231.

Colbert's "Problem with Republicans" quote is from an interview at the John F Kennedy Forum, Kennedy School of Government, Institute of Politics, Harvard University, 12/1/06.

Colbert photo credit: Joel Jefferies via Comedy Central press site.

Use images of certification/endorsement

PetCo.com security images: "Do Security Icons Really Increase Conversions? A/B Test Results from PETCO.com" (`marketingsherpa.com`). May 3, 2006. Retrieved November 2012.

Composite graphic of trust logos: top line: `eagleamerica.com`; bottom line (L to R): `thickquick.com`, `bbb.org`, and `dogstrainingbook.com`.

B.J. Fogg's elements of website credibility: B.J. Fogg. *Persuasive Technology*. Massachusetts: Morgann Kaufmann, 2003. p. 130.

Sites displaying certification are less trustworthy: Benjamin Edelman. *Adverse selection in online trust certifications*. Proceedings of the 11th International Conference on Electronic Commerce. ACM, 2009.

McAfee 12 percent claim: McAfee SECURE Service page (`mcafeesecure.com`). Retrieved November 2012.

Help people complete a set

Codecademy coding challenge: `codeyear.com/stats`. Retrieved February 2012.

Cow Clicker: Ian Bogost. "Cow Clicker, The Making of Obsession" (`bogost.com`). July 21, 2012. Retrieved November 2012.

Zynga 12% of Facebook's 2011 revenue: Facebook S1 (Initial Public Offering) filing with the Securities and Exchange Commission, February 1 2012.

Desire for order

Light switches: "AWARE project." *Swedish ICT Interactive Institute* (`tii.se/projects/aware`) via Dan Lockton. *Exploiting desire for order* (`architectures.danlockton.co.uk`). June 13, 2008. Retrieved November 2012.

Toplinked quote retrieved from the Toplinked.com site November 2008. TopLinked subsequently closed its Top 50 list because it claimed "almost all the people at the top of the list had reached the maximum number of LinkedIn connections." Maybe it's actually because only 4 of the top 10 were actually TopLinked members. (The list was last updated April 23, 2009, when only the top 8 had 30k+ links.)

LinkedIn's philosophy: Patrick Crane. "A guide to building the right connections" (`blog.linkedin.com`). November 9, 2008. Retrieved November 2012.

Manipulating pride to change beliefs

Need for closure associated with dogmatism, need for order, conservatism: Donna M. Webster and Arie W. Kruglanski. "Individual differences in need for cognitive closure." *Journal of Personality and Social Psychology* 67.6 (1994): 1049.

Sloth

Desire lines

Greatest outcome for least work: George Kingsley Zipf. *Human Behavior and the Principle of Least Effort*. New York: Addison-Wesley, 1949.

Desire lines used for redesign of public spaces: Elizabeth Barlow Rogers. *Rebuilding Central Park: A Management and Restoration Plan*. The MIT Press, 1987;

and Christopher Alexander, Murray Silverstein, Shlomo Angel, Sara Ishikawa, and Denny Abrams. *The Oregon Experiment*. New York: Oxford University Press, 1975.

Path of least resistance

F-pattern for reading pages: Jakob Nielsen and Kara Pernice. *Eyetracking Web Usability*. Berkeley: New Riders, 2010.

Fallow areas: The fallow area concept comes from what is called the Gutenberg Diagram, devised by Edmund Arnold. Learn more in Colin Wheildon's book *Type & Layout: Are You Communicating or Just Making Pretty Shapes*. Victoria, Australia: The Worsley Press, 2005.

Mike Dean quote: Stephanie Clifford. "The High Cost of a 'Free Credit Report.'" (`nytimes.com`). August 4, 2008. Retrieved December 2012.

Credit CARD act of 2009, Title II, Section 205 *Prevention of deceptive marketing of credit reports*.

Advertising statistics: Tony Mecia. "'Free' credit report sites switch to offering 'free' scores." (`creditcards.com`). April 5, 2010. Retrieved December 2012.

Reduced options and smart defaults

Toothpaste statistics: Ellen Byron. "Whitens, Brightens and Confuses." (`wsj.com`). February 23, 2011. Retrieved December 2012.

Confuse number of options with importance: Aner Sela and Jonah Berger. "Decision Quicksand: When Trivial Choices Suck Us In." *Journal of Consumer Research* 39 (August 2012).

Fewer options

Choice paralyzes us: Barry Schwartz. *The Paradox of Choice—Why More Is Less*. Harper Perennial, 2004.

Choice can be demotivating: Sheena Iyengar and Mark Lepper. "When Choice is Demotivating: Can One Desire Too Much of a Good Thing?" *Journal of Personality and Social Psychology* 79 (2000): 995–1006.

Present compatible choices: Jonah Berger, Michaela Draganska, and Itamar Simonson. "The Influence Of Product Variety On Brand Perception And Choice." *Marketing Science* 26.4 (2007): 460–472.

Recommendation engines: Xavier Amatriain and Justin Basilico. "Netflix Recommendations: Beyond the 5 stars (Part 1)" (`techblog.netflix.com`). April 6, 2012. Retrieved December 2012.

Pre-pick your preferred option

Priming: Wikipedia provides a great introduction and launching off point at `en.wikipedia.org/wiki/Priming_(psychology)`.

Disclosure: I worked on the user experience for XP Service Pack 2, used as an example here.

Make options hard to find or understand

PC Pitstop EULA: Larry Magid. "It Pays To Read License Agreements." (`pcpitstop. com`). Undated. Retrieved December 2012.

NebuAd: Ed Markey. "Key Lawmakers Question Local Provider Over Use of NebuAd Software Without Directly Notifying Customers" (`markey.house.gov`). July 15, 2008. Retrieved December 2012.

Embarq's two responses: Letter from David W. Zesiger, SVP Regulatory Policy & External Affairs, Embarq, July 21, 2008; and letter from Tom Gerke, president and CEO, Embarq, July 23, 2008, to the Committee on Energy and Commerce.

Facebook privacy: Mark Zuckerberg interview with Michael Arrington at the 2010 "Crunchie" awards, San Francisco.

Privacy setting stats: Mary Madden and Aaron Smith. *Reputation Management and Social Media*. Pew Internet and American Life Project, 2010.

Negative options: Don't not sign up!

E-mail opt-in rates: Steven Bellman, Eric J. Johnson, and Gerald L. Lohse. "On site: to opt-in or opt-out?: it depends on the question." *Communications of the ACM* 44.2 (2001): 25–27.

FTC report: *Negative Options: A Report by the staff of the FTC's Division of Enforcement*. Federal Trade Commission, January 2009.

Class Action Lawsuit: Complaint document, Martha Cornett v. Direct Brands Inc. and Bookspan, United States District Court, Southern District of California. Filed Aug 4, 2011.

Scholastic's $710,000 fine: "Children's Book Publisher to Pay $710,000 to Settle Charges It Violated Commission's Negative Option and Telemarketing Sales Rule." *Federal Trade Commission* (`ftc.gov`). June 21, 2005. Retrieved December 2012.

Discount clubs: "Senate Commerce, Science & Transportation Committee report on Aggressive Sales Tactics on the Internet and Their Impact on American Consumers" (`commerce.senate.gov`). Nov 17, 2009. Retrieved December 2012; and "Senate Commerce, Science & Transportation Committee Supplemental Report on Aggressive Sales Tactics on the Internet" (`commerce.senate.gov`). May 19, 2010. Retrieved December 2012.

List of discount club partner sites: Ben Popken. "88 Big Sites Earning Millions From Webloyalty Scam." *The Consumerist* (`consumerist.com`). November 18, 2009. Retrieved December 2012.

Is it worth the effort?

401k contribution: Brigitte C. Madrian and Dennis F. Shea. "The Power of Suggestion: Inertia in 401(k) Participation and Savings Behavior." *Quarterly Journal of Economics* 116.4 (2001): 1149–1187.

Multiple decisions: Jonathan Levav, Mark Heitmann, Andreas Herrmann, and Sheena S. Iyengar. "Order in product customization decisions: Evidence from field experiments." *Journal of Political Economy* 118.2 (2010): 274–299.

Gluttony

Thomas Aquinas quote: Joseph Rickaby. *St. Thomas Aquinas, Aquinas Ethicus: or the Moral Teaching of St. Thomas. A Translation of the Principal Portions of the Second part of the Summa Theologica, with Notes*. London: Burns and Oates, 1892.

Deserving our rewards

Presence of healthy options: Keith Wilcox, Beth Vallen, Lauren G. Block, and Gavan J. Fitzsimons. "Vicarious Goal Fulfillment: How the Mere Presence of a Healthy Option Leads to a Very Unhealthy Decision." *Journal of Consumer Research* 36 (2009): 380–393.

Portion size increase: "The new (Ab)Normal." *Centers for Disease Control and Prevention* (`makinghealtheasier.org`). Undated. Retrieved December 2012.

Gluttony pants: `betabrand.com/gluttony-pants.html`.

Women's clothing sizes: "Daily Chart: Size Inflation. Why a size 10 is really a size 14." *The Economist Online* (`economist.com`). April 4, 2012. Retrieved December 2012.

Men's clothing sizes: Abram Sauer. "Are your pants lying to you? An investigation." *Esquire* (`esquire.com`). September 7, 2010. Retrieved December 2012.

Make customers work for a reward

Canadian Tire money used to buy mower: Jasmine Franklin. "Man saves Canadian Tire money for 15 years, buys mower." *Toronto Sun* (`torontosun.com`). July 13, 2011. Retrieved December 2012.

Corin Raymond: "Don't Spend It Honey!" *Corin Raymond's Live Album Fundraiser* (`dontspendithoney.com`). Retrieved December 2012.

Seth Priebatsch coupon value: Seth Priebatsch. "How 'Game Mechanics' Can Help Your Startup." *Huffington Post* (`huffingtonpost.com`). March 11, 2010. Retrieved December 2012.

Consider a small reward rather than a big one

Mechanical Turk is addictive: personalbugmenot. "Is turking addictive?" *Turker Nation forum* (`turkernation.com`). October 7, 2012. Retrieved December 2012.

Earnings analysis: Compiled from information supplied by forum contributors at `turkernation.com` and `turkers.proboards.com/`. Obviously, one way to verify the majority of this information would be to run an HIT that requires Turkers to paste their earnings record into the results.

Cognitive dissonance between effort and return: Leon Festinger and James Carlsmith. "Cognitive consequences of forced compliance." *The Journal of Abnormal and Social Psychology* 58.2 (1959): 203–210.

Hide the math

Stats from 166,000 Swoopo auctions (he *doesn't* hide the math!): Ned Augenblick. *Consumer and producer behavior in the market for penny auctions: A theoretical and empirical analysis.* Unpublished manuscript, 2009.

List of penny auction sites: Charnita Fance. "Best Online Penny Auction Sites Reviewed And Compared." *To Muse* (`tomuse.com`). Undated. Retrieved December 2012.

Irrational escalation of commitment: Barry M. Staw. "Knee-deep in the Big Muddy: A Study of Escalating Commitment to a Chosen Course of Action." *Organizational Behavior and Human Performance* 16(1) (1976): 27–44.

Show the problems

Machiavelli quote: Niccolò Machiavelli *The Prince*, 1532 (via Project Gutenberg, `gutenberg.org`)

Trustworthiness study: Graham Dietz and Nicole Gillespie. *Building and Restoring Organisational Trust.* London: Institute of Business Ethics, 2011; and Graham Dietz and Nicole Gillespie. *The Recovery of Trust: Case studies of organisational failures and trust repair.* London: Institute of Business Ethics, 2012.

Cost per customer: "2012 Data Protection & Breach Readiness Guide." *Online Trust Alliance* (`otalliance.org`). Retrieved December 2012.

Blumenthal letter to Sony: Senator Richard Blumenthal. "Blumenthal Demands Answers from Sony over PlayStation Data Breach." (`Blumenthal.senate.gov`). April 26, 2011. Retrieved December 2012.

Sony's admittance of a breach: Patrick Seybold. "Update on PlayStation Network and Qrocity." *PlayStation Blog* (`blog.us.playstation.com`). April 26, 2011. Retrieved December 2012.

University of Michigan Health System statistics: "Full Disclosure of Medical Errors Reduces Malpractice Claims and Claim Costs for Health System." *Agency for Healthcare Research and Quality Innovation Exchange (part of the U.S. Government*

Department of Health and Human Services) (`innovations.ahrq.gov`). June 23, 2010. Retrieved December 2012.

Lexington KY VA Medical Center statistics: "Proactive Reporting, Investigation, Disclosure, and Remedying of Medical Errors Leads to Similar or Lower Than Average Malpractice Claims Costs." *Agency for Healthcare Research and Quality Innovation Exchange* (`innovations.ahrq.gov`). June 23, 2010. Retrieved December 2012.

Escalating commitment

80 percent of donations used for marketing: "Millions in Future Donations to Vets Charity Will Pay Debt Owed to Vendors." *American Institute of Philanthropy* (`charitywatch.org`). August 2010. Retrieved December 2012.

Foot-in-the-door

Fill in a survey: Nicolas Guéguen. "Foot-in-the-door technique and computer mediated communication." *Computers in Human Behavior* 18.1 (2002): 11–15.

Door-in-the-face

"Guilt": The term "guilt" is used here as a layman's synonym for "reciprocal concession," but there is a thread of discussion in the literature that clearly distinguishes guilt from reciprocal concessions. See, for example, Daniel O'Keefe and Marianne Figgé. "A Guilt-Based Explanation of the Door-in-the-Face Influence Strategy." *Human Communication Research* 24.1 (1997): 64–81.

Door-in-the-face described: Robert B Cialdini, Joyce E. Vincent, Stephen K. Lewis, Jose Catalan, Diane Wheeler, and Betty Lee Darby. "Reciprocal concessions procedure for inducing compliance: The door-in-the-face technique." *Journal of Personality and Social Psychology* 31.2 (1975): 206–215.

Second request must be a smaller version of the first one: John C. Mowen and Robert B. Cialdini. "On Implementing the Door-in-the-Face Compliance Technique in a Business Context." *Journal of Marketing Research* 17.2 (1980): 253–258.

Evidence that door-in-the-face works in virtual worlds: Paul W. Eastwick and Wendy L. Gardner. "Is it a game? Evidence for social influence in the virtual world." *Social Influence* 4.1 (2009): 18–32.

Present hard decisions only after investment

90210 ZIP code: Chris Nodder. "Gaining User Trust: Research and a Secret." *User Experience Magazine* 11.4 (2012): 10–13.

Scarcity and loss aversion

Dollar bill experiment: Baba Shiv, George Loewenstein, Antoine Bechara, Hanna Damasio, and Antonio R. Damasio. "Investment behavior and the negative side of emotion." *Psychological Science* 16.6 (2005): 435–439. It's possible to "lose" (earn less than $20 after 20 rounds) only 13 percent of the time if you always gamble.

Loss twice as "powerful" as gain: Daniel Kahneman and Amos Tversky. "Prospect Theory: An Analysis of Decision under Risk." *Econometrica*: *Journal of the Econometric Society* 47 (1979): 263–291.

The Tom Sawyer effect

Tom Sawyer quotes: Mark Twain (Samuel Clemens). *The Adventures of Tom Sawyer*. The American Publishing Company, 1884.

Instill doubt to prevent cancellations

Statistics on BSE: Wikipedia `en.wikipedia.org/wiki/Bovine_spongiform_encephalopathy`. Retrieved December 2012.

Nearly 50 billion burgers/year in the USA: Ellen Rolfes. "The Hidden Costs of Hamburgers." *PBS Newshour "The Rundown" blog* (`pbs.org`). August 2, 2012. Retrieved December 2012.

Impatience leads to compliance

People become more conservative under time pressure: Mark Hwang. "Decision making under time pressure: A model for information systems research." *Information & Management* 27 (1994): 197–203.

Self-control: Gluttony's nemesis

Self-regulation failure: Roy F. Baumeister and Todd F. Heatherton. "Self-Regulation Failure: An Overview." *Psychological Inquiry* 7.1 (1996): 1–15.

Spring break becoming tamer: Lizette Alvarez. "Spring Break Gets Tamer as World Watches Online." *The New York Times* (nytimes.com). March 16, 2012. Retrieved December 2012.

Anger

Emily Dickinson quote from *XLII. Time's Lesson*, in Mabel Loomis Todd and T. W. Higginson (Eds.) *Poems by Emily Dickinson, Second Series*. Boston: Roberts Brothers, 1892.

Anger's effects on decision making: Jennifer S. Lerner and Larissa Z. Tiedens. "Portrait of the angry decision maker: How appraisal tendencies shape anger's influence on cognition." *Journal of Behavioral Decision Making* 19.2 (2006): 115–137.

Use humor to deflect anger

Smiling puts people in a better mood: Many people can't move their eyelid-eyebrow muscle (orbicularis oculi, pars lateralis) voluntarily, so that little test may not have worked for you. Robert W. Levenson, Paul Ekman, and Wallace V. Friesen. "Voluntary facial action generates emotion-specific autonomic nervous system activity." *Psychophysiology* 27.4 (1990): 363–384.

Use whimsical rather than hostile humor: Robert A. Baron and Deborah R. Richardson. *Human Aggression*. New York: Springer, 2004.

Tumbeasts image: © Matthew Inman, *The Oatmeal* (theoatmeal.com). CC BY 3.0.

Avoid overt anger with a slippery slope

Netflix reversion: Stu Woo. "Under Fire, Netflix Rewinds DVD Plan." *The Wall Street Journal* (`wsj.com`). October 11, 2011. Retrieved January 2013.

Netflix details: "Global Internet Phenomena Report: Fall 2011." *Sandvine* (`sandvine.com`). December 2012. Retrieved January 2013.

Qwickster quote: Jason Gilbert. "Qwickster Goes Qwickly: A Look Back At A Netflix Mistake." *Huffington Post* (`huffingtonpost.com`). October 10, 2011. Retrieved January 2013.

Boiled frog anecdote is false: "Boiled Beef." (`Snopes.com`). January 12, 2009.

Facebook comic: © Matthew Inman, *The Oatmeal* (`theoatmeal.com`).

Use metaphysical arguments to beat opponents

Intelligent design: Strictly, intelligent design is seen by its proponents as a form of "evidence-based scientific theory," but it does require the acceptance of certain supernatural explanations (theistic science) that are not necessarily testable using regular scientific methods. In other words, it resorts to metaphysical explanations.

Scientific Impotence: Geoffrey D Munro. "The Scientific Impotence Excuse: Discounting Belief-Threatening Scientific Abstracts." *Journal of Applied Social Psychology* 40 (2010): 579–600.

Pratkanis' techniques: Anthony R. Pratkanis. "How to Sell a Pseudoscience." *Skeptical Inquirer* T9 (1995).

Tim Cook quote: Goldman Sachs Technology and Internet conference, February 12, 2013.

BBC Superbrands documentary: Alex Riley and Adam Boome. "Superbrands' success fuelled by sex, religion and gossip" *BBC* (`bbc.co.uk`). May 16, 2011. Retrieved December 2012.

Kirsten Bell's observations: Francie Diep. "Why Apple Is the New Religion." *TechNewsDaily* (`technewsdaily.com`). Oct 23 2012. Retrieved December 2012.

Apple as religion: Pui-Yan Lam. "May the Force of the Operating System be with You: Macintosh Devotion as Implicit Religion." *Sociology of Religion* 62:2 (2001): 243–262.

Every iKeynote ever comic: Ray, Raf, and Will. (`thedoghousediaries.com`).

Embracing anger

An example of the coverage of Mary Bale's cat trashing from two UK tabloid newspapers: Andrew Parker. "It's a fur cop." *The Sun* (`thesun.co.uk`). January 12, 2011. Retrieved January 2013; and Claire Ellicott. "What's all the fuss? It's just a cat, says woman seen on CCTV shoving tabby in wheelie bin." *The Mail Online* (`dailymail.co.uk`). August 25 2010. Retrieved January 2013.

4-chan description: Nick Douglas. "What The Hell Are 4chan, ED, Something Awful, And /b/?" (`Gawker.com`). January 18, 2008. Retrieved January 2013.

Use anonymity to encourage repressed behaviors

Stanford prison experiment: A good introduction is available on the Stanford Prison Experiment site at `prisonexp.org`.

Deindividuation: Philip Zimbardo. "The human choice: Individuation, reason and order vs. deindividuation, impulse and chaos." In W. J Arnold and D Levine (Eds.), *Nebraska Symposium on Motivation* 17 (1969): 237–307.

Online disinhibition: John Suler. "The Online Disinhibition Effect." *CyberPsychology & Behavior* 7.3 (2004): 321–326.

Disqus data: Daniel Ha. "Pseudonyms." *Disqus blog* (`blog.disqus.com`). January 10, 2012. Retrieved January 2013. There are some potential sampling issues here: People may choose to stay anonymous just because it's simpler than signing up/in rather than because they have any particular desire to mask their commentary. People who choose pseudonyms may also be generally more tech savvy/entertaining and therefore more likely to garner positive reviews and more responses.

EFF's response to the Nymwars: Jillian C. York. "A Case for Pseudonyms." *Electronic Frontier Foundation* (`eff.org`). July 19, 2011. Retrieved January 2013.

Real-time chats are more balanced: Antonios Garas, David Garcia, Marcin Skowron, and Frank Schweitzer. "Emotional persistence in online chatting communities." *Scientific Reports* 2.402 (2012).

Situational norms: Tom Postmes and Russell Spears. "Deindividuation and antinormative behavior: A meta-analysis." *Psychological Bulletin* 123.3 (1998): 238–259.

Give people permission

Milgram's experiment: Stanley Milgram. "Behavioral Study of Obedience." *Journal of Abnormal and Social Psychology* 67.4 (1963): 371–378.

Milgram quotes: Stanley Milgram. *Obedience to Authority: An Experimental View.* New York: HarperCollins, 1974. p. 6.

Not a one-off event: Thomas Blass. "The Milgram paradigm after 35 years: Some things we now know about obedience to authority." *Journal of Applied Social Psychology* 29.5 (1999): 955–978.

Moral disengagement: Albert Bandura. "Moral disengagement in the perpetration of inhumanities." *Personality and Social Psychology Review.* [Special Issue on Evil and Violence] 3 (1999): 193–209.

Water fountain photo credit: Chris Nodder.

Scare people (if you have the solution)

Roy H. Williams quote: Roy H. Williams. "Why We Buy." *The MondayMorningMemo* (`mondaymorningmemo.com`). December 4, 2006. Retrieved January 2013.

Fabric conditioner: For a full breakdown of the ingredients of fabric conditioner, see Patrick Di Justo's article, "What's Inside – Downy Coats Briefs With Horse Fat." *Wired Magazine* 16.2 (November 2008).

Take positive preventive action: Anthony Pratkanis and Elliot Aronson. *Age of Propaganda: The everyday use and abuse of persuasion.* New York: Holt, 2001.

Difficulty with complexity: Gordon Hodson and Michael Busseri. "Bright Minds and Dark Attitudes: Lower Cognitive Ability Predicts Greater Prejudice Through Right-Wing Ideology and Low Intergroup Contact." *Psychological Science* 23.2 (2012): 187–195.

TASER sales figures: 255,000 private sales. "TASER to Release Fourth Quarter 2012 Earnings on February 21, 2013." *TASER International*, February 13, 2013. Retrieved February 2013.

TASER business statistics: TASER 2011 annual report.

Using anger safely in your products

Anger's effects on decision making: Jennifer S. Lerner and Larissa Z. Tiedens. "Portrait of the angry decision maker: How appraisal tendencies shape anger's influence on cognition." *Journal of Behavioral Decision Making* 19.2 (2006): 115–137.

Envy

Deuteronomy 5:21 quoted from King James Bible "Authorized Version", Pure Cambridge Edition.

Benign envy: Mark D Alicke and Ethan Zell. "Social Comparison and Envy" in Richard Smith (Ed.) *Envy: Theory and Research*. New York: Oxford University Press, 2008. p. 88.

Evolutionary background to envy: Antonio Cabrales. "The causes and economic consequences of envy." *Series – Journal of the Spanish Economic Association* 1.4 (2010): 371–386.

Destructive envy: Susan Fiske. *Envy Up, Scorn Down*. New York: Russell Sage Foundation, 2011.

Manufacturing envy

Publicity quote: John Berger *Ways of Seeing*. New York: Penguin, 1972. p. 131.

Create desirability to produce envy

iPhone muggings: Keith Wagstaff. "Muggers Demand iPhone, Turn Down Android." *Time Tech* (`techland.time.com`). December 15, 2011. Retrieved February 2013.

Bloomberg's comments: Michael M. Grynbaum. "Crime Is Up and Bloomberg Blames iPhone Thieves." *The New York Times City Room* (`cityroom.blogs.nytimes.com`). December 28 2012. Retrieved February 2013.

Create something aspirational

Upwardly Mobile magazine: *Upwardly Mobile, the magazine of mobile, manufactured and modular home living* (`umhmag.com`).

Scorn: Susan Fiske. *Envy Up, Scorn Down*. New York: Russell Sage Foundation, 2011.

Make people feel ownership before they've bought

Don Norman: Don Norman. *Emotional Design: Why We Love (or Hate) Everyday Things*. New York: Basic Books, 2005.

Biolite: `biolitestove.com`.

Spore sales figures: Second quarter FY09 from Electronic Arts' investor relations site.

Spore top-10 game: NPD Group/Retail Tracking Service.

38% efficiency: Will Wright made this quote at the Electronic Entertainment Expo in July 2008.

Create status differences to drive behavior

Bruce Schneier: "E-Mail After the Rapture." (`schneier.com/blog`). June 2, 2008. Retrieved February 2013.

Eternal Earth-bound Pets: `eternal-earthbound-pets.com`.

Bart Centre quote: Mike Di Paola. "Caring for Pets Left Behind by the Rapture." *Bloomberg Businessweek* (`businessweek.com`). February 11, 2010. Retrieved February 2013.

Emphasize achievement as a form of status

Two clipped: Joseph C Nunes and Xavier Dreze. "The endowed progress effect: How artificial advancement increases effort." *Journal of Consumer Research* 32.4 (2006): 504–512.

Large numbers of points: Rajesh Bagchi and Xingbo Li. "Illusionary Progress in Loyalty Programs: Magnitudes, Reward-Distances, and Step-Size Ambiguity." *Journal of Consumer Research* 37 (2011): 888–901.

Achievement unlocked comic: Derek Lieu. (`kickinthehead.org`). Jan 18, 2011.

Encourage payment as an alternative to achievement

WOW subscriber numbers: Adam Holisky. "World of Warcraft subscriber numbers dip 100,000 to 10.2 million". *WOW Insider* (`wow.joystiq.com`). February 9, 2012. Retrieved February 2013.

World Bank report: Vili Lehdonvirta and Mirko Ernkvist. *Converting the Virtual Economy into Development Potential: Knowledge Map of the Virtual Economy*. Washington, DC: infoDev/World Bank, 2011.

Blizzard's philosophy on out-of-game gold trading and power leveling: "The Consequences of Buying Gold." (`battle.net`). Retrieved February 2013.

Cory Doctorow quote: Lisa Poisso. "15 Minutes of Fame: Cory Doctorow on gold farming, part 2." *WOW Insider* (`wow.joystiq.com`). August 4, 2010. Retrieved February 2013.

Gympact quote: `Gympact.com` home page, retrieved January 2012.

Offer of payment: Dan Ariely. *Predictably Irrational: The Hidden Forces That Shape Our Decisions*. New York: HarperCollins, 2008.

Let people feel important

Mary Kay Ash quote: Mary Kay Ash. *The Mary Kay Way: Timeless Principles from America's Greatest Woman Entrepreneur*. New Jersey: Wiley, 2008. p. 21.

Dale Carnegie: Dale Carnegie's *How to Win Friends and Influence People* has been in print since 1936. The 1981 revised edition is published by Simon & Schuster.

Warhol quote: Ralph Keyes. *The quote verifier: who said what, where, and when*. New York: Macmillan, 2006. p. 288.

Famous for fifteen people: Nick Currie (Momus). "POP STARS? NEIN DANKE! In the future everyone will be famous for fifteen people...." *I Momus* (`imomus.com`). 1991. Retrieved February 2013.

Zappos photos: `about.zappos.com/our-unique-culture/zappos-furry-customers`.

Threadless quotes: "The Threadless Story: How an Internet T-Shirt Company went XXL." *Motherboard* (`motherboard.vice.com`). September 9, 2010. Retrieved February 2013.

Threadless statistics: William C. Taylor. "The Company as Community: Threadless Puts Everyone in Charge." *Fast Company* (`fastcompany.com`). January 6, 2011. Retrieved February 2013.

Lust

Mason Cooley. "City Aphorisms: Eighth Selection." New York, 1991.

Creating lust: Using emotion to control behavior

Dating science not so scientific: Aimee E. King, Deena Austin-Oden, and Jeffrey M. Lohr. "Browsing for love in all the wrong places: Does research show that Internet matchmaking is more successful than traditional dating." *Skeptic* 15 (2009): 48–55.

Unachievable expectations: Eli J Finkel, Paul W. Eastwick, Benjamin R. Karney, Harry T. Reis, and Susan Sprecher. "Online Dating: A Critical Analysis from the Perspective of Psychological Science." *Psychological Science in the Public Interest* 13.1 (2012): 3–66.

Say "I love you"

Flattery: Elaine Chan and Jaideep Sengupta. "Insincere flattery actually works: A dual attitudes perspective." *Journal of Marketing Research* 47.1 (2010): 122–133.

Computers can deliver the flattery: B.J. Fogg and Clifford Nass. "Silicon sycophants: The effects of computers that flatter." *International Journal of Human-Computer Studies* 46.5 (1997): 551–561.

Be the second best

Avis statistics: Avis website (`avis.com`)

Aronson's original *pratfall effect* work: Elliot Aronson, Ben Willerman, and Joanne Floyd. "The effect of a pratfall on increasing interpersonal attractiveness." *Psychonomic Science* 4 (1966): 227–228.

Subsequent refinements: Robert Helmreich, Elliot Aronson, and James LeFan. "To err is humanizing sometimes: Effects of self-esteem, competence, and a pratfall on interpersonal attraction." *Journal of Personality and Social Psychology* 16.2 (1970): 259–264.

How we rate and who we date: Kenneth C. Herbst, Lowell Gaertner, and Chester A. Insko. "My head says yes but my heart says no: Cognitive and affective attraction as a function of similarity to the ideal self." *Journal of Personality and Social Psychology* 84.6 (2003): 1206.

Dating meta-analysis: Alan Feingold. "Matching for attractiveness in romantic partners and same-sex friends: A meta-analysis and theoretical critique." *Psychological Bulletin* 104.2 (1988): 226.

OkCupid statistics on male reaction to beauty, described as game theory: Christian Rudder. "The mathematics of beauty." *OKTrends* (`blog.okcupid.com`). January 10, 2011. Retrieved March 2013.

Frame your message as a question

Dan Morales State Attorney General story: Sheila Kaplan. "Tobacco Dole." *Mother Jones* (`motherjones.com`). May/June 1996. Retrieved March 2013.

Entire push-poll: "Public Opinion Strategies Push Poll." *Mother Jones* (`motherjones.com`). May/June 1996. Retrieved March 2013.

Public Opinion Strategies quote: "About Our Firm." *Public Opinion Strategies* (`pos.org`). Retrieved March 2013.

Asking suggestive questions of eyewitnesses: Elizabeth F. Loftus. "The malleability of human memory." *American Scientist* 67 (1979): 312–320.

Create an in-group

Supporting the school team: Robert B. Cialdini, Richard J. Borden, Avril Thorne, Marcus Walker, Stephen Freeman, and Lloyd Sloan. "Basking in reflected glory: Three (football) field studies." *Journal of Personality and Social Psychology* 34 (1976): 366–375.

Trash talk: Robert B. Cialdini and Kenneth D. Richardson. "Two indirect tactics of image management: Basking and blasting." *Journal of Personality and Social Psychology* 39 (1980): 406–415.

Favor members of own group: Henri Tajfel. "Experiments in intergroup discrimination." *Scientific American* 223.2 (1970): 96–102.

Maximize reward difference: Henri Tajfel, M.G. Billig, R.P. Bundy, and Claude Flament. "Social categorization and intergroup behaviour." *European Journal of Social Psychology* 1 (1971): 149–178.

Generalization and stereotyping: Marilynn B. Brewer. "In-Group Bias in the Minimal Intergroup Situation: A Cognitive-Motivational Analysis." *Psychological Bulletin* 86.2 (1979): 307–324.

Texas A&M claims trademark to the 12th Man term, which is used under license by the Seahawks.

Give something to get something

The norm of reciprocity: Alvin W. Gouldner. "The norm of reciprocity: A preliminary statement." *American Sociological Review* (1960): 161–178.

Buying a soft drink: Dennis T. Regan. "Effects of a favor and liking on compliance." *Journal of Experimental Social Psychology* 7 (1971): 627–639.

Amount is proportional: Dean G. Pruitt. "Reciprocity and credit building in a laboratory dyad." *Journal of Personality and Social Psychology* 8.2p1 (1968): 143.

Make something free

Amazon.com quote: SEC Form 10-Q 10/26/2012, Page 27 *Marketing*.

e-commerce statistics: Andrew Lipsman. "Free Shipping for the 2010 Holiday Season." *ComScore Insights* (`comscore.com`). November 22, 2010. Retrieved March 2013.

Cheap to free: Dan Ariely. *Predictably Irrational: The Hidden Forces That Shape Our Decisions*. New York: HarperCollins, 2008.

Instagram terms of service: Bryan Bishop. "Instagram's new terms of service: from overreaction to retraction." *The Verge* (`verge.com`). December 20, 2012. Retrieved March 2013.

Chad's garage comic: "Instagram" © Randall Munroe, xkcd.com.

Sell the intangible value

Goldhut photo credit: Chris Nodder.

Problems of perception: Rory Sutherland "Perspective is everything" Ted talk, (`ted.com`).

Make a request in order to be seen more favorably

Benjamin Franklin quote: *The Autobiography of Benjamin Franklin*. Boston: Houghton Mifflin & Co., 1906. p. 107.

Return the money you won: Jon Jecker and David Landy. "Liking a person as a function of doing him a favour." *Human Relations* 22.4 (1969): 371–378.

Lustful behavior

Third person effect: Richard M. Perloff. "Third-person effect research 1983–1992: A review and synthesis." *International Journal of Public Opinion Research* 5.2 (1993): 167–184.

Sleeper effect: Anthony R Pratkanis, Anthony G. Greenwald, Michael R. Leippe, and Michael H. Baumgardner. "In search of reliable persuasion effects: III. The sleeper effect is dead: Long live the sleeper effect." *Journal of Personality and Social Psychology* 54.2 (1988): 203.

Materialistic customers: Marsha L. Richins. "When Wanting Is Better Than Having: Materialism, Transformation Expectations, and Product-Evoked Emotions in the Purchase Process." *Journal of Consumer Research.* 40.3 (2013): 1-18.

Greed

Trump quote: Donald Trump with Tony Schwartz. *Trump: The Art of the Deal*. New York: Ballantine Books, 1987.

Higher social classes are less ethical: Paul K. Piff, Daniel M. Stancato, Stéphane Côté, Rodolfo Mendoza-Denton, and Dacher Keltnera. "Higher social class predicts increased unethical behavior." *PNAS* 109.11 (2012): 4086–4091.

Higher social classes are less compassionate: Paul K. Piff, Michael W. Kraus, Stéphane Côté, Bonnie Hayden Cheng, and Dacher Keltner. "Having less, giving more: The influence of social class on prosocial behavior." *Journal of Personality and Social Psychology* 99.5 (2010): 771–784.

Higher social classes are more selfish: Jennifer E. Stellar, Vida M. Manzo, Michael W. Kraus, and Dacher Keltner. "Class and compassion: Socioeconomic factors predict responses to suffering." *Emotion* 12.3 (2012): 449–459.

Learning from casinos

Monty Hall Problem: en.wikipedia.org/wiki/Monty_Hall_problem.

Lottery sales and gambling income data: North American Association of State and Provincial Lotteries. *Lottery Sales and Profits* (naspl.org).

60 percent of adults report playing at least once per year: *National Gambling Impact Study Commission staff-generated report on lotteries* (1999).

72 percent of all gambling: The majority of gambling income comes from casinos (41 percent) and lotteries (31 percent). These figures don't include tribal casinos. *United States General Accounting Office report to the Honorable Frank R. Wolf: Impact of Gambling: Economic Effects More Measurable Than Social Effects* (2000) GAO-GGD-00-78.

North Carolina lottery repeat numbers (in a lovely introspective journal article written in the first person): Leonard A. Stefanski. "The North Carolina Lottery Coincidence." *The American Statistician* 62.2 (2008): 130–134.

Bulgarian lottery repeat numbers: Carl Bialik. "Lottery Math 101." *The Numbers Guy* (blogs.wsj.com). September 22, 2009. Retrieved March 2013.

Israel National Lottery repeat numbers: Mark Weiss. "Israel lottery draws same numbers as three weeks before." *The Telegraph* (telegraph.co.uk). October 18, 2010. Retrieved March 2013.

Use a partial reinforcement schedule

Game design seen through an operant conditioning lens: John Hopson. "Behavioral Game Design." *Gamasutra* (gamasutra.com). April 27, 2001. Retrieved January 2013.

Dog photo credit: Chris Nodder.

Make it into a game

Volkswagen's Fun Theory promotion: `thefuntheory.com`.
Fold It: Protein folding game online at `Fold.it`.
DigitalKoot: The Finnish National Library DigitalKoot project page at
`digitalkoot.fi`.
Google Image Labeler: Now offline.

Customers should "win" rather than "finishing" or "buying"

fMRI images: Mauricio R. Delgado, Andrew Schotter, Erkut Y. Ozbay, and Elizabeth
A. Phelps. "Understanding Overbidding: Using the Neural Circuitry of Reward
to Design Economic Auctions." *Science* 321.5897 (2008): 1849–1852.
J.C. Penney: J.C. Penney revives "clearance" sales." *CBS News* (`cbsnews.com`). July 26
2012. Retrieved December 2012.
Paco Underhill "sales are like heroin": Anne D'Innocenzio. "Discount, deal junkies
hurting stores' profits." *USA Today* (`usatoday.com`). September 2, 2012. Retrieved
September 2012.
TechCrunch analysis of Groupon: Rocky Agrawal. "Why Groupon Is Poised For
Collapse." *TechCrunch* (`techcrunch.com`). June 13, 2011. Retrieved September
2012.
Fast company report: "Do Groupon And LivingSocial Do More Harm Than Good?"
Fast Company (`fastcompany.com`). March 19, 2012. Retrieved September 2012.

Further inflate people's feelings of skill and mastery

Bertrand Russel quote: Bertrand Russel. *New Hopes for a Changing World*. New
York: Simon & Schuster, 1951.
Dunning & Kruger's research into illusive superiority: Justin Kruger and David
Dunning. "Unskilled and unaware of it: how difficulties in recognizing one's
own incompetence lead to inflated self-assessments." *Journal of Personality and
Social Psychology* 77.6 (1999): 1121.
A primer on the derivatives market: `en.wikipedia.org/wiki/Derivative_`
`products`.

24option.com quote: `24option.com`. Retrieved January 2013.

Buffet quote: Berkshire Hathaway Annual Report 2002, page 15.

Make rewards seem due to skill, not luck

Skinner's superstitious pigeons: W.H. Morse and B. F. Skinner. "A Second Type of Superstition in the Pigeon." *The American Journal of Psychology* 70.2 (1957): 308–311.

Create a walled garden

YouTube search engine information: "comScore Releases November 2008 U.S. Search Engine Rankings." *comScore* (`comscore.com`). December 19, 2008. Retrieved January 2013.

Anchoring and arbitrary coherence

Arbitrary coherence: Dan Ariely. *Predictably Irrational: The Hidden Forces That Shape Our Decisions*. New York: HarperCollins, 2008.

Gas pump photo credit: Chris Nodder.

Historical gas prices: *Weekly Retail Gasoline and Diesel Prices*. United States Energy Information Administration. Independent Statistics and Analysis reports average prices of $0.907/gallon on Monday, February 22, 1999, and $4.114/gallon on Monday, July 7, 2008 for regular gasoline. U.K. gas prices from `whatgas.com` report £1.19/liter in July 2008. One U.S. gallon is 3.785 liters. The USD/GBP exchange rate was ~1.5, so UK gas prices equate to $6.50/US gallon.

TARDIS/Time Lord: If the references are unfamiliar, search for "Dr. Who," a British science fiction television program.

Own the anchor

Social Security numbers can create an arbitrary anchor: Itamar Simonson and Aimee Drolet. "Anchoring Effects on Consumers' Willingness-to-Pay and Willingness-to-Accept." *Journal of Consumer Research* 31.3 (2004): 681–690.

Move from money to tokens

Senator Mark Pryor's letter to the FTC: Mark Pryor. "Prior to FTC: Protect Families from Deceptive Purchases Embedded in Kids' Games." (`pryor.senate.gov`). February 8, 2011. Retrieved March 2013.

FTC report: *Mobile Apps for Kids: Current Privacy Disclosures are Disappointing.* Federal Trade Commission Staff Report, February 2012.

Apple's class action settlement for "bait apps": U.S. District Court Northern District of California San Jose Division. No. 11-CV-1758-EJD. March 1, 2013.

Encourage breakage

Spend additional 40 percent: Kelli B. Grant. "Why Amazon Wants Your Old CDs." *SmartMoney* (`smartmoney.com`). April 11, 2012. Retrieved March 2013.

Best Buy $53 million income from unredeemed cards, $41bn total value of unredeemed cards from 2005–2011: Phil Izzo. "Number of the Week: Billions in Gift Cards Go Unspent." *The Wall Street Journal* (`wsj.com`). December 24, 2011. Retrieved March 2013.

10–19 percent of gift cards are unredeemed: *Gift cards: Opportunities and issues for retailers.* Grant Thornton LLP, March 2011.

Expiration dates: "Gift Card Report 2012." *Scripsmart* (`scripsmart.com`). November 26, 2012.

Make it expensive

Consumers prefer cheaper wines in blind tastings: Robin Goldstein, Johan Almenberg, Anna Dreber, John W. Emerson, Alexis Herschkowitsch, and Jacob Katz. "Do More Expensive Wines Taste Better? Evidence from a Large Sample of Blind Tastings." *Journal of Wine Economics* 3.1 (2008): 1–9.

fMRI shows pleasantness increases with cost: Hilke Plassmann, John O'Doherty, Baba Shiv, and Antonio Rangel. *Marketing actions can modulate neural representations of experienced pleasantness.* Proceedings of the National Academy of Sciences 105.3 (2008): 1050–1054.

Paying cash leads to more indulgent purchases: Rajesh Bagchi and Lauren G. Block. "Chocolate Cake Please! Why Do We Indulge More When it Feels More Expensive?" *Journal of Public Policy & Marketing* 30.2 (2011): 294–306.

The halo effect was first described in: Edward L. Thorndike. "A constant error in psychological ratings." *Journal of Applied Psychology* 4.1 (1920): 25–29.

Show your second-best option first

Length of road lines: Dennis M. Shaffer, Andrew B. Maynor, and Windy L. Roy. "The visual perception of lines on the road." *Perception & Psychophysics* 70.8 (2008): 1571–1580.

Real Estate agents: Robert Cialdini. *Influence: The psychology of persuasion.* Collins Business, 2007. p. 14.

Break coherence to justify prices

Metrication in the UK: *The Great Metric Rip-Off.* British Weights and Measures Association (`bwmaonline.com`). Retrieved March 2013.

Summary

Should you feel bad about deception?

Grocer's store photo: Courtesy of J. E. Nodder.

There's no such thing as monsters: Liat Sayfan and Kristin Hansen Lagattuta. "Scaring the Monster Away: What Children Know About Managing Fears of Real and Imaginary Creatures." *Child Development* 80 (2009): 1756–1774.

Bus Stop: Simone Thies. "Kein Bus wird kommen." *Der Westen* (`derwesten.de`) February 14, 2008. Retrieved March 2013. and Harry de Quetteville. "Wayward Alzheimer's patients foiled by fake bus stop." *The Telegraph* (`telegraph.co.uk`) June 3, 2008. Retrieved March 2013.

Dove "real beauty" campaign video: `youtube.com/watch?&v=m0JF4QxPpvM`

Should you feel bad about using the principles in this book?

Principles of Persuasive Technology Design: Daniel Berdichevsky and Erik Neuenschwander. "Toward an ethics of persuasive technology." *Communications of the ACM* 42.5 (1999): 51–58.

Feel good that you provide a service

Don Norman. *Emotional Design: Why We Love (or Hate) Everyday Things*. New York: Basic Books, 2005.

Index

Gummer, John, 96–97
GymPact, 17, 18, 158–159

H

halo effect, 240
hiding the math, 75–78
high-end anchors, 230–232
HITs (Human Intelligence Tasks), 72–74
Hodson, Gordon, 130
Hopson, John, 209
hubris, 1, 35
Human Intelligence Tasks (HITs), 72–74
Humble Bundle, 94–95
humor, avoiding anger with, 104–107

I

identity, 138, 140, 141, 182
illusive inferiority, 217
illusive superiority, 217–219
Image Labeler, 212
impatience, 99–101
in-app purchases, 233
in-group bias, 183–185
in-groups, 182–185
inequality averse, 137
inertia, 36–37, 57–58
innuendo, 113
Instagram, 193
intrinsic motivation, 209, 248
irrational escalation of commitment, 77
"It's all in my head" factor, online disinhibition effect, 120
"It's just a game" factor, online disinhibition effect, 120
Iyengar, Sheena, 45

J–K

justifications
    for small rewards, 72–74, 102
    moral, 128
Kickstarter, 148–149

L

Lagattuta, Kristin Hansen, 251
Lazarchik, John, 22

Lepper, Mark, 45
Lerner, Jennifer, 134
lifestyle images, 5
lifestyle magazines, 140
LinkedIn, 13, 32–34, 173
LinkWorth, 9
Lockton, Dan, 32
logos, of trust certification, 22–24
loss aversion, 96–99
lotteries, 206–208
    vs. competitions, 214–216
low-end anchors, 232
Lowes, 3–4
lust
    gaining commitment, 185–186
        encouraging reciprocity, 186–190
        offering free gifts, 190–194
        requesting favors, 198–201
        selling intangible value, 195–198
    references, 287–290
    shaping behavior, 169–170
        appeals to self-esteem, 174–178
        flattery, 170–174
        in-groups, 182–185
        push polls, 178–182

M

Machiavelli, Niccolò, 249
maximizers, 45–49
McAfee, 24
Mechanical Turk, 72–74
messages
    personal, hitting home with, 11–16
    positive, repeating, 7–10, 261
metaphysical arguments, 112–117
metrics
    as comparison points, 246
    of success, 18
Microsoft Points, 234
Milgram, Stanley, 7, 124–125
misplaced pride, and cognitive dissonance, 1–5
mommy blogs, 8, 10
Monty Hall problem, 205–206
moral disengagement, 125
Morales, Dan, 179–180
Mozy, 106